Courage and Determination

Technical Support in Laboratory Education for a Visually Impaired Student

Edited by
Administration and Technology Management Center for Science and Engineering,
Waseda University

Waseda University Press

Courage and Determination
Technical Support in Laboratory Education for a Visually Impaired Student

Edited by Administration and Technology Management Center for
Science and Engineering, Waseda University

Translation cooperation by Crimson Interactive Japan Co., Ltd.

First published in 2025 by
Waseda University Press Co., Ltd.
1-9-12 Nishiwaseda
Shinjuku-ku, Tokyo 169-0051
www.waseda-up.co.jp

© Waseda University 2025

All rights reserved. Except for short extracts used for academic purposes or book reviews, no part of this publication may be reproduced, stored in a retrieval system or transmitted in any form whatsoever—electronic, mechanical, photocopying or otherwise—without the prior and written permission of the publisher.

ISBN978-4-657-25002-5

Printed in Japan

Introduction

In April 2019, Makoto Amakawa, a completely blind student was enrolled in the School of Advanced Science and Engineering at Waseda University. Ms. Amakawa, who lost her sight completely when she was in the second grade of elementary school, attended the junior high school of the Special Needs Education School for the Visually Impaired, University of Tsukuba and a metropolitan high school before applying to Waseda University. She passed the university's entrance examination in her first attempt.

After she was accepted, we, the staff at the Administration and Technology Management Center for Science and Engineering of Waseda University (Science and Engineering Center) faced a major challenge—How do we encourage a totally blind student to take up multiple courses that require performing experiments, which is typical of the Waseda University's practical education? This was an almost unprecedented challenge in higher engineering education in Japan and elsewhere.

We worked closely with her and sought the cooperation of internal and external stakeholders to address the unimaginable challenge of providing laboratory education to a totally blind student. We sometimes struggled with what we wanted her to learn through each experimental subject while considering the content of the experiments.

Indeed, it is possible for a totally blind student to receive practical laboratory education at the university level if they are up to the challenge. We, the staff of the Science and Engineering Center, responded courageously by taking on this unprecedented challenge and were determined to ensure that the visually impaired student completed the program in the same way as sighted students. To achieve this, we conducted three years of laboratory education, including during the COVID-19 pandemic.

This document is a record of the challenges faced by the staff at the School of Advanced Science and Engineering at Waseda University, with the respect to examing and preparing the contents of 38 experiments accross the four laboratory courses that Ms. Amakawa took from her first to the third year in the university. Because we had this precious experience, we believe it is our mission to record it with courage and determination.

This document shows that visually impaired students can independently take courses that require experiments, and we believe that this document will be a source of hope for visually impaired students who wish to study science and engineering. In addition, we will be delighted if this document helps in the education of visually impaired students and the practice of laboratory education in higher education.

Administration and Technology Management Center for
Science and Engineering, Waseda University

Checking microscopic images in the laboratory (painting by Ken Yabuno)

Table of Contents

Introduction
Administration and Technology Management Center for Science and Engineering, Waseda University

Part 1
People Involved in Providing Technical Assistance in Laboratory Education for Visually Impaired Students

011

1. Admission of Visually Impaired Students in University Science Departments
— Achievements and Challenges ———————————— 012

Yoshiko Toriyama
Former professor at University of Tsukuba with many years of experience teaching at a school for the visually impaired (Department of Disability Science, Human Science) with Director of Division for the Department of Braille Transcription for Entrance Examinations, National Association of Upper Secondary School Principals

2. Experience at the Special Needs Education School for the Visually Impaired, University of Tsukuba and Challenges at the Faculty of Science and Engineering, Waseda University ———————————— 027

Shizuko Hamada
Former teacher at the Special Needs Education School for the Visually Impaired, University of Tsukuba/Senior Adviser for the Department of Braille Transcription for Entrance Examinations, National Association of Upper Secondary School Principals

3. Implications of Accepting the Visually Impaired Students at the Faculty of Science and Engineering, Waseda University ———————————— 036

Yuji Takagi
Senior Director and Administrative Director of Administration and Technology Management Center for Science and Engineering, Waseda University

4. We Learned with Her — 041
Takafumi Jigami
Manager of Education and Research Support Section (4th section),
Technology Management Division of the Administration and Technology
Management Center for Science and Engineering, Waseda University

5. Ms. Amakawa from the Viewpoint of the Academic Staff — 046
Takuro Katsufuji
Professor, Department of Physics, School of Advanced Science and
Engineering/Department of Pure and Applied Physics, Graduate School of
Advanced Science and Engineering, Faculty of Science and Engineering, Waseda
University

6. They Let Me Experience All Experiments
— What I Learned from It — 051
Makoto Amakawa
Laboratory of Cosmology, Graduate School of
Advanced Science and Engineering, Waseda University

Part 2
Background, Summary and Issues in the Entrance Examination to Technical Assistance
057

1. Entrance Examination Process — 058
2. From Entrance Examination to Admission — 068
3. 1st Year (Basic Experiments in Science and Engineering 1A and 1B) to 3rd Year (Experiments in Applied Physics A) — 074
4. After Supporting Experiments — 080

Part

Record of Technical Support in Laboratory Education

083

❶ Basic Chemistry ─────────────────────── 085

- ❶-1 Water Quality Analysis
  (Basic Experiments in Science and Engineering 1A) ── 086

- ❶-2 Extraction of Caffeine
  (Basic Experiments in Science and Engineering 1A) ── 094

- ❶-3 Synthesis of Nylon
  (Basic Experiments in Science and Engineering 1A) ── 103

- ❶-4 Atomic Emission Spectra
  (Basic Experiments in Science and Engineering 1B) ── 110

- ❶-5 Synthesis of Pharmaceuticals
  (Basic Experiments in Science and Engineering 1B) ── 117

- ❶-6 Inclusion of a Molecule into Cyclodextrin
  (Basic Experiments in Science and Engineering 1B) ── 124

- ❶-7 Synthesis and Electrochemical Measurement of Ferrocene
  (Basic Experiments in Science and Engineering 2B) ── 131

- ❶-8 Separation and Molecular Weight Measurement of Proteins
  (Basic Experiments in Science and Engineering 2B) ── 135

- ❶-9 Synthesis of a Titanium Oxide Photocatalyst by the Sol-Gel Method and Scientific Information Search Using a PC
  (Basic Experiments in Science and Engineering 2B) ── 141

- ❶-10 Synthesis of Polystyrene by Suspension Polymerization and Its Recycling
  (Basic Experiments in Science and Engineering 2B) ── 148

❷ Basic Physics ─────────────────────── 155

- ❷-1 Making a Lens
  (Basic Experiments in Science and Engineering 1A) ── 156

❷-2 Simulation of Physical Phenomena
(Basic Experiments in Science and Engineering 1A) —— 162

❷-3 Estimation of Measurement Uncertainty
(Basic Experiments in Science and Engineering 1A) —— 166

❷-4 Electric Guitar
(Basic Experiments in Science and Engineering 1A) —— 172

❷-5 Capacitor Design and Radio Reception
(Basic Experiments in Science and Engineering 1A) —— 178

❷-6 Electromagnetic Induction
(Basic Experiments in Science and Engineering 1A) —— 183

❷-7 Oral Examination
(Basic Experiments in Science and Engineering 1A) —— 189

❷-8 Brownian Motion
(Basic Experiments in Science and Engineering 1B) —— 190

❷-9 The Physics of Air Hockey
(Basic Experiments in Science and Engineering 1B) —— 194

❷-10 Electronic Circuit Workshop
(Basic Experiments in Science and Engineering 1B) —— 198

❷-11 Light and Waves
(Basic Experiments in Science and Engineering 1B) —— 202

❷-12 Measuring Divices
(Basic Experiments in Science and Engineering 1B) —— 207

❷-13 Heat and Motion of Gas Molecules
(Basic Experiments in Science and Engineering 1B) —— 211

❷-14 Presentation and Discussion
(Basic Experiments in Science and Engineering 1B) —— 216

❸ Basic Life Science —— 217

❸-1 Microscopic Observation of Cells
(Basic Experiments in Science and Engineering 1A) —— 218

❸-2 Extraction and PCR Amplification of DNA
(Basic Experiments in Science and Engineering 1B) —— 226

④ Basic Engineering — 233

④-1 Elasticity and Viscoelasticity
(Basic Experiments in Science and Engineering 2B) — 234

④-2 Resonant Circuits and Vibration Systems
(Basic Experiments in Science and Engineering 2B) — 242

④-3 Automatic Measurements Using a Computer
(Basic Experiments in Science and Engineering 2B) — 257

④-4 Thermal Conductioin and Diffusion
(Basic Experiments in Science and Engineering 2B) — 265

④-5 Laser and Holography Interference
(Basic Experiments in Science and Engineering 2B) — 272

④-6 Optical and Electron Microscopes
(Basic Experiments in Science and Engineering 2B) — 278

⑤ Applied Physics — 289

⑤-1 X-ray Diffraction
(Experiments in Applied Physics A, Physical Properties) — 290

⑤-2 Logic Circuit
(Experiments in Applied Physics A, Electricity) — 297

⑤-3 Optical Circuit Elements
(Experiments in Applied Physics A, Electricity) — 314

⑤-4 Magnetization Measurement
(Experiments in Applied Physics A, Physical Properties) — 321

⑤-5 Infrared Absorption Spectroscopy
(Experiments in Applied Physics A, Physical Properties) — 329

⑤-6 High-Temperature Superconductivity
(Experiments in Applied Physics A, Physical Properties) — 334

Main Support Equipment Used in Experiments — 346

\<Original Authors of Part 3 in Japanese edition>

❶ Basic Chemistry
Takasumi Hattori, Kazuhito Umezawa, Yuki Tsuzuki, Shigeru Uchida, Aya Matsubara
❷ Basic Physics
Shohei Sakata, Yuki Nishi, Yuki Tsuzuki, Akihiro Ueyama, Yasuji Nishino, Sho Nakagawa
❸ Basic Life Science
Takasumi Hattori
❹ Basic Engineering
Jun Tanaka, Kazuo Harashima, Kazuma Yoshino
❺ Applied Physics
Daichi Itaki, Takeshi Yamamoto, Toshiyuki Akanuma, Moemi Takano, Toshiyuki Ito

\<On notation>

Waseda University has experienced teaching staff in each field of study to provide education and conduct research in undergraduate schools, graduate schools, and research institutes. In this document, "Faculty of Science and Engineering in Waseda" includes the following three undergraduate schools and three graduate schools (1) the Undergraduate and Graduate Schools of Fundamental Science and Engineering, (2) Undergraduate and Graduate Schools of Creative Science and Engineering, and (3) Undergraduate and Graduate Schools of Advanced Science and Engineering.

"Science and Engineering Center" refers to the Administration and Technology Management Center for Science and Engineering, Waseda University and "Technology Management Division" refers to the Technology Management Division of the Administration and Technology Management Center for Science and Engineering, Waseda University.

"Sighted person" and "sighted student" refer to a person or student without visual impairment.

Part 1

People Involved in
Providing Technical
Assistance in
Laboratory Education
for Visually Impaired
Students

1 Admission of Visually Impaired Students in University Science Departments — Achievements and Challenges

Yoshiko Toriyama

Former professor at University of Tsukuba with many years of experience teaching at a school for the visually impaired (Department of Disability Science, Human Science) with Director of Division for the Department of Braille Transcription for Entrance Examinations, National Association of Upper Secondary School Principals
(Chairperson of the Board of Directors of the Division at that time)

In this section, we asked Prof. Yoshiko Toriyama, a pioneer in education for the visually impaired, about (1) the historical background on the inclusion of visually impaired students in university science departments (primarily in International Christian University and the University of Tokyo), (2) the characteristics of Waseda University that accepted Ms. Makoto Amakawa, and (3) the challenges and prospects of visually impaired students entering university science departments.

▶ Admission of visually impaired students to university

―――― Before we discuss the admission of visually impaired students to science departments, please tell us about the inclusion of visually impaired students in universities in general.

Toriyama Special Needs Education School for the Visually Impaired, University of Tsukuba (formerly, The School for the Blind, University of Tsukuba), where I worked as a science teacher for more than 20 years until 1998, was established in 1876 (in the 9th year of the Meiji era) as the Rakuzenkai School for the Blind and the Deaf after a delegation dispatched to England in 1868 was impressed by the education provided to the blind and deaf students there. It was decided that it is necessary to establish a school for the blind and deaf in Japan too. Before World War II, it was called National Tokyo School for the Blind, which was under the direct control of the national government; after the war, it was affiliated with the Tokyo University of Education and later with the University of Tsukuba.

Currently, it is called Special Needs Education School for the Visually Impaired, the only national school for the blind affiliated with the University of Tsukuba (hereinafter, "School for the Visually Impaired at the University of Tsukuba"). Currently, the enrollment capacity of the high-school general education course divided over two classes is 16 students per grade. Students are selected from all over Japan through an entrance examination, and many of them live in dormitories. Although there are special support schools for the visually impaired (hereinafter, "schools for the visually impaired") in each prefecture, the number of students enrolled in schools for the visually impaired is very small because visual impairment is the least common disability among all disabilities, along with a declining birth rate. Thus, the main problem for students is that they have very few friends in the same grade. Under these circumstances, students from all over the country come to our school in search of an environment where they can learn and work hard with their classmates. Many of our high school students in the general course aspire to go to university. Nationally, about 30 visually impaired students go to university each year, implying that half of them are from our school.

Sometimes, Western academics say that the number of visually impaired students who go to university in Japan is too small considering the country's level of education. In this regard, I must explain the characteristics of Japanese schools for the visually impaired. Japanese schools for the visually impaired offer a three-year vocational program called the "Specialized High School Course." The goal of this course is to enable students to become a massage therapist, an acupuncturist, or a moxibustion therapist (these three occupations are collectively referred to as "ahaki"), which are traditional occupations for the blind. After three years of study, students obtain the basic qualifications needed to take the national examination, which is the same as the national examination for general applicants. After passing the national examination, they obtain a license. Many visually impaired people take this course, obtain an ahaki license, and go on to work or start their own practice. The ahaki profession was established by the visually impaired in Japan in the Edo period (1603–1868) and from the mid-Edo period, and it has been recognized as a job for the visually impaired under the protection of the Shogun. Although the industry struggled to survive because of a ban on Chinese medicine during Meiji Restoration and a move to ban acupuncture and moxibustion by GHQ after World War II, it has become quite competitive now with the entry of sighted people into the industry. However, ahaki remains the main profession of visually impaired people in Japan.

Although, technically, the Specialized High School Course is a high-school program, it is the same as a junior-college course because it is a three-year vocational course after three years of high school. If we include those who study the Specialized High School Course, most people with simple vision impairment have already received higher education. Those who join university are the ones who seek a different career path. Thus, the vocational background described above is unique to Japan, and universities are not the only places of higher education for high school graduates in Japan.

▶ Why do so few students enter science departments?

———— Why is it that the number of visually impaired students who study science is lower than those who study humanities?

Toriyama Mathematics is the most popular science subject. The first visually impaired student to study mathematics joined the Tokyo University of Education in 1950s At that time, however, the path to the Department of Mathematics in the Faculty of Science was closed, and the student had to enroll in the Department of Special Education in the Faculty of Education and subsequently take courses in the Department of Mathematics in the Faculty of Science to obtain a teaching license. However, after this student performed exceptionally in the mathematics course and was hired as a mathematics teacher at the School for the Blind at the Tokyo University of Education, other completely blind students started to enroll in university mathematics courses and the number of universities accepting visually impaired students increased. Then, in 1986, a visually impaired student who wished to major in mathematics was admitted to the Science Course 1 of the College on Arts and Sciences at the University of Tokyo. During the 30 years of the Heisei era, about 30 students were enrolled in the mathematics major. A total of 30 students over a span of 30 years means that about one student per year got enrolled in the mathematics department. I do not think that this number is particularly small considering the number of students enrolled in schools for the visually impaired; however, it is small compared with the number of students that join liberal arts schools.

There are several reasons for this. First, mathematics courses use extensive graphical representations, such as mathematical formulas, graphs, and geometric figures. Graphical representations converted into "tactile diagrams" that can be understood using touch are studied by visually impaired students who use Braille. However, reading tactile diagrams is more difficult than reading and writing Braille, and it is necessary to develop this skill through systematic instructions from an early age. Even so, reading tactile diagrams by a proficient Braille reader takes more time than reading and writing Braille texts. In other words, graphical representation is not a suitable tool for visually impaired students. Nevertheless, they cannot be avoided in mathematics and science.

Second, learning mathematics without relying on sight is not popular enough in schools for the visually impaired. For example, when solving a mathematical equation, a sighted person solves the problem by comparing the left and right sides of an equation. However, in Braille, the area that can be read at one time is small, so the entire left and right sides cannot be recognized simultaneously with one's fingertips. Therefore, a student has to construct the equation as a single formula in their mind to recognize and memorize it successively. The method of teaching mathematical formulas to visually impaired students in mathematics and arithmetic classes in schools for the visually impaired gained attention only after the visually impaired who uses Braille was hired as mathematics teachers in such schools and gained teaching experience. Until then, this systematic teaching of solving mathematics problems was not widely recognized.

Meanwhile, there were those who demonstrated their mathematical talent through their own ingenious methods. One of them was Ikuzo Ozeki. He joined the Department of Special Education at the Tokyo University of Education in 1950s and studied mathematics at the Department of Mathematics in the Faculty of Science as a main subject for acquiring a teaching license. After graduating from university, Mr. Ozeki worked at the then School for the Blind, Tokyo University of Education, where he taught mathematics to a large number of students (his juniors at the school he studied). Out of these students came the next generation of visually impaired students who became mathematics teachers at the School for the Visually Impaired at the University of Tsukuba. Today, at the school's junior and senior high schools, mathematics teachers who use Braille play a central role in teaching students to learn mathematics without depending on sight. Most visually impaired students who enrolled in university science programs are graduates of this school. I believe that this shows that students are taught a mathematics learning method that does not rely on visual images. Although this method has been taught throughout the country through workshops, it is still not widely adopted. If students cannot learn mathematics in a way that suits them, it is no wonder that many of them think, "I am not good at mathematics," and few students want to pursue a career in the science field. (Note that Mr. Ozeki received doctorate in mathematics from Kyoto University after his retirement. He was an extraordinary person. The Department of Braille Transcription for Entrance Examinations of the National Association of Upper Secondary School Principals was conceived by Mr. Ozeki out of a desire to "guarantee a decent Braille exam to those who study properly." He served as the first Director General of the division after his retirement.)

Earlier, universities did not allow visually impaired students to enroll in science courses, except mathematics, because performing physics and chemistry experiments was considered impossible for the visually impaired. For example, the University of Tokyo opened its doors to visually impaired students majoring in mathematics much later than other universities. The reason for this was that even mathematics major students were required to take classes in physics and chemistry experiments in the College of Arts and Sciences, and it was difficult for students to complete them. The University of Tokyo changed its policy after a visually impaired student enrolled in International Christian University (hereinafter "ICU") in 1983 as a physics major and completed physics and chemistry experiments. In 1986, for the first time, it admitted a completely blind student as a mathematics major. This shows how the achievement of one university encourage other universities to take such steps.

> ### ▶ Admission to an undergraduate school where students must take part in physics and chemistry experiments

——————— How can a visually impaired student be accepted into an undergraduate school where they must take perform physics and chemistry experiments?

Toriyama In 1950s, performing science experiments in schools for the visually impaired was considered almost impossible, but by 1970s, thanks to the efforts of the Ministry of Education, in addition to the research-based practices of dedicated teachers in the field, science classes focusing on experiments in physics and chemistry were being conducted. The basic ideas are to 1) utilize all senses other than sight, 2) produce teaching materials and equipment that do not rely on sight so that visually impaired students can master their operation, and 3) identify the essence of the course content and develop methods for experimentation and observation that allow visually impaired students to work on their own, instead of using the same methods and seeking the same results as sighted students. In 1966, I received an internship at the Lower secondary department, School for the Blind, Tokyo University of Education, to obtain a license to teach at a school for the visually impaired. My research class had an experiment on gas generation to be conducted in the first-grade class for completely blind students in the junior high school. Later, at the Okazaki School for the Blind in Aichi prefecture, where I was assigned from 1969, I conducted classes that incorporated student experiments as much as possible. Furthermore, at the University of Tsukuba School for the Visually Impaired, where I was assigned to teach chemistry in 1978, I focused on student experiments at the junior high and high school levels. My colleague, a physics teacher, was also enthusiastic about developing teaching materials and conducting student experiments almost every hour. Thus, in physics and chemistry, we teachers took pride in the fact that we were conducting experiments that students should be doing in high school. Therefore, when visually impaired students asked us whether they could pursue higher level education in physics or chemistry, we did not think it was "impossible" for them. Of course, the school for the visually impaired has many ingenious methods for experimentation and observation as well as laboratory equipment. So, it was interesting to see how the university evaluate our methods and laboratory equipment.

Perhaps it was the physics and chemistry experiments performed at high school that gave him confidence, but in 1982, Yohei Yagi, a third-year student at the high school, expressed desire to study physics at the university level. I told him there was no precedent for that and that it would be a difficult career path for him. However, because of his determination to pursue physics and academic ability, the guidance department enquired whether any university would accept him, but none did. As a science teacher, I visited several universities and pleaded with the respective deans to consider accepting visually impaired students, but was turned down at every turn.

▶ Pioneering achievements — The case of ICU

Under these circumstances, ICU allowed him to take the entrance examination.

Toriyama In the absence of a precedent in Japan, we relied on an article in a special issue of the *Journal of Chemical Education* (March 1981), one of the official journals of the American Chemical Society, which the library of the University of Tsukuba School for the Blind subscribed to, entitled "Teaching Chemistry to Physically Handicapped Students." The article included information on teaching chemistry to visually impaired, hearing impaired, and physically handicapped students in universities. The results in reports varied due to differences across universities in the U.S., but some results were very informative, containing details about teaching materials and ingenious equipment used for laboratory work in universities.

The ICU was the only Japanese university that showed significant interest in the article in the special issue of the *Journal of Chemical Education* (March 1981).

The ICU had been accepting completely blind students in humanities, but a visually impaired student wanting to major in physics was a surprise to them. Mr. Yagi was an excellent student and scored 100 points in most science subjects of the Common First Test (at that time). However, at that time, neither the Tokyo Institute of Technology nor University of Tokyo, which Mr. Yagi hoped to attend, allowed visually impaired students to take the entrance examination, even for mathematics majors.

The ICU was founded by Americans after World War II and uses English and Japanese as the medium of instruction. Initially, faculty members were split on whether to allow the student to take the entrance examination. However, the university set up a project team partly because of the enthusiasm of an American physics professor who asked, "Why can't we do in Japan what we do in the U.S.?" The faculty members visited the School for the Blind, University of Tsukuba, to observe experimental physics and chemistry classes and researched academic materials describing precedents in the U.S. We were informed through a letter addressed to the principal of the University of Tsukuba School for the Visually Impaired that Mr. Yagi was given "permission to take the examination." The letter came just two weeks before the entrance exam. After few days of hectic preparation, Mr. Yagi successfully passed the exam. At the ICU, a project team was formed at short notice to prepare for the course. We, the science teachers of the School for the Blind, University of Tsukuba, and science lecturers of ICU, also held meetings to discuss ideas.

After enrolling in the university, Mr. Yagi used quantitative pipettes (micro-pipettes and macropipettes) for measurements in basic chemistry experiments, whereas other students used volumetric pipettes and other ingenious methods, such as a light probe and a hot-plate melting point apparatus, to measure the melting point of organic compounds. Moreover, I received permission from the school for the visually impaired and went to the ICU once a week to assist in chemistry experiments.

Physics was Mr. Yagi's major; therefore, there were many experiments in addition to basic experiments. He had enthusiastic helpers, and various innovative ideas were used in terms of equipment and methods for experiments. I was told that a combination of a laser beam and a light probe was frequently used to capture visual changes in various experiments. However, at that time, analog equipment was the norm, and Mr. Yagi could not use many precision-measuring instruments. In such cases, his laboratory partner would conduct measurements and Mr. Yagi would record it. When his partner read out values, Mr. Yagi would answer, "Yes, I think that's about right." Even though Mr. Yagi could not read the scale, he understood the laboratory equipment and predicted the measurement results.

At that time, there were few Braille transcribers in the science field, so sometimes experiment protocols could not be transcribed into Braille in time. I am sure that Mr. Yagi faced a great deal of hardship. But as a former teacher at a school for the blind, someone recently told me that Mr. Yagi said, "I am very happy that I was able to follow the path I wanted to follow." I was relieved to hear that. After studying in a graduate school in the U.S., Mr. Yagi returned to Japan and has been working for the National Space Development Agency of Japan (now the Japan Aerospace Exploration Agency (hereinafter, JAXA)) since 1999. To date, about 10 people have studied physics at the university level.

Some of them now work in the corporate sector. We feel that these people have opened a path for others.

In the ICU case, it was the physics and chemistry faculty members in the science department who consistently took the lead to accept students. In the "Editor's Postscript," the then Associate Professor Koa Tasaka of the Department of Science, who was in charge of editing two booklets compiled after Mr. Yagi's graduation, wrote, "Although accepting a visually impaired student (completely blind) in the science department was regarded a "wise decision" outside, for those involved at the ICU, it was, at first, a "cross we were forced to bear." However, with the help of the teachers at the School for the Blind, University of Tsukuba, and many others, we could realize what at first seemed impossible, and our labors gradually turned to joy." I believe that this feeling is shared to some extent by those who were later involved in the University of Tokyo and Waseda University. Indeed, as a teacher at a school for the visually impaired, it was a valuable experience for me to share the challenge with Mr. Yagi and learn from the collaboration with the teachers at the ICU, which could not have been possible at the school for the visually impaired.

▶ First achievements in the department of chemistry — The case of the University of Tokyo

————I understand that the first visually impaired student got enrolled in chemistry major at the university level much later than in physics major.

Toriyama Yes. In chemistry, Mr. Urano enrolled in the Science Course 1 (Chemistry) of the College on Arts and Sciences at the University of Tokyo in 1999, 16 years after a visually impaired student had enrolled in physics major. In Mr. Urano's case, he started from a point where even we, the teachers at the school for the visually impaired, had difficulty deciding whether a visually impaired person could major in chemistry. Therefore, we decided to determine if there were any completely blind students majoring in chemistry in other countries.

I had a thick list of names, biographies, types and degrees of disabilities, and the age of the onset of disabilities for disabled researchers in the U.S., which I had received during a visit to the Center for Students with Disabilities at the University of California. I searched this list for people who had lost their sight before the age of 17, were completely blind, and were currently working in the field of chemistry; I found two people. So, with the guidance of our English teacher, I asked Mr. Urano to send an e-mail to these two chemistry graduates. One of them responded and was quite supportive of Mr. Urano's aspirations. In addition, a Singaporean friend of Mr. Aomatsu, who was a completely blind teacher in charge of career guidance at the school for the visually impaired and had graduated from Worcester School for the Blind in England, told me that two completely blind students, who were his juniors at the Worcester School for the Blind, had studied chemistry at Cambridge University and Southampton University. Therefore, Mr. Aomatsu, who is fluent in English, and I took the lead in planning a private study trip to England with Mr. Urano and other students.

At Cambridge University, we met the students and their teachers, lab assistants, librarians, and others involved in the project and asked them about how they conducted experiments, exams (especially how to handle complex structural equations and other graphical representations and how to extend the exam time), and other issues. Additionally, we visited Worcester School for the Blind and asked how chemistry experiments were conducted in high school. In the U.K., there is no same-day entrance examination system like in Japan. Instead, students are assessed based on predefined criteria set by high school teachers working in schools that have attained grant A-level certification (advanced level of general education) and students apply to universities with these A-level qualifications after their studies. The Worcester School for the Blind is accredited as an A-level high school.

After returning to Japan, I compiled a report on the reality of completely blind students majoring in chemistry at Cambridge University and submitted it to the University of Tokyo and two private universities in Tokyo to which Mr. Urano had applied. I was sure that all universities would be puzzled that a completely blind student wanted to major in chemistry, but based on the experiences of Cambridge University, all three universities decided to conduct the entrance examination in Braille. As a result, Mr. Urano was accepted by the University of Tokyo. After joining the university, one of the teaching assistants (now an assistant professor) became his dedicated lab assistant, and Mr. Urano was provided numerous digital equipment that was deemed necessary for the visually impaired. This was only possible because of the University of Tokyo's budget. By then, fifteen years had passed since Mr. Yagi had enrolled in the ICU, and laboratory equipment had changed from analog to digital. Visually impaired students cannot use analog instruments unless they are modified to allow them to touch the scale; however, digital instruments use electrical signals, so results are produced as an audible or a visual output. A special pocket PC was built for Mr. Urano so that he could take readings from digital measuring instruments. When the pocket PC was connected to a digital measuring instrument, measured values could be heard through the earpiece. I found out that thanks to this device, Mr. Urano conducted most experiments himself. Fortunately for visually impaired students, shortly before Mr. Urano joined the university, the College of Arts and Sciences had modernized its student experiments, which resulted in the elimination of classic experiments, such as those involving glasswork, and the increased use of digital measuring instruments. They also prepared a large Braille display, which is an instrument for reading diagrams using fine pins lined up on a diagram plane. The pins pop out as shown in the diagram. This instrument was developed for Mr. Yagi when he started working for JAXA, and although it was very expensive, the University of Tokyo made a copy.

In his third year, Mr. Urano enrolled in the Department of Applied Chemistry in the Faculty of Engineering, majoring in theoretical chemistry and completed a master's degree in graduate school.

> ▶ **The Technology Management Division extended considerable help to visually impaired students in their experiments — The case of the School of Advanced Science and Engineering, Waseda University**

——————— What is unique about the third case of Waseda University?

Toriyama Makoto Amakawa, who enrolled in the School of Advanced Science and Engineering, Waseda University in 2019, is the first student from a metropolitan high school to do so. However, she studied at the University of Tsukuba School for the Visually Impaired from the fifth grade of elementary school until junior high, so she had a good foundation in academics as a visually impaired person. The university decided that it was important to have a lab assistant for experiments, so Ms. Shizuko Hamada, a retired science teacher from Ms. Amakawa's junior high school, was assigned by the National Association of Upper Secondary School Principals, the Department of Braille Transcription for Entrance Examinations to serve as an experiment advisor. I will leave the details to Ms. Hamada and others from Waseda University, but I want to highlight the role played by the Technology Management Division of Waseda University.

All faculty members at the Technology Management Division have an academic background. They designed and prepared experimental courses together with the faculty and supervised students during experiments. Furthermore, they know all laboratory equipment because they prepared them. Additionally, they modified equipment for visually impaired students. The fact that Ms. Amakawa could perform experiments as well as her sighted classmates was attributed largely to the Technology Management Division, which provided support behind-the-scenes. Of course, the top management of the university was quite motivated, which inspired the people working in the Technology Management Division.

As I mentioned earlier, when I was a teacher at the School for the Blind, University of Tsukuba, I visited the chemistry and physics departments at various universities and requested them to accept visually impaired students. At that time, the department heads told me that they wanted their young researchers to publish papers, so they did not have time to care for disabled students. Waseda University accepted Ms. Amakawa based on the opposite approach and allowed her to take the same courses as sighted students, achieve the goals of the department, and graduate. I hope that Ms. Amakawa's example will not be a unique case and will pave the way for more visually impaired students to join universities.

▶ What is the objective of conducting scientific experiments?

——————— The aforementioned three universities have made me think about the purpose of conducting experiments. Do differences exist among universities in terms of the purpose or objective of conducting scientific experiments?

Toriyama All the three universities are leaders in higher education. It is closely related to the educational goal, that is, the educational objective of a university is to nurture people who will occupy a position in society. For example, consider the issue of measurement accuracy. Visually impaired students cannot read fine scales on measurement instruments, but in the case of the aforementioned three universities, the goal of education is not to read numbers on the scale but to understand the purpose of the instrument and be able to estimate values that will be obtained in a given experiment under certain conditions. Therefore, the fact that visually impaired students cannot take measures by themselves is not a problem in itself.

By contrast, if, for example, the goal is to produce engineers who can work in the field, it is important that they should be able to use measuring devices according to the respective manuals, and those who cannot do this cannot become specialists and thus will not be allowed to take the course.

▶ Pros and cons of inclusive education

——————— What are your thoughts on inclusive education in terms of allowing visually impaired students to study in university science departments?

Toriyama Inclusivity is a social philosophy that believes that people should not be excluded, rather should be included and supported. However, the term "inclusive education" does not have a definition. In general, it is often used to indicate that children with disabilities should be allowed to study in a regular school with children without disabilities.

Here, I want to consider the three cases that I mentioned above from the perspective of inclusive education. Mr. Yagi and Mr. Urano came from a school for the visually impaired, but Ms. Amakawa, who joined Waseda University, came from a metropolitan high school, so her high school was an inclusive school. While there were students in regular high schools in what was called integrated education at the time Mr. Yagi and Mr. Urano were studying, there was no precedent for visually impaired students studying science. I think it is a good thing that Ms. Amakawa's case came to light. I think things have improved now. The success of Ms. Amakawa's case proves that it is possible for a visually impaired student to enroll in a university science course with inclusive education under right conditions; it also shows that "right conditions" is a high hurdle to cross.

Comprehensively analyzing "right conditions" in Ms. Amakawa's case, first, it is necessary to mention her ability to learn being a visually impaired person. Her ability includes the reading and writing speed and searching skills in Braille, reading and writing tactile diagrams and graphs, understand the teacher's verbal explanations despite not being able to see the blackboard, calculation skills, basic observation and experimentation skills, and communication skills. She studied at the University of Tsukuba School for the Visually Impaired till junior high level and acquired sufficient basic learning skills.

Second, there is the problem of transcribing teaching materials and exams into Braille. In Ms. Amakawa's case, the Department of Braille Transcription for Entrance Examinations of the National Association of Principals of Senior High Schools in Japan was responsible for transcribing teaching materials into Braille and transcribing Braille into written texts at the request of the metropolitan high school, and the teachers at the high school helped in preparing a draft of teaching materials promptly so that they could be transcribed into Braille on time. Naturally, a budget was allocated for Braille and written Japanese transcriptions.

Third, the school for the visually impaired provided full cooperation to high school teachers struggling to teach visually impaired students.

Preparing for these three conditions was not an easy task. If these conditions are met, it is possible for visually impaired students to enroll in the science departments of universities through inclusive education. In other words, the problem is not the place of learning, but conditions and the environment provided for learning.

Note that even with inclusive education, the existence of schools for the visually impaired as centers of expertise is important, and the option to study at schools for the visually impaired for highly specialized education is available. The experience in European countries where inclusive education is the basis of their education varies. Instead of thinking about inclusive education as "everyone learning under one roof," we should think of it in terms of "freedom of choice of educational setting" for children with disabilities and "the right to receive a high level of support from professionals in any setting."

> ▶ **Will the Act for Eliminating Discrimination against Persons with Disabilities and "reasonable accommodation" increase the number of students pursuing higher education?**

——————— Will the ratification of the UN Convention on the Rights of Persons with Disabilities and enactment of the Act for Eliminating Discrimination against Persons with Disabilities and other domestic laws positively impact the enrollment of visually impaired students in science departments at the university level?

Toriyama Certainly. In 2021, the Act for Eliminating Discrimination against Persons with Disabilities made it obligatory to provide "reasonable accommodation" to persons with disabilities, which until then was only required of the national and local governments and was merely an "effort" from private businesses (private universities and companies). It is said that all universities can no longer deny admissions on the basis of disability.

However, I do not think that this issue is simple. This is because simply admitting students to a university does not solve the problem; it is necessary to create a human and material environment that ensures that they can complete their studies at the university.

Until now, two main reasons prevented universities from allowing visually impaired students to enroll in science courses. One is the lack of knowledge about how visually impaired students can take science courses, and the other is the lack of support in terms of human and material resources.

First, I want to ask you to consider the first issue in detail by studying the above-mentioned cases. Every university has its own characteristics and strengths. Courses cannot be completed without the concerted efforts of all people concerned, including students, in a way that utilizes the unique characteristics of each university. However, universities that have accepted visually impaired students so far have told us that "it was easier than they thought it would be" and that "it was not as bad as they had feared." When a visually impaired student enrolls in a university to study science, teachers do not have to go abroad to do research, as in the past. Precedents are available in Japan. I hope this Waseda University report will be a reference for such cases in the future.

The second issue is improving the human and material environment, and I think it is important to consult with a specialized organization based on previous cases. However, financial resources are needed to make this happen. In the past, those universities have considered, and in some cases managed to receive, external grants in addition to their own budgets. Financial support is necessary to provide "reasonable accommodation." I want the national government to take initiatives in this aspect.

Even today, visually impaired students in the science field are a rarity in any university. Even if you have expensive equipment and ingenious devices for visually impaired students, it is unlikely that you will continue to use them at the same university. Is it possible to collect, store, and manage this equipment somewhere and make it a "common property" that can be used by any university that needs it? Otherwise, it would be a waste.

Therefore, I believe that "reasonable accommodation" is meaningful only when the human and material environment is prepared properly.

2. Experience at the Special Needs Education School for the Visually Impaired, University of Tsukuba, and Challenges at the Faculty of Science and Engineering, Waseda University

Shizuko Hamada
Former teacher at the Special Needs Education School for the Visually Impaired, University of Tsukuba/Senior Adviser for the Department of Braille Transcription for Entrance Examinations, National Association of Upper Secondary School Principals

▶ **"A world where we are equal to those who can see" has become a catalyst**

"Even those who can see do not have a clear view of the universe. Molecular biology is no different. In molecular biology, which attempts to elucidate life phenomena at the molecular level, it is not possible to see subjects with the naked eye. In other words, the very large and very small objects remain invisible to even the sighted, so those who can see and cannot are equal."

I often told my students the above when I was a science teacher at the Special Needs Education School for the Visually Impaired, University of Tsukuba (hereinafter, the "University of Tsukuba School for the Visually Impaired"). I started by mentioning two former completely blind students who are very active in the science field.

The two students are Mr. Yohei Yagi and Mr. Morimitsu Urano. Mr. Yagi graduated from the International Christian University (ICU) in 1983 with a physics major. He then graduated from the University of Texas, U.S., where he studied astrophysics, and started working at the Japan Aerospace Exploration Agency (JAXA). He currently works as a translator for specialized literature. In 1999, Mr. Urano enrolled in Science Course 1 at the University of Tokyo's College of Arts and Sciences to study chemistry, with a major in molecular biology. Majoring in chemistry, which involves handling dangerous chemicals, is even more challenging than majoring in physics. Both students went into fields in which "the blind and sighted are equal," and both showed us that it is possible to Excel despite being completely blind.

At first, students think that this is just a dream, but when they hear more about the Mr. Yagi's and Mr. Urano's stories, it becomes more realistic, and they are motivated to do something to work on an equal footing with those who can see instead of relying on the sighted. I use this as a metaphor for career paths in general, but I will be happy if it was taken literally. I am very happy that Ms. Makoto Amakawa was motivated to pursue a career in physics.

Ms. Amakawa stated that she first became interested in studying physics in her second year of junior high school at the University of Tsukuba School for the Visually Impaired, after reading a book on relativity and the universe, and wanted to think about the world from a different perspective. She has been a hard worker since the time she was in junior high school. I taught her chemistry, and she wrote a detailed report for all experiments on her own.

She planned to study physics in university. She was afraid that it would be difficult to take the entrance examination at a school for the visually impaired due to its curriculum, so she joined a metropolitan high school that was a "Super Science High School" and provided excellent education in mathematics, science, and technology. For three years, she took on various challenges among sighted students, and her dream of becoming a researcher grew. As a result, she successfully passed the entrance examination of the School of Advanced Science and Engineering at Waseda University in 2019. Further, she went on to enroll in the university.

▶ Ms. Amakawa's support at the university was based on "pre-experiment"

I retired from the University of Tsukuba School for the Visually Impaired in 2019 after completing my re-appointment. The Waseda University's School of Advanced Science and Engineering asked the Department of Braille Transcription for Entrance Examinations of the National Association of Upper Secondary School Principals (hereinafter, the "Department of Braille Transcription for Entrance Examinations") for a specialist in education for the visually impaired to support Ms. Amakawa in experiments at the university. The Department of Braille Transcription for Entrance Examinations asked me, and I took the job without even a second thought.

My first suggestion to the university was to always conduct a "pre-experiment" with Ms. Amakawa before the day of the actual experiment. The purpose of this is to enable Ms. Amakawa to understand in advance what she can and cannot do on her own and prepare for the actual experiment. If I were suddenly asked to support her in an experiment, I would only be doing for her what she cannot do, and that will be meaningless.

The university readily accepted this suggestion, and we decided to conduct "pre-experiments" before each experiment. Before this "pre-experiment," I participated in a trace experiment for teaching assistants (hereinafter, TA: graduate students who assist in experiments), who support all students on the day of the experiment. Based on the outline of the experiment, I suggested experimental methods and apparatus that can be used/performed without relying on visual sense. For example, when handling liquid nitrogen, which is a hazardous substance, I suggested the use of bamboo tweezers to touch objects inside liquid nitrogen so that she can feel it. When students have to "see" an electron microscope, I suggested to ask the student to trace the monitor screen with her fingers. When making a tactile copy, I suggested to make lines thinner so that it will be easier to understand. The staff at the Technology Management Division accepted these suggestions readily. In addition, before each "pre-experiment," we put stickers on the labware and prepared a tactile copy of the labware so that she can touch them with her hand. Additionally, we borrowed a balance with a readout function from the University of Tsukuba School for the Visually Impaired and arranged for the Braille graph papers.

In these "pre-experiments," Ms. Amakawa, the TA, and I conducted experiments under the guidance of the staff at the Technology Management Division in charge of the experiment, and I encouraged Ms. Amakawa to confirm the flow of the experiment and position and use of experimental equipment and discussed difficult operations each time. We also repeatedly tried to convert "invisible" into "visible."

Naturally, there must have been a big gap between "blindness" and "experiments" for the people in the Technology Management Division. In the beginning, I had to take lead in designing experiments. However, the gap between the "blindness" and "experiments" gradually narrowed with each experiment. In the summer of 2019, four months after Ms. Amakawa enrolled, Waseda University provided the staff an opportunity to narrow that gap substantially. That is, they requested me to speak at a workshop about my experiments at the University of Tsukuba

School for the Visually Impaired. I believe that it is important for the people to experience something to be truly convinced. So, in September 10, 2019, I organized a workshop entitled "Science through the Five Senses." In Room 201 of Waseda University Building No. 57, about 80 people from the Technology Management Division worked in pairs to conduct three experiments (1) determining volume change in gases with one's fingertips, (2) investigating the heat of reaction without smelling (ammonia), and (3) blind and deaf students learning to generate gas by observing gas generation in a plastic pack. This workshop helped everyone understand the concept of "enjoying experiments with nonvisual senses" and made them realize that in this way, we can compensate for visual impairment and conduct experiments. Since then, more and more often, people in the Technology Management Division have come forward with ideas, without any prompting from my side. I thought to myself, "That's what being a professional technician is all about."

> ### ▶ Axes of support are "do everything you can" and "making visible what cannot be seen"

In summary, my evaluation of Ms. Amakawa in experiments is that she could gain experimental experience comparable to that of sighted students. As I mentioned earlier, the staff at the Technology Management Division, the TAs, Ms. Amakawa, and I conducted "pre-experiments" before actual experiments, which was an efficient way to "visualize" the "invisible" parts of an experiment.

However, the key factor that made this possible without delay was Ms. Amakawa's high "spatial perception." Once she was in the laboratory and after I had guided her to desks and lab equipment, she could picture the layout of the room in her mind. Further, when "pre-experiment" started, she instantly understood the position of laboratory equipment and tools. Furthermore, when she touched a piece of laboratory equipment to confirm its shape, she could memorize its details, such as the position of switches. All experiments were conducted on the basis of her high spatial perception.

Looking back on the three years of experiments, all of us, together with the staff of the Technology Management Division, tried to be innovative while asking ourselves the following questions. "Are there any alternative devices that can support operations that will be difficult or dangerous without sight?," "How can we avoid difficulties and dangers?," and "What operations does she have to perform by herself in experiments?" Briefly, we designed experimental methods based on the principle that "she will do everything she can do herself" and "if she cannot do something, we will think of alternative means." Some experiments were conducted in collaboration with classmates, but all experiments were basically conducted by Ms. Amakawa herself.

Let me explain using the example of an experiment called "Making a lens" (an experiment to verify the phenomena of light and properties of lenses and produce an aspherical lens) in the Basic Physics course.

In this experiment, Ms. Amakawa shared roles with her co-experimenter and did "what she could do" to the best of her ability. In the first half of the experiment, Ms. Amakawa encountered difficulty with respect to setting the angle of incidence of the laser light and reading the settings; therefore, her co-experimenter performed those tasks, and she calculated trigonometric functions using BrailleSense (a display device for document creation using a Braille keyboard). In the second half of the experiment, a nonspherical lens was fabricated by shaving an acrylic cylinder with a blade. However, using a blade without preparation can be dangerous. Therefore, the staff of the Technology Management Division used a 3D printer to create a plastic blade that cannot cut. During "pre-experiment," Ms. Amakawa used this alternative blade to identify dangerous points on the blade. This allowed her to handle the blade with confidence during the actual experiment.

Starting with this experiment, she conducted experiments by employing various innovative solutions, such as applying stickers to labware to identify scales and points, using a light probe so that changes can be read by sound, preparing a tactile copy of the graph to read by hand, and making support equipment.

In fact, these methods were an upgrade of the experimental methods employed at the University of Tsukuba School for the Visually Impaired as Ms. Amakawa had acquired the basics of these methods during her junior high school days.

> ### Foundation of "experiments for the visually impaired"
> ▶ **— Experience at the University of Tsukuba School for the Visually Impaired**

When visually impaired people conduct experiments, it is important for them to (1) recognize what they cannot see using senses other than sight and (2) understand and grasp risks involved in experiments. Experiments performed at Waseda University were prepared following these two points.

As mentioned earlier, Ms. Amakawa had already acquired the basics of these skills during her junior high school. Let me introduce these experiments here,

(1) Visual impairment is compensated by other sensory functions

The first example is the first experiment conducted in the first year of junior high school, namely, "Matter and Object," (an experiment to learn about materials around us) in which "hands are made to thoroughly touch so that they become 'eyes'" and "an alternative device (light probe) is used for invisible parts."

Students were given a milk carton, a plastic bottle, a glass bottle, an aluminum can, and a steel can and asked, "All five are beverage containers, but what is their difference?" Students then responded that "materials may be different." We explained to students that "things that exist in a concrete form are called 'objects,' and their materials are called 'substances'"; further, we handed each of the five types of substances shaped into a "board" to students. We let them touch it carefully and asked questions, such as, "what happens if you try to bend it?," while letting them feel the difference between each material. After touching a thick glass board, if students commented that glass is hard and cannot be broken, we would give them a thin cover glass and let them experience firsthand that glass can be broken when pressure is applied to it.

When students touch the five types of "boards" one after the another, some of them, who can see little light, sometimes notice that "the aluminum can is not transparent, but the plastic bottle is transparent." Then, we let everyone check the degree of "transparency" using a light probe. Specifically, when a "board" with the attached light probe is moved from the black desk to the white paper, audio changes from a low to a high if the board is transparent. Meanwhile, the sound does not change if the "board" is not transparent, thereby indicating the degree of transparency through the sound change.

To teach students that metal conducts heat easily and stretches when struck, we ask them to strike a copper wire with a hammer. After striking the copper wire and stretching it, we let students touch the object again, and they always say, "It's warm." Only those who could experience through practice can understand that temperature. That is what "doing" means.

(2) "Lighting a fire using a match" is not scary when safety is considered

The second example is "using a match to light a Bunsen burner," which teaches safety considerations. There is zero risk if the experiment is conducted by the teacher alone and if the experiment and phenomena are conveyed to those who cannot see through "live commentary." However, this does not convey the true content and excitement of the experiment. My approach is to teach them of dangers involved, where dangers lie, and how to avoid them so that they can experience the experiment. Fire is dangerous for the visually impaired, but it can be avoided if they can anticipate danger and respond appropriately.

First, let us discuss how to light a match. We prepare a tool that we call a "match striker," which is a sticker with the striking surface (the part that ignites matches) attached to a soap holder (a suction cup for fixing the soap). and use it for lighting match. By attaching this match striker to a desk and striking a match, even those who cannot see can safely light a fire.

They light a match, hold the matchstick vertically using their dominant hand with the lit end up, and hold their other hand over the fire (fire will go out after a while). Students understand that "when fire burns, flame and heat spread upward" by experiencing firsthand that while the dominant hand holding the matchstick is closer to the fire, the hand that feels hot is the one that is held over the matchstick. In addition, we teach them that "If you hear about a fire, run downstairs as soon as possible. Never run upstairs because the fire will spread there."

Even more important is learning how to discard a lit matchstick. We tell them to throw away matches into a container filled with water and teach them that "If you put the lit end down, the hand holding the matchstick will be burnt; therefore, you should lay the matchstick horizontally on its side so that flame is not under your hand. Hence, place it on the edge of the container, and then release it."

Close the main valve of a Bunsen burner, disassemble it, and have students touch and carefully observe each part. Then, we explain each part and have students understand its function and mechanism before practicing ignition. The amount of gas emitted and state of air mixing can also be judged by sound.

During this experiment, students sometimes shout "hot" or "ouch," but I believe it is important for them to experience these dangers as well. When it feels "hot," we tell them to cool it. We teach them to quickly reach for the water supply, twist the faucet, and cool the affected area with water. Students listen carefully to warnings and have been so careful and attentive during the experiment that in 18 years, only two or three students have actually experienced "heat" or "pain." When it feels "hot," or chemicals splash on the students' hands, the experiment is conducted in a position where a faucet can be easily reach.

To reiterate, even completely blind people can perform experiments without problems if they take safety precautions. I don't think it was flattery when the staff in the Technology Management Division at Waseda University complimented Ms Amakawa, saying, "she is better at using a Bunsen burner than sighted students."

My "let them experience" principle and Waseda University's principle of "practical education" matched

Ms. Amakawa's spirit and physical memories of these experiments in junior high school were the basis of her experiments at Waseda University, Faculty of Science and Engineering.

I think the reason why we could successfully carry out these experiments was that we "allowed students with visual impairment to conduct experiments," which was the foundation of my educational philosophy, and it matched with the "practical education" component of the Waseda University's "spirit of practical learning" principle, which is the cornerstone of the Faculty of Science and Engineering.

My educational philosophy of "allowing students with visual impairment to conduct experiments" was developed when I was a teacher at the University of Tsukuba School for the Visually Impaired. This philosophy was founded on the practice of conducting experiments at the University of Tsukuba School for the Visually Impaired, which was started in 1970s by Mr. Yoshishige Hayashi (who later became a professor at the University of Toyama) and was extended by Ms. Yuko Toriyama (who later became a professor at the University of Tsukuba; see page 12). I became its third-generation advocate. I hope that students will learn "process to conclusion" and "enjoyable discovery" by actually conducting experiments, rather than by memorizing from textbooks. I hear that the principle of "practical education" followed at the Faculty of Science and Engineering, Waseda University, emphasizes the experience of using one's hands, seeing, investigating, and examining. Various experiments assigned to first- and second-year students will train them to move from "knowing" to "being able to do" what they learn in classrooms.

Although there are differences between junior high and high school education for the visually impaired and general university education, I, as a supporter, and the university faculty had the same educational methodology and we could move forward together with the same goal in mind.

This is a bit of a leap, but I think the challenge for visually impaired students is the same as for anyone else, which is to conduct experiments without taking any shortcuts. Even if science and technology become "cutting edge," if the foundation is not firmly in place, the cutting edge will collapse. Therefore, students should not just memorize chemical reaction formulas and be satisfied with that. They should conduct experiments to confirm chemical reactions with their five senses and understand them before moving on to the next step. I hope that the era of "emphasis on experience" will become reality for all of us.

3 Implications of Accepting the Visually Impaired Students at the Faculty of Science and Engineering, Waseda University

Yuji Takagi
Senior Director and Administrative Director of Administration and Technology Management Center for Science and Engineering, Waseda University
(Director of the Technology Management Division of the center at that time)

> ▸ **Ms. Amakawa's enrollment is the very raison d'etre of the university**

When we learned that Ms. Makoto Amakawa wanted to apply to Waseda University, we thought, "Waseda University will never decide that we cannot accept her." But at the same time, we also thought that although it will be a difficult task, "we, in the Technology Management Division, can provide laboratory education even to completely blind students," without having any solid evidence to back up our claim.

As you know, a university is an institution for academic research and higher education. Article 7, Paragraph 1 of the Basic Act on Education clearly states that the role of a university is to "contribute to the development of society by cultivating advanced knowledge and specialized skills, and comprehensively inquiring about the truth to create new knowledge in oder to broadly offer the fruits of these endeavors to society." Briefly, the raison d'être of a university is to contribute to society through its mission of education and research. If we say, "we cannot accept completely blind people because they are blind," the validity of our existence comes under question.

We must take necessary measures to ensure that completely blind students are not at a disadvantage in the entrance examination compared with other students, and if a student passes the examination, we must guarantee "fairness in education" by employing optimal methods, such as providing specialist support, so that the student can acquire academic learnings. We thought that these were natural steps to take considering a university's raison d'être.

At that time, the Act for Eliminating Discrimination against Persons with Disabilities required private universities, which are private businesses, to "provide reasonable accommodations to the extent that it is not too burdensome when a person with a disability conveys their need for such an accommodation (reasonable accommodation);" however, they were only required to make an effort. Nevertheless, instead of making it obligatory to comply with these requirements, we decided to actively accept them out of a "sense of mission" and a "passion for education" under a university's raison d'être.

After making the admission decision, I told the division director's committee, which comprised the directors of the university's staff divisions, "We ask for understanding and cooperation of everyone working in various divisions as there are few such cases in the world." I also reported on the progress in the subsequent supports offer to her, as well as in her learning at that time. There were no negative comments, and I believe that the entire staff understood and agreed with our position.

▶ Sense of mission among technical staff

Initially, we had to ask ourselves, "What is the disadvantage of Ms. Amakawa, who is completely blind, in laboratory education?" In the case of classroom lectures, it is a matter of understanding the contents of lectures. In experimental courses, she must operate, measure, and observe equipment, and there are limitations with respect to what a completely blind student can do. Therefore, we felt it was necessary to reconfirm what we want the student to learn and understand from experiments and the knowledge and skills we want them to acquire. The focus was to provide support in such a way that this objective would be satisfied.

I mentioned that we accepted Ms. Amakawa because of our "sense of mission" and "passion for education" under the university's raison d'etre; however, they are also linked to our motivation to "support her because there is probably no record of a completely blind student entering the Faculty of Science and Engineering at Waseda University, and this is a rare case in the world." Everyone became proactive and enthusiastic, saying, "This is an opportunity for us to offer our fullest support."

I was one of the people who made a toctile 3D model of the Waseda Science and Engineering's campus when Ms. Amakawa got enrolled in the university. Unlike high school, students in a university need to move from one building to another for classes. To help her understand the location of classroom buildings and the layout of classrooms, where students have to move frequently, I decided to make the 3D model. This was partly motivated by the fact that we had prepared a "tactile copier" that could prepare black lines and black dots in tactile shapes, and we wanted to try it. So, I drew a part of the science and engineering campus and showed the route from Building No. 56, where Ms. Amakawa's room was located to Buildings No. 52–54, where classrooms were located, along with the location and direction of the stairs in each classroom building. I also studied the basics of Braille, attached the building numbers in Braille to the model, and made the model in the size of a single A4 sheet of paper. I gave it to her, saying, "This may be unnecessary."

I was happy when she said, "Thank you very much." But the truth is, I enjoyed making it because "as a maker," I am driven by attaining small joy from making things.

These activities could be described as leisure-time activities, but the people in the Technology Management Division demonstrated these abilities in the field of experimentation.

▶ The Technology Management Division is a cross-faculty education and research support organization

The Technology Management Division of the Administration and Technology Management Center for Science and Engineering, which supported Ms. Amakawa in her experiments directly and indirectly, is a unique staff organization of the Faculty of Science and Engineering, Waseda University. To explain how it works, I will start with its history.

The Waseda University's Department of Science and Engineering was established in 1908 and was set up as an independent campus at its current location (Okubo, Shinjuku-ku, Tokyo) in 1967, during the later period of rapid economic growth. An increase in the number of students from approximately 1,200 to approximately 1,700 per academic year led to the establishment of "common laboratories" that could be used by multiple departments and the organization of more than 100 technical staff, who had previously been affiliated with different departments, into one group. A steering committee consisting of academic and technical staff from all departments that use the common laboratories was established for each laboratory, and since then, the technical staff has been assisting the academic staff in conducting experiments and practical training courses with a large number of students, which was the beginning of the current Technology Management Division. In other words, technical staff who previously belonged to laboratories of different departments were grouped into several "sections" and specialized in different fields, for example, the common laboratory of mechanical, chemical, or electrical sciences. Additionally, a training system was introduced to deepen their specialized knowledge and a system was developed for designing laboratory courses together with the academic staff for teaching actual experiments was developed.

In 2007, after the 40th anniversary of the independent campus, and just before the 100th anniversary of the founding of the Department of Science and Engineering, the department was divided and re-organized into three departments and graduate schools—Fundamental, Creative, and Advanced. The organization that promotes these independent and integrated educational and research activities is the Faculty of Science and Engineering. With more than 10,000 undergraduate and graduate students at the Faculty of Science and Engineering and with the academic field becoming more advanced and interdisciplinary, the purpose of this project was to take advantage of the larger scale of the university and number of students to achieve much higher development. As many of you may recall, the trisection of the existing science and engineering departments attracted a great deal of attention because it was extremely rare. Before re-organization, the staff, including that of the Technology Management Division, was re-organized as the Administration and Technology Management Center for Science and Engineering in 2005.

One of the important duties of the current technical staff is to provide students with an educational and research environment that enables them to link theory and practice in collaboration with the academic staff in the three departments of science and engineering (School of Fundamental Science and Engineering, School of Creative Science and Engineering, and School of Advanced Science and Engineering) and emphasize on practical "laboratory education" that allows students to touch things and experience phenomena as the starting point of education. For example, in the basic science and engineering experiments that must be performed by all first-year students in the three undergraduate schools, the technical staff that specializes in chemistry are in charge of chemistry experiments for the students of the chemistry department and other departments; similarly, the technical staff specializing in physics are in charge of physics experiments for students in all departments and in the physics department. In other words, the technical staff is a "cross-departmental, cross-disciplinary laboratory education group." We are closest to students to guide them. We offer support in diverse fields, including basic science and engineering, mechanical and material science, earth and environmental science, electrical science, electronics and telecommunications, chemistry and physics, and life sciences.

Currently, there are about 100 technical staff working full-time and part-time in the center. Some are new graduates, while others are former graduates who have worked in corporate laboratories or manufacturing sites, and they are aged 20s to above. What we all have in common is a high level of "educational passion" based on our "love of experiments" and "joy in helping others grow." All of us are eager to take on any challenge and are passionate about passing on our wisdom to future generations.

Although the academic staff are in charge of experimental courses, the technical staff support them in developing the contents of laboratory education and providing detailed instructions at laboratories. In these roles, everyone involved became very proactive because they considered it as their mission to accept Ms. Amakawa.

I believe that the Waseda University's traditions make the Technology Management Division what it is. These traditions are "Independence of Scholarship," "Practical Application of Scholarship," and "Fostering of Good Citizens," which were adopted as its educational philosophy by the then President Shigenobu Okuma at the 30th anniversary celebration of the founding of Waseda University in 1913. To instill a spirit of independence and self-reliance, to conduct scientific education and research uninfluenced by authorities or current trends, to make practical use of learning, as well as to produce global citizens who have a rich sense of humanity are also the goals of the Technology Management Division. I envision that a large number of students will grow through interactions with the faculty and staff. We train students to go from "understanding" and "knowing" through academic study to "being able to do" in practice. I want to add that thorough practical education, in which the Technology Management Division plays a key role, is the lifeline of the Faculty of Science and Engineering.

4 We Learned with Her

Takafumi Jigami

Manager of Education and Research Support Section (4th section), Technology Management Division of the Administration and Technology Management Center for Science and Engineering, Waseda University
(Manager of Education and Research Support Section (1st section) at the time)

▶ Ms. Amakawa's determination motivated me

I first met Makoto Amakawa on the day of the entrance examination for the School of Advanced Science and Engineering at Waseda University in February 2019. I was in charge of the room where the staff of the Department of Braille Transcription for Entrance Examinations, National Association of Upper Secondary School Principals was transcribing examination questions into Braille and her answer sheets in Braille back into written Japanese. Since December of the previous year, we had been preparing for the Ms. Amakawa's entrance examination and her enrollment and had formed an image of what type of person she would be. I still remember the time when I went to visit Ms. Amakawa during the examination in between transcribing the exam into Braille.

The number of papers required for transcribing exam questions into Braille was three to four times the usual amount. She was reading questions with her fingers and then typing her answers on the Braille typewriter with determined finger movements. Unlike normal PC keyboards, Braille typewriter keys are quite loud. I was overwhelmed by the sight of her, making noises as she typed out answers with all her energy, and I thought to myself, "I will do my best to support this student once she joins the University." Of course, at that point, we could not know whether she would pass or fail or whether she would enroll.

My image of 18-year-old Ms. Amakawa was "a visually impaired person who wanted to pursue a science career," So, she voluntarily entered a metropolitan high school and worked hard to achieve this goal. I think, I was impressed because, behind the typewriter, I sensed perseverance that far exceeded what we could have imagined. As she read, solved, and drafted her answers for the entrance exam questions, I was in awe of her drive, passion, and effort. In other words, as I witnessed her "drive," "passion," and "effort," I felt a strong desire to do my best to create an environment in which she can learn to the fullest at our university. I think that her efforts on the day of the entrance exam ignited a fire in my heart.

▶ Boundaries between people with and without disabilities

I had never interacted with people with disabilities until I met Ms. Amakawa. Perhaps, because of this, I was only vaguely aware that there was a "boundary" between the worlds of able-bodied and people with disabilities—a world that we know of and a world that we don't know of.

However, I had never really been aware of this basic information. Although I knew that "normalization" means creating an environment in which people with disabilities are considered equal to able-bodied people and that their lives and rights are guaranteed, it was just theoretical knowledge. I did not know how to go back and forth between "here," the perspective I have and "there," the perspective that people with disabilities inhabit. However, through interacting with Ms. Amakawa, we unexpectedly connected with people who we thought inhabited the "other" world in the academic environment of Waseda Science and Engineering. As I got to know Ms. Amakawa better with Basic Experiments in Science and Engineering, I began to think that it might be wrong to distinguish between "here" and "there." The sense that there was something wrong grew with time, and I began to think that "here" and "there" are not separate, and the reason I thought of them as separate was because I was thinking too much from the "here" side.

▶ Tremendous performance with just a little support

I mentioned at the beginning that I was impressed by Ms. Amakawa's hard work on the day of the entrance examination. As I got to know Ms. Amakawa better after she enrolled in the university, I saw her hard work up close. I played the role of coordinator, transcribing text into Braille for experiments and organizing trace experiments, pre-experiments, and actual experiments for each experiment.

We, the technical staff, worked for three years to enable Ms. Amakawa to conduct experiments in Basic Experiments in Science and Engineering 1A and 1B in the first year, Experiments 2B in the second year, and Experiments in Applied Physics A (her elective) in the third year. It was challenging to redesign experiments in such a way that she could "see" and "perform" with her tactile and auditory senses instead of the visual sense (see Part 3 for how each experiment was addressed).

Most of the support she needed was for performing experiments. She performed some experiments with the support of others, while some other operations, she did by herself, such as analyzing and simulating experimental data and summarizing results in reports and other documents. She answered oral examinations on experiments satisfactorily. Her performance in most of these steps was comparable to those of other students, and my impression of her was that Ms. Amakawa had a good understanding of the theory underlying experiments. She was no different from other students, except the fact that she was completely blind. She could attain the same goals as other students or even exceed them with the support of those around her. Because of her accomplishments, I realized that there are no boundaries separating a sighted person from a visually impaired one. I also realized the obvious fact that she was a student first and a visually impaired person second. Hence, I believe that Ms. Amakawa had allowed us to achieve deeper recognition.

▶ What I learnt from Ms. Amakawa

Ms. Amakawa brought fresh perspective to our laboratory education. I realized once again that the academic staff, technical staff, and other instructors use many demonstrative pronouns, such as "that," "this," and "those," in the classroom without even thinking about them. When we reviewed how Ms. Amakawa executed experiments, we could determine the essential parts of experiments and organize our minds by considering parts of experiments that were important and necessary for Ms. Amakawa to focus on to achieve her goals. Moreover, explanatory materials we normally use contained numerous figures and tables and were entirely dependent on visual perception. When we read them aloud, we realized how much we rely on students' visual understanding even in our regular classes. This made us understand the importance of using appropriate words to communicate.

It is better not to use demonstrative pronouns to convey contents correctly even when talking to sighted people. Of course, usual explanatory materials and their oral and accurate presentation made us very conscious of the essence of what we wanted to teach in class. We now apply these insights to our regular laboratory education.

In addition, I participated in off-campus events and workshops related to education for the visually impaired, such as "Jump to Science" (a workshop for visually impaired junior- and high-school students), "Inclusive Academia Project" (a research project organized by the Research Center for Advanced Science and Technology at the University of Tokyo), and "Sight World" (an exhibition specializing in supporting the visually impaired), as much as I could to understand if such event help, the technical staff, for supporting visually impaired students in any way. By participating in these events, I learned that education for the visually impaired is advancing slowly and that the world of people with disabilities is not too different from the world of the able-bodied and is not a special world.

This is entirely a personal issue, but in 2022, I became a volunteer guiding runners in the blind marathon (marathon for the visually impaired). Had I never known Ms. Amakawa, I would never have been interested in such activities.

Lastly, my encounter with Ms. Amakawa has given me more opportunities to search for information related to the visually impaired. For example, new business opportunities could be explored with respect to customizing devices for the visually impaired that were developed for the general public with a little creativity and developing technologies that increase real-world accessibility and quality of life for the visually impaired.

Through the researchers themselves are unaware of it, numerous researches conducted at various universities could create something that would be more convenient for people with disabilities with addition of a few more ideas. It is important for the university to become aware of such seeds of resources, explore their possibilities of their usage, and connect them with places where such technology is needed. This is true for Waseda University and other universities and research institutes in Japan and around the world. I hope that new technologies are being developed through this new awareness of researchers. I learned a lot from my interactions with Ms. Amakawa, and I am grateful for having met her.

5 Ms. Amakawa from the Viewpoint of the Academic Staff

Takuro Katsufuji
Professor, Department of Physics, School of Advanced Science and Engineering/Department of Pure and Applied Physics, Graduate School of Advanced Science and Engineering, Faculty of Science and Engineering, Waseda University

▶ **Ms. Amakawa's admission process went smoothly**

I first heard that Ms. Makoto Amakawa, a visually impaired person, was interested in applying to the School of Advanced Science and Engineering at Waseda University at the faculty meeting of the Physics and Applied Physics Departments in December 2019. It was mentioned that she wanted to enter the Department of Physics or Department of Applied Physics. I remember thinking that theoretical physics may be an appropriate choice for a visually impaired person because it does not require experiments.

In the faculty meetings, one of the faculty members told us about the remarkable achievements of two visually impaired people.

One was Dr. Chieko Asakawa, Director of the National Museum of Emerging Science and Innovation (Miraikan) and an IBM Fellow, the highest technical position at IBM. She earned her doctorate from the Graduate School of Engineering, University of Tokyo, and in 1997, she developed the world's first practical voice-based web browser "Home Page Reader," which reads text information on the web aloud. She also worked on a suitcase-shaped autonomous robot called "AI Suitcase."

The other was Prof. Lev Pontryagin, a Russian mathematician. He graduated from Moscow State University and received the Lenin Prize, Stalin Prize, and USSR State Prize for his numerous mathematical achievements, including the development of the theory of topology.

"If there have been universities that accept completely blind persons, then Waseda University will can do the same." Optimistic, perhaps, but "we will accept Ms. Amakawa." became consensus among faculty members.

▶ Securing the support she needs after entering university

Preparation for providing her support was led by the members of the Academic and Student Affairs Section, and we, the academic staff, followed the instructions and schedule given by them. As an academic staff in charge of laboratory courses in the Advanced School of Science and Engineering, which Ms. Amakawa was about to enroll in, my first involvement was a visit with our technical staff to the University of Tsukuba School for the Visually Impaired that she joined prior to the university. We learnt about two important tools that enable us to support people with visual impairments there.

The first is Braille. At first, we thought that it would be more efficient to use a speech-to-text conversion tool to read written materials, but we learned that Braille is the most appropriate tool because, with Braille, it is easy to re-read parts of a text that have already been read, which is not easy with speech-to-text conversion tools. Therefore, we decided to transcribe all classroom textbooks and laboratory manuals into Braille.

The second is TeX, which is a text-formatting system created by computer scientist Donald Knuth. TeX was not developed for the visually impaired, but for a sighted person, and it has been widely used since the days when regular writing software could not write complex mathematical formulas. This turned out to be an effective tool for the visually impaired to communicate mathematical formulas. A professor in the mathematics department volunteered to teach her how to use TeX so that all professors in the Ms. Amakawa's class can provide her text with complete mathematical formulas.

During our visit to the University of Tsukuba School for the Visually Impaired, we met Ms. Shizuko Hamada. She gave us insights into education provided at the school and enthusiastically spoke about how serious and studious Ms. Amakawa was when she was a student there in the junior high school. At that time, we came up with the idea of asking Ms. Hamada to support us in laboratory courses.

The laboratory courses, which had originally been designed for sighted students, had to be re-designed so that they could be conducted by Ms. Amakawa on her own. The technical staff were creative in their efforts. Usually, for each experiment, one research associate and two teaching assistants (TAs) teach 40 students, but we decided to assign another TA only for Ms. Amakawa.

▶ Ms. Amakawa showed us what students should do

I want to share two instances involving Ms. Amakawa after she entered Waseda University.

The first is from a professor who taught her first class. Ms. Amakawa was given materials that had been transcribed into Braille for her to study before the class. After the class, the professor asked Ms. Amakawa, "How was the class?" Ms. Amakawa replied, "I understood very well as it was the same as what I had read beforehand."

The professor said "She did nothing special, she had read the material given to her before the class and came prepared. She reminded me of what students should do."

The other instance took place during the COVID-19 pandemic when she was in her second year. During the pandemic, all classes were conducted online, and we prepared lecture materials for online classes. Additionally, we conducted a make-up class for Ms. Amakawa because we were afraid that she was at a disadvantage compared with other students in online classes. Back then, one of my colleagues asked her, "Did you find anything difficult?", and he was surprised when she pointed out materials that lacked clarity and were even inadequate. This again showed us that she took her classes seriously and prepared for them well. Of course, her suggestions improved the class.

I too encountered a similar situation. In her third year, she took a laboratory course where after completing each experiment, she has to give an oral exam with other students.

Actually, students were given a 20-page document to read in advance, and most questions in the oral exam were related to the content presented in the first two or three pages of the document. Nevertheless, many students could not answer my questions.

However, Ms. Amakawa answered all questions and asked me, "Is this answer really OK?" as if she was suspicious because my questions were too easy. I told her, "Of course it is OK, but remember, that other students could not answer."

Thus, Ms. Amakawa showed us what students are supposed to do—prepare for class, take class seriously, and review after class. Ms. Amakawa reminded us of the importance of allowing students who have not done so to do so.

▶ Three advices for accommodating visually impaired people

In the spring of 2023, Ms. Amakawa graduated from the undergraduate school with excellent grades. Ms. Amakawa's admission to Waseda University became one of the successful cases of a completely blind person studying science- and engineering-oriented courses including laboratory courses. We had decided to accept Ms. Amakawa after learning about Dr. Chieko Asakawa and Prof. Lev Pontryagin, and in a similar manner, Ms. Amakawa's case may serve as a good example for other universities that are considering the enrollment of visually impaired students in the future. I want to give three advices to such universities.

(1) Administrative staff should take the lead

There is no chain of command within the academic staff at universities. Therefore, I think that it is difficult for the academic staff to take the lead on a project like this one, but the administrative staff should take the lead. In this respect, Waseda University had good administrative staff and technical staff, who worked together to build a relationship based on trust. This led to the successful completion of the project.

(2) Multiple points of contact between students and schools

Universities are an organization that comprises numerous people helping each other. Therefore, it is desirable to provide multiple points of contact to students. If there is only one staff member that acts as the point of contact and a student does not get along with that person, it may be difficult to receive full support.

If there are multiple staff members that serve as a point of contact, it is possible to get help from an appropriate person at any time.

(3) Classes that students with disabilities can understand are easy for able-bodied students to understand

As mentioned above, we had many opportunities to hear from Ms. Amakawa about laboratory courses and classroom lectures. Many of the things she pointed out to us as being "difficult to understand" had been assumed by us as being "obvious." I believe that careful examination and improvement of these points will lead to the better education of not only impaired students but also other students. Ms. Amakawa provided us such insights.

We hope that universities that decide to accept visually impaired students will use our experience as a guide and provide them with a better education.

6 They Let Me Experience All Experiments — What I Learned from It

Makoto Amakawa
Laboratory of Cosmology, Graduate School of Advanced Science and Engineering, Waseda University

> ▶ Admitting "a visually impaired person in a science course" with few precedents

I became interested in astrophysics when I was in junior high school. My interest was initially triggered by fantasy; however, after reading various books on the subject, my interest in physics grew and I began to think, "To understand the vastness of the universe, I must also know about things at a very small scale, such as elementary particles, and it is physics that reveals everything."

At that time, I remember that Ms. Shizuko Hamada and other teachers at the University of Tsukuba School for the Visually Impaired encouraged me by saying, "Even sighted people cannot see things on a very large or very small scale, so visual impairment is not a handicap in this field."

I chose a career in science because I wanted to conduct such type of research at university.

When I applied to the School of Advanced Science and Engineering at Waseda University, I had assumed that I would have to conduct experiments as it is a science major. But, it was after my enrollment that I learned that a total of 22 basic science and engineering experiments were be performed in the first and second years. There are few visually impaired students in the science field, and I was the first in Waseda University.

Speaking of experiments, when I was a student at the Junior High School of the University of Tsukuba School for the Visually Impaired, I performed experiments arranged for visually impaired students, and I loved doing experiments since then.

However, in high-school experiment classes, a science teacher who had time to spare, often sat next to me and verbally explained the experiment; this method was quite effective. However, I wanted to experience for myself the university experiments, which are more advanced than high-school experiments, because there is something to learn by conducting the process myself.

I was concerned about the kind of support I will get for all required experiments, given the lack of precedent for visually impaired students in the science field. Thankfully, these pre-admission fears were unfounded.

Before admission, my high-school teachers and I had a discussion with the university staff regarding the Braille transcription of teaching materials, campus mobility assistance, the use of TeX (a document formatting program), and a special room for storing Braille teaching materials. Around that time, it was also decided that Ms. Hamada would be appointed as a supporter during experiments. I am thankful for the strong support system the university put in place.

▶ Conduct the same experiments as other students using a bit of ingenuity

I mentioned that I liked experiments since my junior high school days at the University of Tsukuba School for the Visually Impaired, but experiments in the junior high-school level are drastically different from those at the university level. The experiments at the University of Tsukuba School for the Visually Impaired are designed in such a way that they can be conducted by visually impaired students. However, the university experiments are designed for sighted students, so it was necessary to find creative ways for a completely blind person to operate, measure, and observe. In other words, modifications had to be made so that I can use tactile, auditory, and other nonvisual senses instead of the visual sense during experiments.

I don't think it was easy to be creative. I thought that I would have to conduct some experiments by listening to a verbal explanation of the procedure as if it were a "live broadcast," as I did in my high-school laboratory classes. However, thanks to the ingenuity and consideration of the staff at the Technology Management Division and Ms. Hamada, I did not have to perform a single experiment that way, and I am grateful that I could conduct all experiments by myself with some modifications, such as using support equipment.

In the first year, basic science and engineering experiments span four classes (6 h) from the second to the fifth classes. The Braille transcription of the text describing the experiment would arrive two weeks before the experiment, and I spent as much time as I could to prepare for the experiment. I believe that a sighted student could understand the arrangement and use of laboratory equipment just by looking at it on the day of the experiment. But that was not possible for me, and I am handicapped in the process of experiments.

For this reason, they dedicated two or three sessions (3–4.5 h) beforehand to conduct a "pre-experiment" for me. I heard that they conducted a "trace experiment" with Ms. Hamada before each pre-experiment, and that pre-experiments were designed based on her suggestions. The staff at the Technology Management Division and Ms. Hamada identified key points in each experiment and then arranged various things, such as "using a quantitative pipette," "using a light probe," "putting a sticker on the scale of the experimental equipment," "cutting an incision in a syringe," etc. before pre-experiments. For some experiments, during pre-experiments, it became clear that further arrangements were required; these were added during the actual experiment. Although the schedule was tight, pre-experiments allowed me to deepen my understanding of the experiment through preparatory study.

Thanks to the support of the staff at the Technology Management Division and Ms. Hamada, all experiments went smoothly and I achieved the required results. However, because I am visually impaired, in some cases, it took me a lot of time to do things that a sighted person could have done more easily. The actual experiments were conducted by two people—me and a co-experimenter. I was often in charge of recording data, but when I used a voice reader to input data and manipulate the respective spreadsheet, it took even more time. For example, when converting a graph into a tactile chart, if the units indicated on the vertical and horizontal axes were written in Kanji, Ms. Hamada would have to convert them into Braille before making a tactile chart, which increased the experimental time. Support equipment that are currently available has limitations, and although it was unavoidable, I felt guilty with respect to burdening my co-experimenter.

> ▶ **Experiment shows the process of arriving at a result**

Experimental results are provided in textbooks. Therefore, some people may say that performing experiments is not necessary as we already know their results. However, I think it is important to conduct experiments with your own hands so that you can understand the "process" of reaching a conclusion. Here are four representative examples of many things that I learned through touch.

(1) Example 1 : Microscopic Observation of Cells

Experiments involving microscopes had the biggest impact on me.

This was in the experiment titled "Microscopic Observation of Cells" in basic life science. In this experiment, animal cells had to be observed under various microscopes to learn the cell structure. To do this, we had to learn the characteristics of these microscopes. They modified the process for me by connecting the microscopes to a PC so that the CCD camera image projected on the microscope was digitized and displayed live on the monitor, which I could then trace with my fingertips. I had already learned what a cell is, so it was not the experiment itself that impressed me but the operation of microscopes that had the greatest impact.

I had never used a microscope before, and this was the first time I had actually touched one. The conceptual diagram of the microscope that I had studied in my mind, in other words a merely abstract concept I learnt verbally, better as more tangible entity by actually touching each part of the microscope, including the cover lens, slide lens, lens barrel, stage, and reflector. I was so impressed that I could understand how a microscope work as if I were holding it in my hands, such as how light shines on the observed object, how the transmitted or reflected light is magnified by an objective lens, and the eyepiece.

(2) Example 2 : Synthesis of Nylon

The second example, which had a great impact on me, was when I had to make an object during the experiment. In the beginning of the first year, we had to synthesize nylon 66 and nylon 6 in an experiment titled "Synthesis of Nylon" in basic chemistry. I vividly remember touching freshly made nylon threads, which were wet, and I was thrilled to learn the process by which they were made. The experimental text did not mention that freshly made nylon is "wet," and it was only by touching it that I was able to know how it felt.

(3) Example 3 : Electronic Circuit Workshop

The third example is the experiment called "Electronic Circuit Workshop" in basic physics. The experimental goal was to fabricate an unstable multivibrator (oscillation circuit) using components commonly used in electronic circuits, such as resistors, capacitors, light-emitting diodes, and transistors, and check its operation; however, it was difficult to construct a circuit by soldering. The staff at the Technology Management Division prepared a very easy-to-understand breadboard for this purpose. The circuit was constructed by assembling each component with a lead leg in a grid pattern, and I could then check the components of the circuit by touching them with my hands.

(4) Example 4 : Logic Circuit

The fourth example is an experiment called "Logic Circuits" in applied physics. For this experiment, I had to use a special logic circuit laboratory apparatus and follow a circuit diagram to connect numerous components and terminals arranged on the apparatus surface using lead wires. They provided me an experiment manual that contains a diagram of the layout of the components used in the experiment as well as other ingenious solutions, such as covering the components of my logic circuit training device that were not used in the experiment with plastic panels to reduce the amount of information on the components and terminals and make it easier to locate those to be used by hand, taping symbols made of wire for logic components on the panels, and attaching the names of components in Braille. In this experiment, I had the real experience of touching a wire that indicated the name of the logic component.

> ▶ **Experience gained from experiments is the basis of my current research**

The COVID-19 pandemic started in the spring of 2020, during my second year. After a state of emergency was declared, Waseda University started online classes, and experiments had to be conducted remotely. The staff at the Technology Management Division conducted experiments assigned to students, and students watched and learnt from the video recordings of the process on their home PCs. For me, understanding via this format was impossible. Because of the university policy, only the first eight weeks of classes in the fall semester were conducted in person and the remainder of the semester was conducted remotely. My course, Basic Experiments in Science and Engineering 2B, was in the fall semester, but the university made a special arrangement (so that I would not be at a disadvantage and could understand the course as well as other students) to allow me to commute to the university after the ninth week and attend laboratory classes in person. I am very grateful for this arrangement. I was also thankful that they reduced the length of pre-experiment in the first year from 2–3 sessions (3–4.5 h) to 1–2 sessions (1 and 1.5–3 h) because I was getting used to experiments in the second year and the number of reports I had to submit became very large because of the remote nature of nonexperimental classes.

Even during my third year, when there were no compulsory laboratory courses, I chose Experiments in Applied Physics A as an elective and conducted six experiments in the fields of physical chemistry and electricity.

Thanks to these experiments, I successfully graduated from the undergraduate program in the spring of 2023, and I am now pursuing a master's degree in cosmology. I am currently studying dark matter in our laboratory; although its existence is confirmed via observations, its true nature is yet to be discovered.

The experience of reading graphs and data comparisons in Braille or printed out as tactile copies for different experiments during my undergraduate days provided a foundation for computer simulations that I am currently conducting. I can say with confidence that the laboratory classes I took as an undergraduate student were very useful.

In addition, those laboratory classes allowed me to understand the "process" of reaching a conclusion—an experience that I would not trade for anything. I believe that this experience will come in handy in many ways in the future.

Part 2

Background,
Summary and Issues
in the Entrance
Examination to
Technical Assistance

1 Entrance Examination Process

A group e-mail asking "Please make reasonable accommodation for a completely blind student taking the exam"
Everyone vaguely understood that "the admission of visually impaired students cannot be refused"

"A completely blind student named Ms. Makoto Amakawa wishes to take the entrance examination for the School of Advanced Science and Engineering. Please make reasonable accommodations for the entrance exam and admission."

This was the first e-mail that we received on this subject at the Technology Management Division of the Administration and Technology Management Center for Science and Engineering (hereinafter, the Technology Management Division) on December 11, 2018. The Admission Center of Waseda University contacted the Admission Office of the School of Advanced Science and Engineering, which sent a group e-mail to the executive staff of the School of Advanced Science and Engineering (including the dean and the associate dean) and other relevant staff, including the Technology Management Division.

We received many requests for consideration from prospective students every year on entrance examination. For example, requests for a single room or a separate room close to a bathroom, and we consider each request on an individual basis. In accordance with the guidelines of the Ministry of Education, Culture, Sports, Science and Technology (MEXT), we extended the duration of the examination for students with severe developmental disabilities and doubled the font size on examination papers for students with poor vision.

Under these circumstances, We think everyone vaguely understood that overall, there is no option to refuse the admission of completely blind people. However, we did realize that there was a possibility that she may not pass even if she took the examination or that she may not enroll in Waseda university even if she passed.

Experiments are designed to be "visible"
Some were puzzled, saying, "Is it realistic?"

The words "reasonable accommodation" in the group e-mail were firmly etched in the minds of those who received it. It indicated that when a person with a disability communicates that they require some kind of accommodation, accommodation should be provided to the extent that it is not too burdensome.

Following the ratification of the United Nations Convention on the Rights of Persons with Disabilities in 2014, the Act for Eliminating Discrimination Against Persons with Disabilities, which aims to "eliminate discrimination based on disability and realize a society in which everyone can live together without discrimination," came into effect in 2016 in Japan; the Act prohibits "discriminatory treatment" and requires "reasonable accommodation." Although private universities were only required "to make efforts" at that time (it became a legal obligation only in 2021), the staff knew that the Waseda University Basic Policy for Supporting Students with Disabilities had been implemented in 2016 under the Act for Eliminating Discrimination Against Persons with Disabilities.

Waseda University Basic Policy for Supporting Students with Disabilities
Article 2: All members of the University shall work to eliminate discrimination on the basis of disability and to ensure that students with disabilities have an equal opportunity to participate in education and research as students without disabilities.
2 : The University will contribute to the realization of a harmonious society by providing an environment in which all students, regardless of disability, respect each other's position and learn from each other.
3: The University will support students with disabilities so that they can become productive and autonomous members of society.

However, the goal of the three schools of science and engineering at Waseda University (School of Fundamental Science and Engineering, School of Advanced Science and Engineering, and School of Creative Science and Engineering) is "practical education" that focuses on enabling students to actually touch things and experience phenomena. Regardless of the department they study in, students must complete basic experiments in a total of 22 subjects (i.e., 14 physics-related, 6 chemistry-related and 2 life science-related experiments) during their first year.

Naturally, all experiments are based on the premise of "vision." How can people without sight conduct these experiments? We had no idea.

We were quite puzzled at the Technology Management Division, wondering if it is too difficult to accommodate a completely blind person.

From confusion to a "sense of mission"
What can each division do for completely blind students?

This was the first time a completely blind student was taking the entrance exam of the Faculty of Science and Engineering. Not only the Technology Management Division, but the other divisions involved were also quite confused. However, it wasn't long before this confusion transformed into a positive desire to take on the challenge. Everyone's feelings changed to "even completely blind students should be able to get education at the Faculty of Science and Engineering." Then, we conducted a simulation with all staff members by putting ourselves in Ms. Amakawa's shoes and asked ourselves "What hurdles will we face when she enters the university? How can we overcome these hurdles?"

Once she passed the entrance examination and wished to enroll, we could never refuse. We started discussing about how to support her in laboratory courses under the assumption that she would pass the exam and enroll in the program. All divisions involved identified issues within their respective missions and thought about "what can we do?" for completely blind people.

The "think while you run" approach and "reasonable accommodation" by the Technology Management Division

We would like to add few words about the University's "reasonable accommodation" for students with disabilities.

Waseda University set up the Office for Students with Disabilities in 2006. The three Schools of Science and Engineering admit ~8–9 students with "special needs" every year. We understood that Ms. Amakawa, who is completely blind, was going to be a student with special needs and that "reasonable accommodations" we had to make for her would be the same as those for other students with special needs. However, as mentioned earlier, it is no exaggeration to say that we had to think about the situation realistically; it is difficult to accommodate her because it is very difficult to interpret "reasonable accommodation" or what falls within the scope of "not too burdensome." There are things that universities can and cannot do for budgetary and personnel reasons, and there are no clear answers with respect to what the scope should be.

In the absence of clear answers, everyone thought that "acceptance is our mission" because the attitude shifted to "think while running" and "find answers while running" by first taking action.

In the business world, there has been an attitude shift from a cautious "take time to think on various cases, formulate a strategy, and implement it," to a more bold approach of "formulate a rough strategy as a hypothesis, test the hypothesis, increase speed, and expand the scale." We can say that we adopted the latter approach.

Our mission was to ensure that Ms. Amakawa will not be at a disadvantage compared with other students in all laboratory courses and to guide her to success-fully complete her courses. I heard that many visually impaired students had given up and dropped out, so I was very keen to avoid such a situation from happening at Waseda University.

How do we go about designing her laboratory classes? In the beginning, we could not imagine what that would even look like.

December 18, 2018: Kickoff meeting to discuss challenges encountered by the Technology Management Division

The kickoff meeting on admittance took place on December 18, 2018, with participation from staff belonging to all related divisions, including the Technology Management Division; this occurred eight days after we received the first e-mail.

At this point, we had no knowledge regarding Ms. Amakawa's walking abili-ty, spatial awareness, or how she had studied up to that point, but we all agreed that the biggest challenge would be supporting her in the compulsory first-year courses. While there were some ideas regarding redesigning the general lecture courses, we had no idea about what to do for laboratory courses, such as how to support her in the first-year basic science and engineering experiments (22 experi-ments in total).

How can a completely blind person operate equipment and analyze data, which are essential steps in these experiments? Each experiment staff member identified issues to be addressed for each experiment subject and presented responses to issues at the meeting. These issues and responses are listed in Table 2-1.

Issues encountered in the laboratory courses can be summarized as follows:

- How to address "looking at a monitor or a microscope?"
- How do we conduct the "look-and-do" tasks?
- How to handle glassware?
- Should we let her use blades or not?

Meanwhile, there were additional issues that should be considered, such as

- Can she move around between classrooms inside a complex science and engineering campus by herself?
- What is the level of her spatial awareness and walking ability?

possible challenges in accessing facilities. It was agreed that all divisions would maintain detailed records and exchange information with each other.

December 27, 2018: Interview with the metropolitan high school to gather information for class support

At the time, the only information we had about Ms. Amakawa's background was that she was a third-year student at a Tokyo metropolitan high school and that she had attended junior high school at the University of Tsukuba School for the Visually Impaired. Our knowledge of "visually impaired people" was poor, and we could not imagine what daily life look like for such people or whether she had performed any scientific experiments in junior high or high school. We could not determine answers to these questions on the internet. For the first time, we became acutely aware of blocks installed at stations and on roads to guide the visually impaired, and we suddenly became concerned about them at the time.

At the time of the kickoff meeting, the entrance exam was less than two months away; so we acted quickly after that.

Initially, we conducted an interview with the metropolitan high school. On December 27, 2018, we visited the high school along with the administrative and academic staff.

This school has been designated as a "Super Science High School" by

Table 2-1 Issues the staff expected a completely blind student taking Basic Experiments in Science and Engineering 1A would face

Field	Subject	Expected Issues	Possible Response
Physics	Making a lens	Use machine tools to make an object (lens). Taking angle and focal length readings when a laser beam is incident on a prism. Caliper reading. Measuring the magnification of the fabricated lens. Creating graphs.	It is difficult for her to make a lens due to safety reasons. Additionally, a significant part of the experiment will be the responsibility of the co-experimenter; therefore, it is a concern whether or not she should be considered to have completed the experiment?
	Simulation of physical phenomena	Observing simulation. Draw lines by hand on the printed sheet from the wave experiment and estimate the angle of incidence and angle of refraction. Handwriting (free form) on the printed sheet.	Simulation has to be described by another person. Handwritten notes on a printed sheet (free form) may be input into the PC and printed out if she can do this.
	Electromagnetic Induction	Check the waveforms displayed on the monitor. Read numerical values on a printed sheet (waveform). Produce graphs.	The waveforms displayed on the monitor have to be explained by another person.
	Estimation of measurement uncertainty	During experiment, the assignment must be recorded in a notebook and inspected by a staff member. Produce graphs (with error bars).	What if the student could not record the assignment in her notebook during experiment?
	Electric guitar	Waveform observation using an oscilloscope. Produce graphs. Observing string vibration.	Is it possible to verbally explain differences between the waveforms displayed on the oscilloscope? The vibration of strings can be described to some extent by touching them.
	Capacitor design and radio reception	Waveform observation by an oscilloscope. Read micrometer values and adjust them to the values specified by the micrometer.	Is it possible to verbally explain what the waveform on the oscilloscope looks like?
	Oral examination	Examination will be conducted by the teacher while showing laboratory notes using a document camera. Prepare notes for examination.	Is it possible to conduct oral examination without preparing notes.
Chemistry	Water quality analysis	Difficult to conduct experiment. Assistance is needed for obtaining results (Observing changes in the color tone and reading out measured data). Assistance is needed to complete the report on time.	Assuming that experiment will be performed by the co-experimenter, we must determine whether the desired educational effect can be achieved by preparing a report based on the results of the experiment conducted by others.
	Extraction of caffeine	It will be very difficult to perform experimental manipulations involving the use of organic solvents and heating operations due to the safety risks involved. Expert assistance is needed for obtaining experimental results (reading balance values, observing shapes, and understanding TLC). Assistance is required to complete the report on time.	Assuming that experiment will be performed by the co-experimenter, we must determine whether the desired educational effect can be achieved by preparing a report based on the results of the experiment conducted by others.

Field	Subject	Expected Issues	Possible Response
Chemistry	Synthesis of nylon	Performing experimental manipulations involving heating operations will be extremely difficult due to the safety risks involved. Expert assistance is required to obtain experimental results (reading balance values and understanding IR). Assistance is needed to complete the report on time.	Assuming that experiment will be carried out by the co-experimenter, we must determine whether or not the desired educational effect will be achieved by preparing a report based on the results of the experiment made by others.
Life science	Microscopic observation of cells	Performing microscopic observations and sketching cells (individual work). Questions to be asked during the oral examination (no questions about observations, only about principles and phenomena).	We must determine whether the experiment should be considered complete only with the final oral examination, without microscopic observations and sketches that account for the majority of the experiment.
General		How to convert experiment manuals into Braille and record notes and data sheets and how should the staff confirm whether the graphs are created by the student? How to submit reports? How to distribute learning management system (LMS) materials transcribed into Braille?	Regarding confirmation by the staff, it is acceptable if it is judged via oral examination that the student understands the contents, except for the items in the report. LMS materials should not be downloaded, but handed directly to the student. All paper materials, such as texts, manuals, data sheets, and LMS materials, must be transcribed into Braille.

Issues the staff expected a completely blind student taking Basic Experiments in Science and Engineering 1B would face

Field	Subject	Expected Issues	Possible Responses
Physics	The physics of air hockey	Entering numerical data into an Excel sheet on a PC (PC operation). Creating graphs.	
	Heat and motion of gas molecules	Real-time graph reading of the measurement data displayed on the data logger (three lines are displayed simultaneously). Reading measured data, such as the internal volume of a cylinder. Operating a device that performs adiabatic compression is challenging because operation is performed while viewing the waveform data displayed on the data logger. Moreover, measurement requires the simultaneous operation of the PC and the device. Dangerous to touch because some equipment can become very hot (up to 100°C).	If she can operate the PC, the co-experimenter can operate equipment that performs adiabatic compression.
	Light and waves	Confirming colors when white light is spectrally divided via diffraction grating. Installing and adjusting cameras for taking photographs. Confirming the diffraction image using laser light. Using the PC to edit photographic images. Measuring the slit width using a microscope.	Equipment has to be adjusted to obtain experimental data (photography). It also plays a major role in the experiment. The co-experimenter could perform a significant portion of the work, including microscopic adjustments.
	Brownian motion	Recording the movement of Brownian particles using a pen on a plastic sheet attached to the monitor. Reading the position (coordinates) of particles recorded on the plastic sheet.	

Field	Subject	Expected Issues	Possible Responses
Physics	Measuring devices	Students must learn to use oscilloscopes, function generators, testers, and other instruments and pass a practical test arranged by the staff to complete the experiment. Creating a semi logarithmic graph.	Practical exams conducted on an individual basis require support, such as staff to explain waveforms displayed on the oscilloscope when the student performs operations. Extend the time limit (normally by 3 min)
	Electronic circuit workshop	Making a circuit using a soldering sheet. Creating graphs.	She cannot make circuits by soldering. Meanwhile, making circuits using a breadboard is possible, but it requires precise work, such as determining length in millimeters, and support.
	Presentation and discussion	Slides for the presentation must be prepared in Powerpoint (by all groups).	It is expected that the co-experimenters will largely handle the preparation of the Powerpoint slides. The presentation itself is possible as it is an oral presentation.
Chemistry	Atomic emission spectra	Difficult to conduct experiment. Expert assistance is needed to obtain results (spectrometer and spectrum readings). Assistance is required to complete the report on time.	Assuming that experiment will be carried out by the co-experimenter, we must determine whether the desired educational effect can be achieved by preparing a report based on the results of the experiment conducted by others.
	Synthesis of pharmaceuticals	Performing experimental manipulations that involve heating operations will be extremely difficult due to the safety risks involved. Expert assistance is needed to obtain results (reading balance values, observing shapes, understanding TLC, reading IR spectra). Assistance is needed to complete the report on time.	Assuming that experiment will be performed by the co-experimenter, we must determine whether the desired educational effect can be realized by preparing a report based on the results of the experiment conducted by others.
	Inclusion of a molecule into cyclodextrin	Difficult to conduct experiment. Expert assistance is needed to obtain results with respect to reading balance values, measurements, and structures from simulation. Assistance is required to complete the report on time.	Assuming that experiment will be carried out by the co-experimenter, we must determine whether the desired educational effect can be realized by preparing a report based on the results of the experiment conducted by others. Among assignments, screen sketches will be difficult to create.
Life science	Extraction and PCR amplification of DNA	Micropipette operation, DNA extraction from human oral epithelial cells, PCR, and electrophoresis (Is it possible to conduct experiment alone by not doing the individual work one part and having the co-experimenter proceed with the other parts of the experiment?)	We must determine whether the experiment should be considered complete only after conducting the final oral examination based on the experimental results heard from co-experimenters.
General		How to record in notes and datasheets and how to check graphs created by the staff? How to submit report items? How to distribute LMS materials transcribed into Braille?	Regarding confirmation by the staff, it is acceptable if it is judged via oral examination that the student understands the contents, except for the items in the report. LMS materials should not be downloaded but handed directly to the student. All paper materials, such as texts, manuals, data sheets, and LMS materials, must be transcribed into Braille.

MEXT as a high school providing excellent education in science, mathematics, and technology. Our visit to this school was nothing short of amazement. we were so impressed with the dedication of the staff that we wondered, "Does "reasonable accommodation" really offer so much?"

"I want to study at a higher level"
We were impressed by the "thickness" of Braille textbooks

When we visited the high school, we asked Ms. Amakawa's homeroom teacher about her academic abilities. We were told that Ms. Amakawa joined the high school because she "wanted to study at a higher level," even though many students from the junior high school of the University of Tsukuba School for the Visually Impaired continued in the same high school. We could see how eager Ms. Amakawa was to study at a higher level.

We were particularly surprised by the quantity of Braille textbooks. We looked at all Braille textbooks, and they were all very thick, with a huge number of pages. The English dictionary alone was about 1-m thick. It was obvious at first glance that this would increase many times over when transcribed into Braille. We also learned that the aforementioned Department of Braille Transcription for Entrance Examinations supported all Braille and written text transcriptions (transcribing Braille into non-Braille (written) characters) for entrance examinations and regular tests.

The Department of Braille Transcription for Entrance Examinations

We want to describe the functions of the Department of Braille Transcription for Entrance Examinations, which we learned during our visit to the metropolitan high school.

The Division for Entrance Examinations Using Braille System is an organization with an office at the University of Tsukuba School for the Visually Impaired. Below is the transcript of the interview with its Executive Director Akiyoshi Takamura.

"It was in 1970s that the visually impaired began to attend universities. At that time, Braille textbooks were produced mainly by Braille transcription volunteers (paid volunteers). These volunteers were well-educated housewives who wanted to do something useful for society and had time on their hands. Braille notation is created using the Japanese Braille System established by the Braille Authority of Japan and symbols and notations used in Braille textbooks for the visually impaired. However, some contents are difficult to represent using Braille, so experience and expertise in the subject matter are required. Braille transcription in the science courses is particularly difficult, and with the help of visually impaired university students, the staff could hone their skills.

After a long period of time, in the late 1980s, there was a growing movement to establish a Department of Braille Transcription for Entrance Examinations. The website of the Department of Braille Transcription for Entrance Examinations states, "Our main mission is to transcribe university entrance examination questions into Braille at the request of universities concerned to contribute to the resolution of various issues related to university entrance for the visually impaired in Japan. We have been active since 1990 to achieve this goal." The Division has been used by most universities and other institutions across Japan that require Braille transcription. We are affiliated with the National Association of Upper Secondary School Principals because we want to maintain our position as a voice in high-school education and other matters.

In addition to entrance examinations (second-stage examinations in national and private university examinations), we transcribe the following examinations into Braille and back into written text.

- University examinations (regular examinations)
- University entrance exam practice tests
- High-school entrance examinations
- Academic achievement tests administered by prefectures, etc.
- Various certification and qualification examinations
- Various employment examinations

The number of housewives who can engage in the volunteer work decreased because of the women's entry into the workforce since around 1990s. Since then, the number of new volunteer transcribers has not increased. Support for Ms. Amakawa could be provided by Braille transcription experts who had many years of experience before they retired."

Entrance Examination Process

2 From Entrance Examination to Admission

Department of Braille Transcription for Entrance Examinations supported the entrance examination

The entrance examination for the School of Advanced Science and Engineering was held on February 16, 2019.

It was conducted with the assistance of the Department of Braille Transcription for Entrance Examinations, which performed Braille and written-text transcriptions. The English, mathematics, and science (physics and chemistry) examination papers took a lot of time to transcribe into Braille, but the science examination papers (physics and chemistry) were especially difficult to transcribe into Braille because of the use of numerous specialized symbols.

The Braille transcription of physics and chemistry texts requires transcribing specialized expressions to conform to the rules of Braille transcription. For example, numbers, such as, 1, 2, 3, and 4, must be preceded by a "number sign" that indicates that "a number comes after the sign." A six-dot Braille expression without the number sign will be indistinguishable from an ordinary alphabet in some cases. There are various rules for the use of such number signs and their expressions. In the case of mathematical formulas, it is essential to use Braille transcriptions that match the rules of expression for each formula.

Chemical formulas are even more difficult to transcribe. For example, if "C_2H_6O" is written on a standard question paper, its meaning cannot be understood unless it is preceded with number signs "two C's," "six H's," and "one O" in Braille.

Braille transcription cannot be done mechanically; it requires meticulous and detailed effort.

The Department of Braille Transcription for Entrance Examinations is truly a professional group. The members of the Department of Braille Transcription for Entrance Examinations re-affirmed to us that "professionals are rewarded by guaranteeing the realization of accurate products through a long process and with much effort and manpower." After the exam, they transcribed all answers of Ms. Amakawa's into written texts, officially sealed the answer sheets, and the lengthy exam was over.

The number of people working in the Department of Braille Transcription for Entrance Examinations has been decreasing due to the aging population. Although IT has advanced, the automation of terminology has not progressed much. It is unreasonable to force a visually impaired person, who has learned using Braille and is accustomed to it, to switch to audio. As a team who has seen how well the Division for Entrance Examinations Using Braille System did Braille and written-text transcriptions, we hope that the techniques and know-how of the Braille transcribers will be passed on to future generations and that a time will come when this work can be automated.

Visit to International Christian University, which accepted a visually impaired student 35 years ago
Documents were old, and no one knew about the case

After the completion of the entrance examination, we again thought to ourselves, "We hope that Ms. Amakawa passes the entrance examination and enrolls in our university." We think that this was because we saw how dedicated she was on the day of the entrance examination.

On February 26, ten days after the entrance examination, the results were announced, and we learnt that Ms. Amakawa had passed.

However, we also learned that she had been accepted into other universities. We did not know whether she would choose Waseda University. However, if we had waited until the confirmation of her enrollment, we would not have been ready. Therefore, we began preparations for her admission under the assumption that she would enroll.

On February 26, we visited International Christian University (hereinafter, ICU) because it had accepted a completely blind student in the Physics Department of its Faculty of Science in 1983. The delegation was led by the Support Office for Students with Disabilities. The Technology Management Division also joined.

ICU is a Christian liberal arts university that provides education to a small group of students, unlike Waseda University, which caters to a large number of students. No completely blind student had been admitted to the science department since 1983; however, completely blind students have been admitted to the liberal arts department, and every year, people with visual impairments other than complete blindness are also admitted. It is the most advanced university in Japan in terms of admitting visually impaired people.

What we in the Technology Management Division wanted to know was how they conducted experiments. However, as it had been more than 30 years since they had accepted a completely blind student in physics, the documents were out of date and none of the faculty members had any knowledge regarding experiments that were conducted at the time. While equipment used at that time was still there, it was no longer usable. Some documents provided certain information on the thoughts of the teachers at that time, such as the creation of project teams in the Science department, assignment of "experiment helpers," and decision-making mechanism, including replacing equivalent experimental methods as much as possible based on the essence of science education without changing the original experimental theme. It was a small gain for us to be able to read the thought process of the teachers at that time and their decision-making mechanism.

Unfortunately, we could not shake off the impression that their structure was different from that of our university. ICU had a permanent support office for students with disabilities, which was linked to the library and an on-campus team with some Braille transcription capability. ICU had accumulated the know-how and had a support system in place.

This renewed our belief that "we have to build our own accommodation system."

Interview with Ms. Amakawa
Seven days later, we received a "Declaration of Intent to Enroll"

On March 4, 2019, the day to meet Ms. Amakawa arrived.

It is no surprise that Ms. Amakawa was just as anxious about attending university as we were. We met Ms. Amakawa, who came with her high-school homeroom teacher, in the office of the Dean of the Faculty of Science and Engineering.

We had only seen Ms. Amakawa on the day of the entrance examination, so this was the first time we met her properly. Despite this, it did not seem as if we were meeting her for the first time, probably because we had been thinking about her since December when we first learned that she was going to take the exam.

"In the second year of junior high school, I read a book about relativity and the universe, and I became interested in the idea of thinking about the world from a different perspective than what is commonly understood. This was the beginning of my desire to study physics at university. I went from the junior high school of the University of Tsukuba School for the Visually Impaired to a metropolitan high school because I understood that the curriculum at the high school of the School for the Visually Impaired would make it difficult for me to pursue a university major in physics." (Ms. Amakawa)

As Ms. Amakawa spoke about her reasons for studying physics, her desire to study at the university became clearer. When she came to the open campus at Waseda University, she thought it was a good university and decided to apply because the Support Office for Students with Disabilities was very attentive to her needs.

There were concerns regarding facilities on campus and provision for Braille transcription. That day, she voiced all her concerns, such as the installation of guide blocks and Braille transcription of textbooks; we re-assured her that the university would take care of such matters, We thought that "Ms. Amakawa had studied and progressed this far with the support of many people. The next stage of support will be provided by our university."

On March 11, she announced that she would enroll in Waseda University.

We visited the University of Tsukuba School for the Visually Impaired and saw a demonstration of a chemical experiment to get an idea regarding what we could do and prepare

On March 12, 2019, we visited the University of Tsukuba School for the Visually Impaired. It turned out to be the day after Ms. Amakawa's had announced her intention to enroll in our university, but we had already made an appointment to visit the school by then. Nine people visited the school, including physics and chemistry teachers and staffs. We were greeted by the vice principal, who had been Ms. Amakawa's homeroom teacher when she was in junior high school, and teachers in charge of mathematics, social studies, physics, and chemistry.

The University of Tsukuba School for the Visually Impaired is located near the Gokokuji Temple in Bunkyo-ku, Tokyo. This was our first visit to a school for the visually impaired. When we entered the school building, we were shocked to see students with visual impairments walking around normally. Chimes rang. It was recess, and junior high students were walking to and from their classrooms. It seemed as though they could see. Everyone walked normally, turned the corner when they needed to turn, and entered the classroom they needed to enter.

2　From Entrance Examination to Admission

A young teacher told us, "Students have a good grasp of space. It varies from person to person. Some students learn to walk easily in a week, while others take six months, but none of them use a white cane when they are in the school."

Imagining Ms. Amakawa's junior high school days, we discarded the stereotype that sighted people have of visually impaired people and learnt what "spatial awareness ability" means.

We wanted to know how physics and chemistry experiments were conducted at the University of Tsukuba School for the Visually Impaired. How could we ensure the safety of visually impaired people, and what types of experimental methods can be performed?

Ms. Shizuko Hamada, Ms. Amakawa's science teacher in junior high school, guided us. On the day of our first meeting with Ms. Hamada, who later became Ms. Amakawa's laboratory supporter at Waseda University, we were taken to the chemistry classroom on the second floor.

There were four desks that can accommodate about six people comfortably, and each desk had a sink with running water at the end. There were lockers on the back wall that stored various laboratory equipment. The rule is that when students enter this classroom, the first thing they should do is grasp the space.

Ms. Hamada started by saying, "I make them do experiments that are a little hot or painful," and pointed to the water sink, "I rigorously teach them that if they feel 'hot' from using fire, they must immediately run to that water tap, turn on the faucet, and cool themselves under running water; so, they will be fine, and there is nothing to worry about."

She gave a demonstration of what they do in the first semester of the first year of junior high school, such as letting everyone learn to light a match and handle an alcohol lamp using a "light probe" to understand differences in color and transparency and weighing using a balance with a weight-readout function instead of a scale. Although all of this was beyond our imagination and we could not fully absorb it at the time, we understood that Ms. Amakawa had first-hand experience of conducting such experiments and that we had to think of ways to replace "invisible" parts with support devices. It gradually dawned on us how we could support her.

With the cooperation of the Department of Braille Transcription for Entrance Examinations, the basic policy of experiments was decided and a TeX training course was held

On March 15, 2019, three days after we saw Ms. Hamada's chemistry experiment demonstration at the University of Tsukuba School for the Visually Impaired, we received an offer of a comprehensive support "package" from the Department of Braille Transcription for Entrance Examinations that included providing the Braille transcriptions of textbooks and other materials related to experiments and experiment supporters. We immediately went to a meeting two days afterward. The reason for this was that it would be more convenient for the university and Department of Braille Transcription for Entrance Examinations to share information on actual experiments and work together to provide support for the transcription of textbooks, experiment manuals, and other materials. We requested an estimate for the required transcription of the related contents of experiments. It was perfect timing for Ms. Hamada as she was due to retire from the University of Tsukuba School for the Visually Impaired and become a member of the Department of Braille Transcription for Entrance Examinations.

The two weeks leading up to enrollment passed in the blink of an eye. We communicated with Ms. Hamada almost every day and decided on a basic policy for Ms. Amakawa's experiments. For example,

- Experiment subjects or methods will not be changed for Ms. Amakawa.
- Use equipment and instruments normally available in the laboratory as much as possible.
- She should be allowed to experience the entire process.
- Maximize the use of alternatives to the visual sense.
- Reports should be submitted in a form that can be read by the staff.
- The laboratory instruction manual must be transcribed in Braille beforehand.
- Laboratory must be kept free of obstacles.

Further, we decided that the staff, including Ms. Hamada, would conduct trace experiments before pre-experiments were conducted by Ms. Amakawa and discuss methods to be used for the chemistry experiment, which was the first experiment.

In our second meeting with Ms. Amakawa, We think there was a "welcoming mood" in air. Ms. Amakawa seemed to feel at ease with our university, and the atmosphere was quite friendly. Ms. Amakawa listened with a smile as we told her about the appointment of Ms. Hamada as her support and provided her a report on small details, including the preparation of a dedicated room near the laboratory and changes made to its door lock from a touch-screen type to a cylinder type, which was easier for her to use.

Additionally, we took a course on TeX used by Ms. Amakawa. It was around this time that all of us began to learn the basics of Braille and use of the tactile copy machine we had purchased.

Meanwhile, the hardware on the science and engineering campus was being prepared at a rapid pace. Tactile paving was installed based on the advice of specialists so that she could walk safely without hesitation with a white cane along the escalator, underground passage, and stairs (or elevator) from the on-campus subway station to the dedicated room. Training sessions on navigating the campus were held on March 19 and 25. Furthermore, we confirmed the location of the University Co-op. It was a busy spring break for Ms. Amakawa before she joined the university, but she came to us without a single look of displeasure, which was a tremendous encouragement to us.

On April 2, 2019, Ms. Amakawa attended the entrance ceremony held at the Waseda Arena, and just before the ceremony, she ran into President Aiji Tanaka. He said, "Congratulations on your enrollment, and best wishes for your future." These words from the president were heartwarming to all those who had listened to them.

3 1st Year (Basic Experiments in Science and Engineering 1A and 1B) to 3rd Year (Experiments in Applied Physics A)

Trace experiments and pre-experiments

In April 2019, Ms. Makoto Amakawa enrolled as a first-year student in the School of Advanced Science and Engineering. Basic Experiments in Science and Engineering 1A was held on Wednesdays. Basic Experiments in Science and Engineering is a compulsory course for all new students in the three Schools of Science and Engineering. It is a laboratory education course rooted in the principles of the Faculty of Science and Engineering, in which students experience phenomena by touching things.

As mentioned earlier, we asked the Department of Braille Transcription for Entrance Examinations to transcribe all experimental texts into Braille. In addition, Ms. Hamada was send by the Department of Braille Transcription for Entrance Examinations as an "experiment advisor," and Ms. Amakawa followed the same schedule as a sighted students in principle. Ms. Amakawa fully participated in experiments, working with her hands, obtaining the experimental data, and preparing and submitting reports based on the results. We set up a system where only those operations for which visual impairment is a barrier were to be supported by a co-experimenter, Ms. Hamada, a TA, or the technical staff. We want to explain again how trace experiments and pre-experiments were conducted before the day of each experiment and what we, at the Technology Management Division, did to help.

The Technology Management Division, which belongs to the Science and Engineering Center, is a unique staff organization of the Faculty of Science and Engineering with about 100 technical staff members with expertise in science and engineering (see Part 1 for details). The technical staff designs laboratory courses in consultation with the academic staff and plays a part of the teachers' role in the practical implementation of laboratory education.

First, Ms. Hamada participated in the trace experiment, which was conducted before the day of the actual experiment, to understand the purpose of the experiment and simulate the support needed by Ms. Amakawa. Ms. Hamada instructed the technical staff about necessary support equipment for Ms. Amakawa after determining whether she could do operations herself or with support equipment. (See "Main support equipment used in experiments" at the end of Part 3 for details about specific support devices and their support content.)

Some of the support devices used were as follows:

- The scale on the devices is not visible → Cut stickers from a felt fabric, make labels of the scale, and affix them to the devices
- A metered volume container cannot be used → Cut a slit in syringes so that a fixed volume of solution can be dispensed
- Difficulty in weighing powder reagents → Use a balance with a readout function
- Inability to discern color change → Use a light probe (a device that converts the brightness of light into the pitch of sound) to identify the color change by

the change in sound

- Charts of spectra, etc. cannot be checked visually → Draw tactile charts using a raised line drawing board or a tactile copy machine and turn them into charts that can be touched

In addition, the technical staff came up with the following support measures when conducting trace experiments.

- Provide equipment for taking pictures instead of making sketches or use demonstration equipment by the staff
- Use a 3D printer to modify devices or create mock-ups
- Use micropipettes utilized in life science experiments for quantitative preparative operations in chemistry experiments

After setting up support equipment, Ms. Amakawa and Ms. Hamada would come to the laboratory the day before the experiment, and the technical staff would lead pre-experiment. The reason for doing this on the previous day was to avoid disrupting the other classes of Ms. Amakawa. First, Ms. Amakawa would touch laboratory equipment to grasp its arrangement and shape, and then she would begin the experiment process actually using the instruments that had been prepared by the technical staff after trace experiment.

When we saw Ms. Amakawa operate laboratory equipment effortlessly after grasping the arrangement, we were amazed at her spatial grasp, and we realized that contrary to what we had imagined, challenges associated with conducting experiments may be much lower.

Experiments were lengthy, spanning four classes (6 h from the second to the fifth class). Pre-experiments would be shorter because Ms. Hamada would work on some parts of the experiment, but even so, it took 2–3 h. However, whether it was devising support equipment or conducting trace experiments and pre-experiments, the technical staff worked with dedication and a positive attitude. Ms. Hamada often said to us, "You all seem to be having a lot of fun." The technical staff also felt that through Ms. Amakawa, we learnt a valuable lesson as we conducted experiments.

Table 2-2 List of experiments in the first year (in the order of date)

[Spring Term / Basic Experiments in Science and Engineering 1A]	
April 17	Chemistry: Water Quality Analysis
April 24	Chemistry: Extraction of Caffeine
May 8	Chemistry: Synthesis of Nylon
May 15	Physics: Making a Lens
May 22	Physics: Simulation of Physical Phenomena
May 29	Physics: Estimation of Measurement Uncertainty
June 5	Physics: Electric Guitar
June 12	Physics: Capacitor Design and Radio Reception
June 19	Physics: Electromagnetic Induction
June 26	Physics: Oral Examination
July 3	Life: Microscopic Observation of Cells

[Fall Term / Basic Experiments in Science and Engineering 1B]	
October 9	Life: Extraction and PCR amplification of DNA
October 16	Chemistry: Atomic Emission Spectra
October 23	Chemistry: Synthesis of Pharmaceuticals
October 30	Chemistry: Inclusion of a Molecule into Cyclodextrin
November 6	Physics: Brownian Motion
November 13	Physics: The Physics of Air Hockey
November 20	Physics: Electronic Circuits Workshop
November 27	Physics: Light and Waves
December 4	Physics: Measuring Devices
December 11	Physics: Heat and Motion of Gas Molecules
December 18	Physics: Presentation and Discussion

Keeping a record

The first-year experiments (academic year 2019) are listed by date (Table 2-2).

A great deal of effort was put into documenting Ms. Amakawa's experiments so that they could be referenced in the future. The biggest difference between 35 years ago when the first completely blind Japanese student to major in physics was admitted into ICU and now is that video cameras have become more accessible. The whole experiment could be recorded from various angles, with Ms. Amakawa's consent, using three video cameras—one fixed at her side, another in front of her, and the third held by a staff member. Detailed notes were prepared, with the technical staff in charge of each experiment recording "anything they noticed, even if it was trivial." Video recordings and written notes became the basis for records in Part 3.

Information communication, group training for the Technology Management Division, review meeting

In most experiments, Ms. Amakawa conducted experiments in the same laboratory as other students, with Ms. Amakawa and a co-experimenter. The entire laboratory was supervised by the academic staff, technical staff, and TAs.

The first-year students began their first experiment class with "Water Quality Analysis" during which the staff in charge of the "Capacitor Design and Radio Reception" experiment came to observe. If necessary, other staff would visit the laboratory to check what she could do and the support she needed.

The Technology Management Division conducts group training twice a year. On September 10, 2019, we asked Ms. Hamada to give a lecture entitled "Science Through the Five Senses," which was attended by all technical staff members. The presentation was based on the theory that visually impaired students should be given the same opportunities for conducting experiments as sighted students. In the presentation, a demonstration of experiments conducted at the University of Tsukuba School for the Visually Impaired was shown. Although only about one-fifth of approximately 100 technical staff members was responsible for supporting Ms. Amakawa in laboratory courses, the social significance of dealing with a visually impaired student and experience of Ms. Amakawa's technical staff were shared with many technical staff who were not in charge of experiments conducted by Ms. Amakawa. Furthermore, we realized that experimental methods utilizing all five senses improve the understanding of the experiment and are more effective even for sighted people.

After completing all experiments in the first year, a review meeting was held with the staff members who were in charge of the experiments, Ms. Amakawa, and Ms. Hamada. The staff members responsible for the following year's experiments were also present. The purpose of the meeting was to review the first-year's experiments and improve the management of the second-year's experiments.

Comprehensive decision to allow in-person experiments during the COVID-19 pandemic

In April 2020, Ms. Amakawa became a second-year student and was required to take Basic Experiments in Science and Engineering 2B, a compulsory course for second-year students of the School of Advanced Science and Engineering. It was the same year that the COVID-19 pandemic began. All spring-term classes were taught online, but fortunately, Ms. Amakawa's laboratory course was in the fall term, so she attended the course in person.

As the pandemic continued, the start of classes in April was postponed, and Waseda University decided to conduct all spring-term classes online. Even laboratory courses had to be conducted online. Therefore, in each laboratory, the staff at the Technology Management Division had to perform experiments, record them on videos, create on-demand contents, and teach classes. We remember how difficult this process was. However, the content prepared in such a way cannot be viewed by Ms. Amakawa.

In the fall term of 2020, the university allowed in-person classes to be held only during the first eight weeks of the fall term, so we started in-person experiments while preparing video contents. Ms. Amakawa also conducted in-person experiments first. As in the first year, it was a two-step process: trace experiment with Ms. Hamada and pre-experiment with Ms. Hamada and Ms. Amakawa before the actual experiment. However, after the sixth experiment, we could see that she was under a lot of strain.

After eight weeks, we had to switch experiments to an on-demand format. However, as Ms. Amakawa could not attend the experiment classes online, we decided to continue the class in person based on our comprehensive decision. Pre-experiment duration was shortened and held on the day of the experiment, and the actual experiment was conducted immediately afterward. This decision was made to create special educational opportunities for her "so that she would not be at a disadvantage compared with other students." In other words, from the perspective of educational equity.

The experiments for the second year are listed in Table 2-3.

Table 2-3 List of experiments in the second year (in the order of date)

[2nd year Fall term / Basic Experiments in Science and Engineering 2B	
October 6	Engineering: Elasticity and viscoelasticity
October 13	Chemistry: Synthesis and electrochemical measurement of ferrocene
October 20	Engineering: Resonant circuits and vibration systems
October 27	Chemistry: Separation and molecular weight measurement of proteins
November 3	Engineering: Automatic measurement using a computer
November 17	Engineering: Thermal conduction and diffusion
November 24	Chemistry: Synthesis of a titanium dioxide photocatalyst using the sol–gel method and scientific information search using a PC
December 1	Chemistry: Synthesis of polystyrene by suspension polymerization and its recycling
December 8	Engineering: Lasers and holography interference
December 15	Engineering: Optical and electron microscopes

In the third year, the laboratory courses were elective subjects and not compulsory; nevertheless, Ms. Amakawa wanted to choose a course with experiments. So, she selected Experiments in Applied Physics A.

In the spring term of 2021, even though the COVID-19 pandemic was not yet over, we returned to in-person laboratory courses. The teams from the electrical engineering and physical chemistry laboratories, who are in charge of the course, prepared for in-person experiments and kept contact with Ms. Amakawa. As the experiments of one subject was to be conducted once per week for three times, over the period of three weeks in total, we could design experiments for Ms. Amakawa a little more flexibly than we could in the first and second years. The experiments for the third year are listed in Table 2-4.

4 After Supporting Experiments

Before the entrance examination, we had no clue regarding what to do when we heard that Ms. Amakawa wanted to take the exam. After Ms. Amakawa enrolled in the university, we struggled a bit to keep pace with what was necessary. However, we, the staff at the Technology Management Division, were united in our mission to support Ms. Amakawa so that she would not be at a disadvantage

Table 2-4 List of experiments in the third year (in the order of date)

Experiments in Applied Physics A	
April 15	Physical Chemistry: X-ray diffraction
May 6, 13	Electricity: Logic circuits
June 10, 17	Electricity: Optical circuit elements
October 7	Physical Chemistry: Infrared absorption spectroscopy
November 11	Physical Chemistry: Magnetization measurement
December 2	Physical Chemistry: High-temperature superconductivity

compared with other students in all laboratory courses and ensured that she would master all laboratory courses. The mission, which seemed very difficult initially, gradually became easier during her first year and became difficult again in her second year because of the COVID-19 pandemic. Although there were many challenges, we could accomplish our mission.

The fact that Mr. Amakawa, who is completely blind, enrolled in the School of Advanced Science and Engineering, took various experiments and produced results is a historic achievement for Waseda University and the world. Furthermore, we, the technical staff who participated in this journey, gained important knowledge. This was our main conviction. We could provide technical support through the Technology Management Division and enabling smooth cooperation with other divisions within the university and with the Department of Braille Transcription for Entrance Examinations (including Ms. Hamada's assistance).

"Laboratory courses will be the responsibility of the Technology Management Division." It simultaneously feels like it was only a short time ago and a long time ago that we heard such statements from various divisions in the university and were motivated to perform the challenging task at hand.

"We realized that we were wrong to believe that it would be impossible for a visually impaired person to conduct experiments with their own hands."

"We realized that we had unconsciously used many demonstrative pronouns such as, "this" and "that" and understood the need to use precise words to convey information in all situations."

"By considering methods that do not rely on the visual sense, we could re-evaluate the nature of experiments."

"Some experimental methods that use support equipment are easier to understand and applicable even to sighted students."

These were the sentiments expressed by the academic and technical staff who have provided technical assistance to Ms. Amakawa. We conclude this chapter by stating that this experience was invaluable not only for those of us who were directly involved but also for humanity at large.

Part 3

Record of Technical Support in Laboratory Education

Basic Policy for Technical Support

The Technology Management Division of the Administration and Technology Management Center for Science and Engineering at Waseda University provided support for all experiments for four experimental courses: Basic Experiments in Science and Engineering 1A (first-year spring semester), Basic Experiments in Science and Engineering 1B (first-year fall semester), Basic Experiments in Science and Engineering 2B (second-year fall semester), and Experiments in Applied Physics A (third-year full-year)—all of which Ms. Makoto Amakawa took from the academic years between 2019 and 2021.

In principle, the course schedule was the same as that for a sighted student, wherein students performed experiments, obtained experimental data, and prepared and submitted reports based on the acquired results. However, for operations in which complete blindness might be an issue, a support system was established with the help of co-experimenters, Ms. Hamada (who assisted the blind student), and technical staff, including those in the Technology Management Division. In particular, for experiments that require the visual sense, we improved or modified laboratory equipment so that they can be operated through touch and hearing.

[Composition of Part 3]

Part 3, "Record of Technical Support in Laboratory Education," details the record of each experiment and describes "what" and "how" support was provided based on (1) Outline of Experiment, (2) Advance Preparation, (3) Observations on the Experiment Day, (4) How to Confirm Understanding Level, and (5) Comments.

While there were four experimental courses—"Basic Experiments in Science and Engineering 1A," "Basic Experiments in Science and Engineering 1B," "Basic Experiments in Science and Engineering 2B," and "Experiments in Applied Physics A"—as described above, they are re-categorized into five fields of "Basic Chemistry," "Basic Physics," "Basic Life Science," "Basic Engineering," and "Applied Physics" for the better understanding of readers.

1

Basic Chemistry

1–1 Water Quality Analysis
(Basic Experiments in Science and Engineering 1A)

(1) Outline of Experiment

The goal of this experiment is to quantify the iron content in a soft drink pre-pared as an unknown sample using phenanthroline absorption spectrophotometry to facilitate a basic understanding of analytical chemistry. To detect the presence of iron based on color, a chromogenic reagent, 1,10-phenanthroline, is used to change the color of the solution to bright orange-red. In addition to visual confir-mation using the colorimetric method, in which the color intensity is determined in proportion to the iron concentration, a UV–visible spectrophotometer is used to quantitatively determine the color intensity. The measurement principle is based on the Beer–Lambert law; the law is used to determine the correlation between absorbance and a known sample concentration by plotting them for a specific wavelength on a graph to create a calibration curve. Further, the absorbance of a sample with an unknown concentration is calculated from this calibration curve.

In the first half of the experiment, the main tasks are the handling of glass-ware, sample solutions, and reagents to be added to prepare the standard and un-known sample solutions of iron. The key question here is the approach to be taken for Ms. Amakawa, who is completely blind, so that she can quantify the iron con-centration using the colorimetric method.

The second half of the experiment involves operating the UV–visible spec-trophotometer and recording experimental values obtained from spectroscopic analysis. We assumed that the calculation of absorbance would not be so difficult if the calibration curve could be drawn.

(2) Advance Preparation

Because this was Ms. Amakawa's first experiment in Waseda Univeristy, we started from total uncertainty. However, she previously had experience in chemis-try experiments when she was a student at the Special Needs Education School for the Visually Impaired, University of Tsukuba (hereinafter referred to as "University of Tsukuba School for the Visually Impaired"), and we could rely on Ms.

Hamada's abundant knowledge on various preparation methods after the preliminary meeting.

As her personal equipment, she used "BrailleSense," a portable Braille terminal to record experiments by hand, because she could not use a normal notebook, unlike a sighted person. In addition, she used "Braille Label," which is useful for quickly attaching Braille to devices and instruments, and "light probe," an instrument used to detect the color change in solutions by sound as she could not visually confirm the change; these were prepared by the laboratory. Notably, the use of a raised line drawing board (a handmade device made of cardboard, a net with a rough mesh, and a ballpoint pen) for drawing uneven graphs and a plastic tray to prevent glassware from falling over are worth mentioning.

While Ms. Amakawa performed most experiments as planned, the following items, including the aforementioned ones, were changed to alternatives; all of them were prepared prior to the day of the experiment.

- A micropipette was used instead of a volumetric pipette for weighing.
- The alignment of marks on volumetric flasks was performed by the assistant.
- Spectrophotometer was set up by the assistant.
- The transcription of the spectra to the raised line drawing board and reading out of measured values were performed by the assistant.

In addition, to prevent beakers from tipping over, a plastic tray with a hole

Figure 1-1-1 ▸ Measures to prevent beakers from tipping over

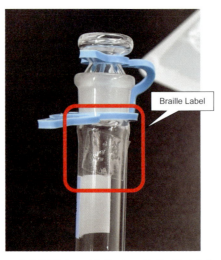

Figure 1-1-2 ▶ Volumetric flasks with Braille labels

drilled in the center and placed upside down was prepared on the day of the experiment (Figure 1-1-1). Furthermore, reagent containers and volumetric flasks were labeled in Braille by Ms. Amakawa (Figure 1-1-2).

(3) Observations on the Experiment Day

◆ Preparation of iron standard solutions for calibration curves and unknown sample solutions

 In the first half of the experiment, the main operations were the preparation of the iron standard solutions and unknown sample solutions of different concentrations. Because this is an analytical chemistry experiment, several liquid handling operations, such as co-washing and dispensing between instruments, must be performed repeatedly.

 Although the dispensing of solutions into a beaker had initially concerned us, we found that while she had no vision, her other senses were heightened and she could grasp the amount of solutions poured to some extent by the temperature change in the side of the beaker. As a result, pipetting could be performed without problems (Figure 1-1-3). Co-washing could also be performed by discarding solutions into a waste beaker while turning them.

 Although a volumetric pipette would normally be used to measure the iron

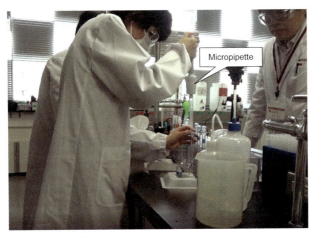

Figure 1-1-3 ▶ Dispensing solution

standard solution, as she cannot confirm its markings, a micropipette was used, as described above. As micropipettes do not require co-washing, the overall operation was performed easily. However, if the micropipette is sucked too forcefully, air bubbles will get inside the tip. The assistant had to point out whether air bubbles had been trapped or not as she could not see this.

◆ **Coloration operation**

The 1,10-phenanthroline solution, used as the coloring reagent, and ammonium acetate solution, utilized as the buffer solution, were taken in a small test tube and transferred to a volumetric flask to prevent mix-up with other solutions. Because pipettes were used to transfer solutions between containers with narrow mouths, it was difficult to insert them inside containers while aligning the tip accurately, and she encountered the difficulty of the easy spilling of pipettes. In some situations, it was necessary to place a finger on the container and let the liquid run down the finger. A container with a wide mouth would have enabled to perform this task easily.

Because volumetric flasks were filled repeatedly, she returned them to the volumetric flask stand after each filling, checking the order of solutions to avoid mistaking for the solution that was filled. The efficiency of this operation increased when two flask stands were used.

◆ Determination of iron(II) ions via colorimetric method

The solution after coloration was analyzed via the colorimetric method to estimate the iron concentration. Because colorimetry involves determining the sample concentration through visual confirmation, it cannot be performed by a completely blind person using the common method. In other words, the information that can be visually obtained by a sighted person must be acquired by the blind person by substituting sight with another sense that can be perceived. Therefore, we decided to use a "light probe" as a device that can detect color changes acoustically (Figure 1-1-4 and Figure 1-1-5). In actual use, the color change is expressed as a difference in the pitch, but the round volumetric flask is curved and intensity of the color differs between the rim and middle of the flask.

Figure 1-1-4 ▶ Light probe

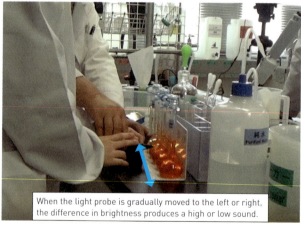

When the light probe is gradually moved to the left or right, the difference in brightness produces a high or low sound.

Figure 1-1-5 ▶ Detection using a light probe

Therefore, it seemed to be very difficult for her to identify the pitch at which she should determine the color. Further, pitch recognition became increasingly difficult owing to the interruption of sound when sliding horizontally between volumetric flasks. Meanwhile, after dispensing solutions into the cell, sound became somewhat more stable due to the flat surface of the cell, and the difference in the pitch was clearer.

◆ Determination of iron(II) ions via absorption spectrophotometry

Apart from the colorimetric method, absorbance was measured using an instrument that is more advanced compared with that used in high schools. The coloration of 1,10-phenanthroline is orange red; therefore, measurement was performed in the visible light range. In the basic chemistry laboratory, each group had its own UV–visible spectrophotometer; therefore, Ms. Amakawa used this device as well.

Initially, the sample had to be dispensed into a 1-cm-wide square glass container called an analytical cell. A glass pipette was used for this task. Initially, this task was difficult for her because she had to collect liquid from a container with a narrow mouth and transfer it to a small container while ensuring that the pipette tip was inside the cell. With Ms. Hamada's advice, she could gradually perform the task smoothly by holding the volumetric flask and cell with one hand.

As for the UV–visible spectrophotometer, Ms. Amakawa checked the device

Figure 1-1-6 ▶ Recording of the measurement results from a UV–visible spectrophotometer with BrailleSense

by touching it and then placed the cell in the spectrophotometer and pressed the start button by herself. The values obtained during the experiment were recorded using BraillSense (Figure 1-1-6).

The spectra of the solution were copied at 200% magnification and transcribed onto a cardboard using the raised line drawing board. Although the general shape of the spectrum could be understood on the cardboard, it was necessary to read out the scale of the spectrum.

◆Cleaning

Ms. Amakawa washed most of the experimental equipment. She performed primary cleaning in the same manner as co-washing and was more careful than sighted students when using a brush and detergent and replacing pure water. However, the process seemed to take a little longer than usual, and at many instances, Ms. Hamada had to take care of equipment as it was difficult to find a place to put them when there were so many items to be washed.

(4) How to Confirm Understanding Level

Experimental reports were prepared in a separate room using the software Microsoft Word (hereinafter referred to as "Word") on a personal computer (hereinafter referred to as "PC") and submitted through e-mail by the next morning deadline. Tables were created using the spreadsheet software Microsoft Excel (hereinafter referred to as "Excel") and formatted for printing by the staff.

However, as we could not prepare the Braille graph paper on the same day, she was allowed to prepare graphs by the next week (Figure 1-1-7).

(5) Comments

The experimental results showed that her measurement accuracy was as good as or better than that of sighted students. Color comparison using a light probe was performed with high accuracy, although it was difficult to handle.

Initially, she was nervous and unfamiliar with some of the operations; however, because many of them were repeated in the "Water Quality Analysis," she became proficient and could perform them smoothly as she understood the arrangement of objects. As a result, her individual operations did not lag far behind those of sighted students.

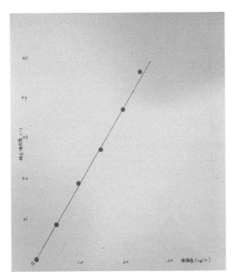

Figure 1-1-7▶ Drawing graphs on a Braille graph paper
(Relationship between the iron concentration and corrected absorbance)
The vertical axis denotes corrected absorbance, and the horizontal axis represents the iron concentration in the solution.

The experiment time was faster than that of sighted students because she could understand operation and instructions clearly and could complete calculations more quickly than sighted students. However, because washing equipment was time-consuming, the total time spent on experiments was almost identical to that of sighted students.

Her understanding of experiments and calculation processes was superior to that of other students, and we felt that she could obtain sufficient learning effect from the experiment subject.

Nevertheless, having a fixed storage place for experimental equipment, including small tools used in experiments, would have been better. She placed used small test tubes, pipettes, etc. in a volumetric flask stand so that they could be easily identified.

In any case, knowledge the support team gained from the first chemistry experiment was remarkable, and there is no doubt that it gave us a good idea regarding how to support completely blind students in laboratory courses.

(Original text by Hattori, with some corrections by Umezawa)

1 -2 Extraction of Caffeine
(Basic Experiments in Science and Engineering 1A)

(1) Outline of Experiment

In this experiment, caffeine from a commercial instant coffee powder is separated and purified. Through this experiment, students learn separation operations, which are the basis of chemical experiments.

Specifically, caffeine was recovered through liquid–liquid separation under basic conditions, and the solvent was evaporated using an evaporator. Caffeine was precipitated from the obtained extract through recrystallization; subsequently, the solid was recovered via vacuum filtration and further purified by sublimation. In addition, the extract, sublimed caffeine, and standard caffeine samples were compared using thin-layer chromatography (TLC).

Because glassware and organic solvents were used in separation and purification, as in the case of "Water Quality Analysis," care was taken to avoid injury due to falls or breakage. In addition, because the process included heating using a hot stirrer, further attention was required to avoid burn injuries.

(2) Advance Preparation

By the day before the experiment, the laboratory was set up, equipment was checked, and instant coffee and magnesium sulfate were measured; some of the preparation was completed during pre-experiment with Ms. Amakawa, while others were performed solely by the staff.

Powder weighing is an easy task for a sighted person as they only need to look at the displayed numbers and make fine adjustments. However, for a completely blind person, reading numbers is an impossible task. Here, a "balance with a readout function (a minimum scale of 0.01 g)" prepared by Ms. Hamada was useful. This device reads out the scale value in real time, allowing the user to check the mass of a material currently on the balance without having to visually inspect it. However, it was necessary to take at least three or four measurements to adjust values, and it seemed to take a little longer for Ms. Amakawa to complete measurements than for a sighted person. In any case, weighing was done successfully. Instant coffee powder was placed in a conical flask to be used on the day, and anhydrous magnesium sulfate was stored in a container with the size of a film case (anhydrous magnesium sulfate absorbs moisture from air, and if it loses its dehydrating power, its usage in the experiment becomes meaningless. Therefore, it cannot be left in the container carelessly and must be stored in a sealable container).

During the experiment, stirring was performed several times in a day; however, the stirring speed (RPM) varied depending on operation. Therefore, it was necessary to know the degree of stirring. Hence, a felt sticker was placed on a part of the scale on the hot stirrer to distinguish between set values (two types).

Felt sticker labels are an effective way to identify differences in values on containers and utensils and can be used in various situations. While there were few instruments to be labeled this time because of the different shapes and sizes of the containers used, Ms. Amakawa labeled the "test tube stand" for holding Komagome pipettes and "spatula/spoon stand" by herself because they were made of the same material and of the same size.

In addition, at Ms. Hamada's suggestion, notches were cut into the handles of plastic syringes (5 and 50 mL) for every 1 or 10 mL to indicate volume (Figure 1-2-1) and a glass pipette was inserted at the tip to take the solution. This method is also used at the University of Tsukuba School for the Visually Impaired because it is sufficient for weighing solutions that need not be highly precise. A beaker and a beaker stand for measuring solutions with a syringe were also prepared, as in the previous experiment.

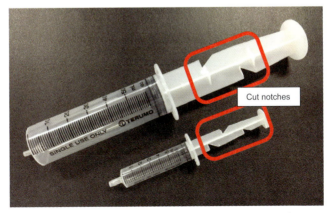

Figure 1-2-1▶ Plastic syringe with notches (5 and 50 mL)

(3) Observations on the Experiment Day

◆ Extraction of caffeine

The coffee solution was prepared in pre-experiment by pouring 100 mL pure water into 10 g coffee powder weighed in a conical flask under stirring with a stirrer. A plastic syringe with notches was used to measure 100 mL pure water. Although notches were used to determine the amount of the solution to be measured, it was difficult to grasp the direction of the solution when pouring; hence, the solution tended to spill out of the container. Moreover, the hot stirrer was employed for two purposes in this experiment: stirring and heating. Therefore, it was necessary to adjust the stirring and heating conditions by turning the knobs. By marking each knob with a felt sticker beforehand and checking in advance that beakers and other objects would be placed in the center, the device could be operated without difficulty on the experiment day.

To the prepared solution, 4 mol/L sodium hydroxide solution was added six times (~4.2 mL) with a dropper to make the solution more alkaline. A pH test paper was used to confirm whether the solution became alkaline or not, but as she could not compare the test paper color with the colorimetric chart, how the color of the test paper changed was checked by the assistant.

Once the solution reached the appropriate pH, 50 mL ethyl acetate (extraction solvent) was added, and the solution was stirred for ~2 min. When measuring ethyl acetate to a beaker, it seemed that its amount could be determined by touch based on the solvent temperature; nevertheless, the assistant ensured that the ethyl acetate amount was sufficient. Because it was difficult to estimate 2 min by a blind person with a special analog watch, she prepared a digital timer to measure time.

At this point, most caffeine had transferred from the initial coffee solution (aqueous phase) to ethyl acetate (organic phase). After stirring, the mixture separated into two layers after standing for a while. The aqueous phase was removed using the Komagome pipette, and only the organic phase was retained (Figure 1-2-2).

Handling a Komagome pipette is extremely difficult for a completely blind person. This was an aspect that was difficult for us to notice before. When handling such instruments, a sighted person naturally determines based on visual information "how much more I have to grasp the rubber ball to suck out the solution" and "what I should do to avoid spilling of the sucked solution," etc. Meanwhile, a completely blind person cannot determine whether the solution is

Fig. 1-2-2 ▶ Liquid separation

being sucked properly or even whether the pipette is in the solution. Therefore, she performed only the main process of liquid separation, and assistants were responsible for detailed works, such as removing few milliliters of the remaining aqueous phase. In practice, although Ms. Amakawa separated liquids to an acceptable degree even without assistance, she still seemed to be facing difficulty in this regard.

Magnesium sulfate which was added to remove water from the organic phase, was weighed in advance, added in its entire amount, and stirred. By making a shape with her hands that was several centimeters larger than the flask and shaking the flask inside the shape, she shaked the flask at a constant width, and stirring was sufficient. The subsequent filtration process was performed without any problems by pouring the solution in the organic phase slowly, while the assistants ensured that the solution did not overflow.

The extraction solvent, ethyl acetate, had to be removed from the dehydrated organic phase. For this purpose, a rotary evaporator was used. While she had to attach the eggplant flask to the evaporator body and operate several knobs, cocks, etc., she could perform all operations by herself because she could assume most of them, including positional relationships, at pre-experiment (Figure 1-2-3).

Although the shape of the extract had to be explained in detail by the assistant, Ms. Amakawa could confirm it by smell and touch.

Figure 1-2-3 ▸ Operation of the evaporator

◆ Recrystallization from extract

This was an experiment performed to obtain the crude crystals of caffeine through recrystallization from the extract obtained in the previous step. First, the extract adhering to the wall of the eggplant flask was peeled off and dissolved in ethanol. Although a curved spatula with a long handle and a curved tip was used for this purpose, it tended to result in rough recovery because she could not visually check whether all of the extract had peeled off. The assistant helped with the final step of dissolving crystals in an eggplant flask, although Ms. Amakawa herself dissolved crystals sufficiently. Ethanol was supplied using a plastic syringe with notches.

The extract dissolved in ethanol was collected in a 30-mL beaker, which was placed on a hot stirrer. A stirring bar was added, and the mixture was heated and stirred. Eventually, the solution started boiling and became more concentrated (Figure 1-2-4). The assistant determined whether the concentration had progressed, and Ms. Amakawa moved the 30-mL beaker into an ice-cooled container when the solution was sufficiently concentrated (reduced to ~5 mL).

Although heating with a hot stirrer poses the risk of burns, she performed operations without causing any particularly dangerous situations by confirming the shape of the device and heat-generating parts in advance.

A solid matter in a solution precipitates when cooled in an ice-cold container

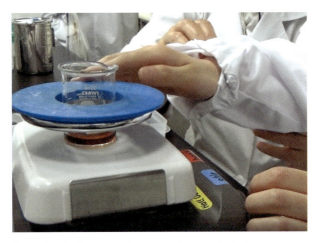

Figure 1-2-4 ▶ Concentration process in recrystallization operation

due to its solubility difference with temperature. This solid matter, in this case, is crude caffeine, which was then filtered by suction in the next step. The obtained crystals were washed with cold ethanol as the last step of filtration, and the assistant confirmed whether washing was sufficient or not.

The initial plan was to collect crystals from the Kiriyama funnel by removing the funnel and placing it upside down on a piece of thick paper, which was used as the thin wrapping paper so that the crystals would come out naturally. In fact, they did not come off this way, and Ms. Amakawa had to use a spatula to peel off the crystals. The crystals were then collected by peeling them off from the Kiriyama filter paper using a spatula.

For yield measurement, a laboratory balance was used, and the assistant read the values out because the commercial electronic balance with a readout function cannot weigh with an accuracy of up to 0.001 g.

◆ Purification of recrystallized caffeine through sublimation

The crude crystals obtained through recrystallization were purified by sublimation. In this process, the crystals were transferred to a petri dish and heated using a hot stirrer. During this operation, the assistant ensured that the crystals were placed in the center of the petri dish for Ms. Amakawa. Subsequently, Ms. Amakawa installed and heated the crystals on the hot stirrer. The assistant checked and informed about the completion of sublimation to remove the petri dish from the hot plate. While this operation also involved the risk of burns due to the handling of the heated petri dish, she handled it without any difficulty because she had practiced this operation in advance.

◆ Confirmation of caffeine using thin-layer chromatography

TLC was used to compare the extract and solid obtained after sublimation with the caffeine standard. Sample preparation and the insertion/removal of the plate into the development chamber were performed by Ms. Amakawa, while spotting and pencil marking on the thin-layer plate were performed by the assistant.

After marking, the assistant made a 200% uneven copy of the silica gel plate by the raised line drawing board, Ms. Amakawa checked the figure of the plate and calculated the R_f value by measuring to the nearest 1 mm using a Braille ruler (Figure 1-2-5 and Figure 1-2-6).

The experimental results showed that her caffeine recovery was comparable to that of sighted students. The TLC result was clear and easy to understand by touch. However, because the Braille ruler was used to measure the distance

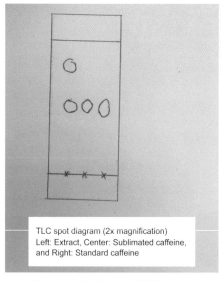

Figure 1-2-5 ▶ Skatch of TLC result

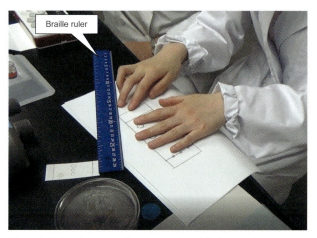

Figure 1-2-6 ▸ Understanding the results of TLC plate development using a Braille ruler
The raised line drawing board was used to identify the spots on the TLC plate by the engraved unevenness of the paper surface.

travelled by the solvent used for calculation of the R_f value, as well as that of each substance, the units were limited to mm and R_f value was calculated in two digits.

As the weighing of crude caffeine was completed in the morning, she took about the same amount of time as other students for the experiment, and at the time of final operation (evaporation and solidification), the time taken was about the average of the entire class. Because some afternoon operations, such as ethanol weighing and preparing suitable volumes, dissolution, and crystal collection, took longer time than other students, she was little behind the schedule. However, after cleaning up, she started writing the report at the same time as 50–65% of the class.

◆ **Cleaning**

Ms. Amakawa cleaned the experimental equipment herself.

(4) How to Confirm Understanding Level

The report was prepared in a separate room using Word. Although the deadline was extended to the next day, she submitted the report at about the same time as other students. The descriptions of charts were read by Ms. Amakawa and transcribed by the staff.

(5) Comments

This experiment involved heating at high temperatures for the first time and even some sighted students suffered minor burns, so we were very careful to ensure her safety. In reality, however, by understanding equipment and operations and confirming dangerous points during trace experiment, no special measures were required during actual heating, and the experiment was completed smoothly. This result greatly changed our awareness, and we felt that she can perform many more operations in future experiments. Meanwhile, numerous operations involving solutions containing organic solvents were difficult or time-consuming, such as checking whether the liquid was being collected properly, whether the pipette tip had reached the container, and whether the entire liquid had been drained. In particular, this experiment involved a greater number of detailed and variety operations than the previous experiment. Therefore, we had the impression that she did not had adequate time for preparation and that it was difficult to follow operations; hence, we keenly felt that preparation time is necessary for a detailed understanding of experiments.

(Original text by Hattori, with some corrections by Umezawa)

1 -3 Synthesis of Nylon
(Basic Experiments in Science and Engineering 1A)

(1) Outline of Experiment

The goal of this experiment is to synthesize the synthetic fibers of nylon 66 and nylon 6 and examine their physical and chemical properties. Specifically, for nylon 66, different forms of thin films, threads, and capsules were synthesized through interfacial polymerization and observed. Thin films were analyzed using infrared (IR) spectroscopy to determine the presence or absence of amide bonds. Nylon 6 was synthesized through ring-opening polymerization, and its tensile strength was estimated to compare with commercially available fishing lines.

Unlike the two experiments discussed earlier, this is an advanced synthesis experiment where synthesis itself, and not only analysis, was conducted. In addition to the use of corrosive chemicals (adipoyl dichloride) in the synthesis of nylon 66, synthesis involved heating using a Bunsen burner; therefore, even greater care was required to avoid burn injuries.

(2) Advance Preparation

The laboratory was set up, equipment was checked, and sodium bicarbonate, sodium chloride, and ε-caprolactam (polyethylene glycol was added at the same time) were weighed by the day before the experiment. The sample weighing 1 g or less was sealed in a 2-cm-diameter sample tube bottle (50 mL volume), and ε-caprolactam was sealed in a 3-cm-diameter screw tube. In this experiment, Ms. Hamada prepared the balance with a readout function that has a minimum scale of 0.01 g for weighing. Braille labels were attached in advance to beakers, sample tube bottles, and screw tubes (Figure 1-3-1). In addition, heating operations were practiced in advance.

As in the previous experiment, notches were cut in the handle of a plastic syringe (50 mL) at every 10 mL to indicate volume. A glass pipette was inserted into the tip so that the solution could be collected, and a beaker stand made of a plastic tray was kept separately.

Ⅰ Basic Chemistry

Figure 1-3-1 ▶ On the side sample tube bottles, screw tubes, etc. with Braille labels

(3) Observations on the Experiment Day

◆ Synthesis of nylon 66 through interfacial polymerization

In this experiment, nylon 66 was synthesized by the reaction of 1,6-hexanediamine with adipoyl dichloride. Prior to synthesis, each substance must be weighed and dissolved in appropriate solvents.

Initially, an aqueous solution of 1,6-hexanediamine had to be prepared by adding 0.50 g sodium bicarbonate weighed in advance to a 50-mL triangular flask with a stopper, which contained 0.70 g 1,6-hexanediamine weighed by the laboratory staff beforehand. Subsequently, 30 mL pure water was added to dissolve substances. Pure water was measured using a plastic syringe with notches cut into it, and although this operation was performed without any problems, finding the solution outlet was difficult and it tended to leak easily. Stirring and dissolving operations were performed easily using a flask with a stopper.

Next, a hexane solution of adipoyl dichloride was prepared. A total of 1.0 g adipoyl dichloride was weighed using the electronic balance with a readout function, and 30 mL hexane was added to dissolve the substance. As micropipettes and syringes were not resistant to organic solvents, the weighing of hexane was done by the assistant by reading the scale on the meter glass.

In this experiment, three types of nylon 66 with different shapes were prepared, and their conditions are listed below.

(1) Preparation of nylon 66 thin film

When a hexane solution of adipoyl dichloride was dropped into an aqueous solution of 1,6-hexanediamine, an oil film was formed on the aqueous solution and a polymerization reaction occurred at the interface, producing nylon 66. If a metal ring for forming a thin film was submerged in the aqueous solution in advance and the thin film was scooped out in the shape of a ring using the goldfish scooping technique, the ring would be covered with a nylon 66 thin film. Normally, the experiment was conducted using a single ring. However, in Ms. Amakawa's case, she could not visually confirm the appropriate position for dripping the hexane solution containing adipoyl dichloride with a dropper. Therefore, rings were stacked on top of each other in a two-level arrangement, and by dripping along the inside of the ring placed on the upper level, it was possible to drip the liquid all over the submerged ring on the lower level (Figure 1-3-2). This operation went smoothly because she practiced it in advance.

As excess reagents and water adhered to the fabricated thin film, it had to be washed with ethanol. No problems were encountered during this process either. However, as she was not sure if she was dropping sufficiently to cover the entire ring area, the dropper dispensed a slightly larger volume and film thickness increased by a little (Figure 1-3-3). While an excessively thick film may affect transmittance in IR measurements, which are to be performed later, this was not a problem as sufficient data were obtained.

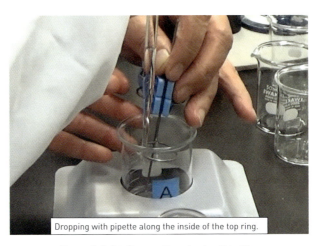

Dropping with pipette along the inside of the top ring.

Figure 1-3-2 ▶ Preparation of nylon thin film

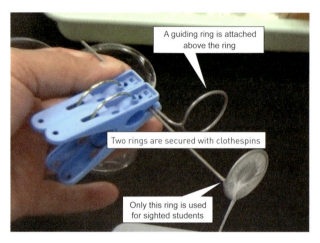

Figure 1-3-3 ▶ Fabricated nylon thin film

(2) Nylon 66 fibers

The principle for fiber formation is the same as that for thin film formation, but here, instead of scooping out nylon obtained through interfacial polymerization as a thin film, it was spun into thread-like fibers.

This time, she inserted tweezers into the solution, pinched them, and guided the thread; subsequently, she touched the finished thread and guided it to a winder. In fact, she produced a long piece of thread than other students by carefully reeling it in. Drying was performed on the winder because it was difficult to peel thin threads by touch without breaking them (threads were sufficiently dry by the afternoon).

(3) Preparation of Nylon 66 capsules

A capsule can be prepared through coloring of an aqueous solution of 1,6-hexanediamine blue by mixing an aqueous solution of trypan blue, and then adding few drops of this solution to a hexane solution containing adipoyl dichloride. The prepared capsules were placed in three solutions: pure water, isotonic solution, and saturated saline solution, and their color change in each solution was monitored.

Although it was difficult to drip the solution with a dropper, she practiced in advance and produced capsules leanly. However, capsules were soft and often broke when removed, making it difficult to confirm the difference by touch.

◆ Measurement of the IR absorption spectrum of nylon 66 (IR measurement)

For IR measurement, Ms. Amakawa set the sample in the instrument and pressed the switch on the instrument to start measurement (however, this was done by opening the larger service window that is not normally used). The results were copied in their original size, and the spectra were traced with the raised line drawing board. The approximate positions of the IR peaks were confirmed by creating axes for each 500 cm^{-1} and 20%T.

◆ Synthesis of nylon 6 through ring-opening polymerization and tensile strength test

Nylon 6 was synthesized by heating ε-caprolactam, polyethylene glycol, and N-acetyl-ε-caprolactam in a test tube to melt the contents and adding sodium *t*-butoxide (base) when the mixture boils. Except for sodium *t*-butoxide addition, which was performed by an assistant, Ms. Amakawa performed the rest of experiments. Ms. Amakawa confirmed the adjustment of the Bunsen burner and boiling of the solution by sound and touch, where she could understand the situation through vibration produced when the mixture boils. Fiber production was also performed without any problems (Figure 1-3-4).

She had the experience of using Bunsen burners at the University of Tsukuba School for the Visually Impaired, and there were no concerns regarding their han-

Figure 1-3-4 ▸ Synthesis of Nylon 6

dling even though we were expecting hazardous situation.

The synthesized nylon 6 fiber was compared with commercially available fishing lines through tensile strength tests. Tensile strength was calculated by dividing the force required to break the thread by the cross-sectional area of the thread. Although the measurement of the cross sectional area of threads was performed using calipers, being not able to check the value was inconvenient for her; therefore, the reading of the caliper value was performed by the assistant. However, Ms. Amakawa inserted threads into the calipers and fixed the threads to the spring scale. The thread is normally pulled vertically until it breaks, but it was difficult to pull it straight vertically without a guide, so it was pulled horizontally along the side of the experimental table.

Regarding the experimental results, the nylon film, capsule, and threads (two types) were prepared without any problems. She was especially careful with the threads and made long threads (Figure 1-3-5). Tensile strength measurements were performed as expected. However, there was an error in the report because the diameter and radius values were incorrect in calculation.

Regarding the experiment time, she finished about 10 min earlier than other students in the morning because the waiting time for explanations was short and she proceeded at her own pace. Further, she proceeded about 10 min earlier in the afternoon and cleaned up first. In the end, she started working on the report when about 25% of the class was ready to do so.

Figure 1-3-5 ▶ Spinning of nylon 66 threads

◆ Cleaning

Ms. Amakawa cleaned experimental equipment.

(4) How to Confirm Understanding Level

The reports were prepared in a separate room using Word and submitted through e-mail by the next day deadline.

(5) Comments

Although there were many difficult operations in this experiment, such as heating and thread production, and we were concerned that there might be problems with the process, she conducted the experiment without any problems by confirming operations the day before. Heating with a Bunsen burner, in particular, was done more skillfully and safely than we had expected. We found out that information that we can obtain through our hearing and touch is much more than we realize. We were also reminded that there is a lot of information to be aware of, such as the sound difference with the shape of the flame, tactile sensation transmitted to the hand due to the boiling of solutions, and difference in the properties of spun thread and thin films due to their tactile feel. In general, she seemed to have done sufficient preparation, understood each experimental operation beforehand, and performed them smoothly, despite the complexity of operations.

(Original text by Hattori, with some corrections by Umezawa)

1-4 Atomic Emission Spectra
(Basic Experiments in Science and Engineering 1B)

(1) Outline of Experiment

In this experiment, students make a simple spectroscope by cutting a piece of cardboard with a blueprint on it using a cutter and a scissor and observe differences in diffracted light from various light sources, such as fluorescent lamps, incandescent lamps, and LEDs. Moreover, the Balmer series spectrum of hydrogen atoms was observed using a small fiber spectrometer. From the observation result, a numerical analysis based on the Bohr's hydrogen atom model was performed to calculate the Rydberg constant and electron energy ranking of hydrogen atom. These experiments facilitate a basic understanding of luminescence and spectroscopy.

We expected that the first half of the experiment, which involved cutting and pasting cardboard to create a simple spectroscope would be feasible. After that, however, a sighted person would have to observe the spectra utilizing the spectroscope and record the observation on a sheet using colored pencils. The key issue was how to implement this part. In the latter half of the experiment, using the small fiber spectrometer, data for numerical analysis were collected using the PC software while taking care to avoid electric shock or burns because the simple luminescence device uses a discharge tube with an accessible high-voltage section.

(2) Advance Preparation

The following preparations were made in advance to create a simple spectrometer.

- The cut and fold lines of the simple spectrometer were traced with a ballpoint pen with force to make concave grooves that clearly indicate the location of printed lines. The cardboard was cut out using a scissor.
- A titration stand and a clamp were prepared as a temporary holder for the simple spectrometer (fixed toward a light bulb), and a digital camera was used to take images through the observation window of the spectrometer. The

images were printed, and the diffracted light images were traced with the raised line drawing board to prepare the spectrum.

- Three types of discharge tubes and three types of light bulbs utilized in the measurement of emission spectra using the small fiber spectrometer were labeled in Braille because of their similar shapes.
- The spectral data obtained from the experiment were printed, and the shape of the spectra was confirmed by creating uneven lines using the raised line drawing board.

In term of sharing responsibilities equally, Ms. Amakawa conducted installing and replacement of the tubes as others would normally do, while the co-experimenter operated the PC software.

However, sketches of the observation on the sheet were omitted.

(3) Observations on the Experiment Day

◆ Measurement of the atomic emission spectra of hydrogen atoms using a compact fiber spectrometer

Owing to the group of the experiment, measurement with the small fiber spectrometer was conducted in the morning and that using the simple spectrometer was performed in the afternoon. Initially, measurement was taken using the small fiber spectrometer. Wavelength calibration was performed using the standard light sources of mercury and neon, and then measurement was taken with a standard light source of hydrogen.

Ms. Amakawa was mainly in charge of installing the luminescent device and replacing the discharge tubes. As tracing was done the day before, operation was completed smoothly and without any major hazards (Figure 1-4-1).

Meanwhile, we warned her that forgetting to turn off the power supply of the discharge tube as she could not visually check if it is off or not may cause the thermal runaway of the measurement device, the deformation of the resin used for the surrounding cover, or even a fire, when she forgot to do so.

During experiment, the co-experimenter noticed an error in reading numerical values (the channel value of the Ne tube) while operating the PC, and re-measurement was necessary. However, re-measurement was completed without any problems due to smooth cooperation with the co-experimenter, including the replacement of the discharge tubes. In terms of the sharing of the measurement data,

Ⅰ Basic Chemistry

Figure 1-4-1 ▶ Replacement of discharge tube

the results were read out by the co-experimenter and recorded, and there were no particular problems.

◆ **Spectral measurements of fluorescent lamps, incandescent lamps, and LEDs using the small fiber spectrometer**

This experiment allowed students to visually understand that even white light bulbs exhibit different spectra when different types of light bulbs are used. In Ms. Amakawa's case, instead of using visual information, she employed tactile information, i.e., figures made with uneven lines.

Ms. Amakawa continued to be in charge of the installation and replacement of the three types of light bulbs and turning the power supply on and off, and operations went smoothly according to trace experiment conducted on the previous day. The height of the optical fiber of the spectrometer needed to be adjusted to observe the appropriate intensity, and this adjustment was done without any problem while talking with the co-experimenter who was checking the intensity on the PC. The PC was operated by the co-experimenter, and the obtained spectral data were printed and processed by an assistant using the raised line drawing board and handed over to Ms. Amakawa (Figure 1-4-2).

◆ **Procedure for fabricating a simple spectrometer**

The simple spectrometer was fabricated by cutting and gluing a piece of

Figure 1-4-2 ▶ Checking spectral data

Figure 1-4-3 ▶ Fabrication of a simple spectrometer

cardboard and incorporating a diffraction grating and a scale into the cardboard. We confirmed during trace experiment on the previous day that she could make it by bending the indented line and cutting the outer frame with a scissor, which she did on the day of the experiment. However, sometimes she cut small parts, such as glue joints, a little too much (Figure 1-4-3). When this was the case, the spectrometer was repaired with a light-shielding tape, so Ms. Amakawa basically did the cutting work.

| Basic Chemistry

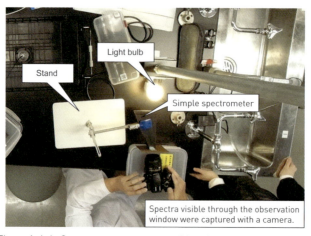

Figure 1-4-4▶ Spectrum measurement with a simple spectrometer

Ms. Hamada offered support by cutting details, such as glue joints, slits, and square windows (two locations), with a scissor and a cutter. Diffraction grating and the fixed position of the scale were important aspects because they affect measurement accuracy. Ms. Amakawa roughly attached them, and Ms. Hamada made fine adjustments to ensure accuracy. We reduced the use of glue to one of the long sides and utilized the light-shielding tape for the other parts to simplify the assembly, which was done by Ms. Amakawa.

Although the resulting spectrometer was slightly twisted, it could still be used for measurements; therefore, we continued to observe the spectra.

◆ Observation of spectra with a simple spectrometer

The spectra were observed using the simple spectrometer in the same way to compare with those obtained using the small spectrometer. The replacement of the three types of light bulbs, turning the power supply on/off, and setting the simple spectrometer on the stand went smoothly as these operations were traced on the previous day.

The spectra were photographed with a digital camera from the observation window of the simple spectrometer and printed in a large size by the assistant and given to Ms. Amakawa after creating uneven lines using the raised line drawing board (Figure 1-4-4).

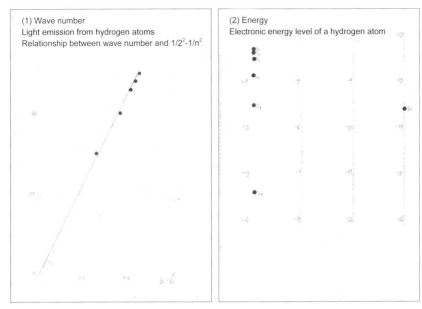

Figure 1-4-5 ▶ Graphs created in "Atomic Emission Spectra" The relationship between wave numbers and $(1/2^2)-(1/n^2)$ in the emission spectrum of hydrogen atom (left), and electron energy levels of hydrogen atom (right)

◆ Spreadsheets, data analysis, and graphing

Data processing was done using Excel to calculate Rydberg constants and energy levels and to analyze the obtained data. Because Excel data sheets are designed for sighted students, it would have been difficult to understand the position of cells, input locations, calculation results, etc., so Ms. Amakawa created data sheets from scratch according to the content of the report (using text-to-speech software (NVDA) to understand the content) and had the data sheet attached to the report as is. (She was allowed to submit the data in her own format rather than using prepared data sheets.)

Ms. Amakawa read the spectral data (waveform shape, spectral range, etc.) of the three types of light bulbs obtained using the small fiber spectrometer and simple spectrometer by touching the spectra converted to uneven lines with her fingers.

Furthermore, she prepared graphs with the help of Ms. Hamada using a Braille graph paper and felt stickers (Figure 1-4-5).

After analyzing and creating these necessary items, the staff checked the data and completed the experiment.

(4) How to Confirm Understanding Level

The report was prepared in a separate room using Word and submitted through e-mail on the day of the experiment.

(5) Comments

Throughout the experiment, she smoothly performed tasks she had traced the day before without any confusion and performed safety-related tasks (e.g., turning the power switch on and off, locking the discharge tube container each time, and supporting the discharge tube container with her body to prevent it from falling to the floor) more carefully than sighted students. While Ms. Amakawa made a simple spectrometer by cutting the cardboard with a scissor as she had requested, she needed Ms. Hamada's assistance and instructions at several steps, and we recognized the difficulty faced by her in the detailed work. However, in the end, she completed the experiment just as well as sighted students, so there was a sense of accomplishment for Ms. Amakawa and relief on the part of the staff. We felt that more work needs to be done in the future for tasks using PCs (including the use of a special software to be used in experiments), such as, for instance, the development of supplementary software.

(Original text by Uchida, partly revised by Umezawa and Hattori)

1-5 Synthesis of Pharmaceuticals
(Basic Experiments in Science and Engineering 1B)

(1) Outline of Experiment

Acetylsalicylic acid is synthesized by the reaction of salicylic acid with acetic anhydride under acid catalyst conditions. The progress of the reaction is confirmed by TLC, and the melting point and IR absorption spectrum of the resulting compound are measured and compared with literature to determine whether the synthesis of the target compound has been achieved.

The first half of the experiment involved synthesis; therefore, handling glassware and reagents was the main task. In the second half of the experiment, the identification of compounds was performed using instrumental analysis, which required dexterity, such as the preparation of samples. By this time, Ms. Amakawa and the faculty members had become accustomed to dealing with this situation based on their previous experience of handling chemical experimental substances. As a result, a method was established in which basic operations were left to Ms. Amakawa, with assistance given only for the more difficult parts of the procedure, which enabled the technical staff to place more emphasis on safety than on the progress of the experiment.

(2) Advance Preparation

The following preparations were made by the week before the experiment.

- The arrangement of glassware, tracing of usage, and handling of the tracing solution for UV–visible spectrophotometer usage were confirmed in advance.
- Braille labels were attached to chemical containers and vial bottles.
- An electronic balance with a readout function was prepared.
- An enamel vat was placed to cover the hot water bath to prevent burns from accidentally touching the hot water bath when feeling around by her hands.

In addition, we decided to provide appropriate assistance for the following

I   Basic Chemistry   117

during experiments.

- Micropipette calibration.
- Spotting of samples on a TLC plate, and the observation of the melting-point analyzer.

(3) Observations on the Experiment Day

◆ Synthesis of acetylsalicylic acid

In the Basic Experiments in Science and Engineering 1A/1B, two students were often seated on each side of the laboratory table and worked in groups. However, during Basic Experiments in Science and Engineering 1A in the spring semester, there were numerous instances where the assistants did not know how to support completely blind persons in their chemistry experiments, so Ms. Amakawa's experiment was separated from the group and the assistants provided full attention to her during experiments. Throughout the three chemistry experiments and experiments in other fields in the spring semester, the significance of allowing Ms. Amakawa conduct parts of the experiments that she could as much as possible and of sharing and discussing the results of experiments through the group were affirmed among the teaching staff. In Basic Experiments in Science and Engineering 1B in the fall semester, groups and tables were set as usual. The "Synthesis of Pharmaceuticals" is basically an individual experiment, but the co-experimenter provided assistance as needed, for instance, by passing reagents and other shared materials.

Acetylsalicylic acid is synthesized by the reaction of salicylic acid with acetic anhydride in the presence of an acid catalyst. The weighing of salicylic acid was performed using a readout electronic balance, and a thick plain paper was used as the packaging paper. One problem we did not foresee was the difficulty in transferring solid powder chemicals into thin tubes such as test tubes (φ16 mm). Though she used a 300-mL conical beaker to fix the test tube and a round piece of paper as a funnel, the task still seemed to be difficult.

A total of 2 mL acetic anhydride and 8 drops of phosphoric acid were added to the test tube and stirred. Liquid reagents were added using micropipettes (Figure 1-5-1).

The assistant observed the inside of the test tube under stirring in the hot water bath from nearby and communicated changes, such as the solid dissolving into

Figure 1-5-1 ▶ The solution is being put into a container using a micropipette

a clear solution.

The reaction was conducted in a hot water bath for 5 min after the disappearance of the solid. Next, 15 mL pure water was prepared in a 100-mL conical beaker, and the entire reaction mixture was added to the beaker. The entire reaction mixture was poured into a 100-mL conical beaker. This resulted in the precipitation of acetylsalicylic acid, which is insoluble in water. A total of 15 mL pure water was measured out twice using a micropipette.

Because suction filtration was already performed in the spring semester, it was carried out as usual. In fact, it seemed that a high recovery rate was achieved as a result of vigorous pouring into the funnel.

The sample was collected from the filter paper by placing the 120-mm filter paper over the funnel and turning it upside down. The remaining sample on the filter paper was collected by the assistant. Ms. Amakawa folded the filter paper and wrote her name on it before drying in oven.

◆ **Confirmation using thin-layer chromatography**

TLC was used to confirm the progress of the reaction. For TLC sample preparation, Ms. Amakawa was responsible for the addition of acetone, while small amounts of acetylsalicylic acid and salicylic acid were collected by the co-experimenter. Ms. Amakawa collected the synthesized acetylsalicylic acid.

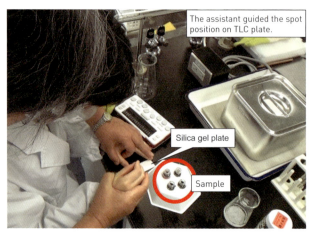

Figure 1-5-2 ▶ Spotting on the TLC plate

Making marking on the TLC plate by a pencil was performed by the assistant. As spotting involved the use of an ultrafine glass capillary tube, it was a very detailed manual process, but Ms. Amakawa performed spotting while the assistant guided her to the correct position (Figure 1-5-2). Ms. Amakawa used tweezers to place and retrieve the TLC plate from the developing chamber.

Ms. Amakawa placed a UV lamp to confirm the position of spots by irradiating the plate with UV light, and the assistant marked the confirmed spots. Ms. Amakawa also sprayed iron chloride with assistance, and after drying, she confirmed the results using a graphical representation prepared utilizing a 200% enlarged copy and the raised line drawing board.

◆ Melting-point measurement

In addition to TLC, two other measurements were performed in this experiment to confirm the synthesize of acetylsalicylic acid: melting-point and IR absorption spectrum measurements. These measurements are described below.

Melting-point measurement is used to confirm a substance. Because each substance has its own unique melting point, the melting point of the tested substance is compared with that of a standard sample, and if there is no difference, it is likely that the tested substance is the target substance.

Before performing the melting-point measurement, it is necessary to remove a small amount of water adhered to the sample during synthesis. During the lunch

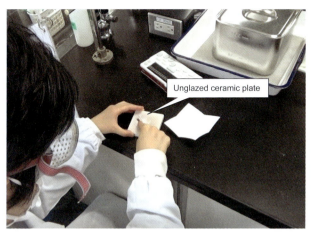

Figure 1-5-3 ▸ Drying operation on an unglazed ceramic plate

break, the powder was kept in oven for drying; however, because the powder cannot be fully dried in 1 h, it was rubbed on an unglazed ceramic plate to form fine particles to remove any remaining moisture.

She seemed to have some difficulty in transferring a part of the sample to the unglazed plate because she could not sense the sample amount on the spatula. The assistant checked whether it was the necessary amount. It was easy to dry the sample uniformly as drying on the unglazed ceramic plate allowed her to feel the change in texture depending on whether the sample was present or not. Ms. Amakawa had gathered the sample in the center of the unglazed ceramic plate and collected it (Figure 1-5-3). Filling the sample into the melting-point measurement tube was also performed without any problem by placing the sample in the center of the tube. Although it was difficult to install thin glass measuring tubes, which are easily broken, inside the melting-point analyzer, it was made possible by having the first one done by the assistant and Ms. Amakawa using it as a guide to insert the other two tubes sideways. Ms. Amakawa operated the melting-point analyzer, and the assistant checked the melting state and read out the temperature at that time.

◆ IR absorption spectrum measurement

The last measurement was IR absorption measurement. IR absorption spectra are used to determine the structure of a target substance utilizing the fact that

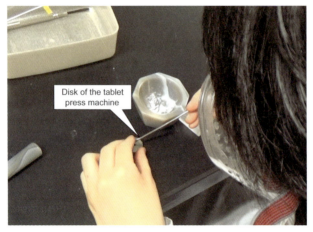

Figure 1-5-4 ▶ Introducing the sample into the disk of the tablet press machine

functional groups and specific bonds contained in a molecule absorb different IR wavelengths. In actual organic synthesis experiments, identification is performed using mass spectrometry and nuclear magnetic resonance (NMR) in addition to other techniques; however, because this was a student experiment, the IR spectrum was analyzed to roughly determine whether or not acetylsalicylic acid was synthesized.

Samples for IR measurement were prepared by mixing a small amount of the sample powder with potassium bromide (KBr). The sample was the powder dehydrated using the unglazed ceramic plate during melting-point measurement. These operations were performed by Ms. Amakawa, starting with the grinding of KBr in a mortar. Although it was little difficult for Ms. Amakawa to transfer KBr to the mortar, she could grind it in the mortar and add the sample to be measured without any problem because she could confirm the difference in the texture of the sample during the grind process through touch. She assembled the disk cosisting of three parts, introduced the samples to it smoothly, and compressed them with the tablet press machine (Figure 1-5-4). However, at one instance, the disk fell apart halfway, and she had to start over. After assembly, Ms. Amakawa compressed the disk using a hand press, set the disk in the IR measurement device, and operated the switch on the main unit to start measurement. The results of IR measurement were enlarged by 141%, printed, and graphically prepared using the raised line drawing board. The axes were appended with Braille labels.

◆ **Cleaning**

Ms. Amakawa cleaned the experimental equipment.

(4) How to Confirm Understanding Level

The report was to be prepared in a separate room using Word and submitted through e-mail by the deadline of the next day.

(5) Comments

Overall, she performed all experiments conducted by sighted people without any changes, except for the observation using the melting-point analyzer. Although there were some detailed tasks, such as spotting the TLC plate and setting up the melting-point measurement tube, they were carried out with the help of the assistant who guided her through the process. Perhaps because many aspects of the experiment were a repetition of operations performed in the spring-semester experiments (extraction of caffeine and synthesis of nylon), she could conduct them smoothly. She finished the experiment at the same time as other students and started writing the report smoothly.

(Original text by Hattori, with some corrections by Umezawa)

1-6 Inclusion of a Molecule into Cyclodextrin
(Basic Experiments in Science and Engineering 1B)

(1) Outline of Experiment

This experiment was performed to observe the inclusion phenomenon of phenolphthalein by β-cyclodextrin through colorimetric and absorbance spectrophotometry. Furthermore, the process of the inclusion of phenolphthalein into β-cyclodextrin was determined using Gaussian, a quantum chemical calculation software, to derive an energetically stable conformation.

We inferred that for the first half of the experiment, she already had a good understanding of the experimental flow as she had already worked on the preparation of β-cyclodextrin solution and phenolphthalein solution, colorimetric method, and spectrophotometer in "Water Quality Analysis" in Basic Experiments in Science and Engineering 1A. However, as structural optimization calculations in the latter half were performed on a PC entirely, Ms. Amakawa naturally could not see screens during the process. Therefore, the co-experimenter operated the PC and shared the obtained results; at the same time, it was very difficult to explain differences in the results before and after performing structural optimization.

(2) Advance Preparation

In the first half of the experiment, the following preparations were made based on previous experimental experience.

- The arrangement of glassware, tracing of equipment usage, and handling of the tracing solution for the UV–visible spectrophotometer usage were confirmed in advance.
- Braille labels were attached to chemical containers and vial bottles.
- As in previous experiments, holes were drilled in a plastic tray to hold beakers.

Meanwhile, structural optimization simulation using a PC needed to be handled separately by the staff, so the following two methods were used to check the

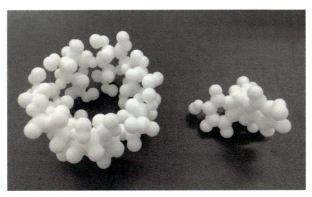

Figure 1-6-1 ▶ 3D printer models of β-cyclodextrin (left) and phenolphthalein (right) as filled models

results.

- Make a tactile copy from the displayed figures, and check the calculated structure.
- The optimized models obtained from calculations are prepared in advance using a 3D printer (filled model and stick model) and confirmed on the day by Ms. Amakawa through touch, enabling her understanding of the characteristics of the molecular model (Figure 1-6-1).

In addition, the following experimental modifications were offered by assistants as required in the same manner as in previous experimental tasks.

- Micropipette calibration
- Confirmation of UV–Visible spectrophotometer operation

(3) Observations on the Experiment Day

The experimental modifications on the day of the experiment were conducted as follows.

◆ Preparation of β-cyclodextrin solution

The β-cyclodextrin solution was prepared by co-experimenters, and Ms.

Figure 1-6-2 ▶ Addition of buffer solution

Amakawa prepared the phenolphthalein solution. A micropipette was used to measure 5 mL phenolphthalein solution, and the buffer solution was measured with a dropper that holds ~10 mL per dose, which was then poured to a volumetric flask (Figure 1-6-2).

The volume of the solution in the volumetric flask was subsequently measured by placing a finger on the neck of the flask and estimating its height by temperature sensation, similar to the approach employed in the "Water Quality Analysis." Further, pure water was poured from washing bottles up to the neck of the flask. Subsequently, pure water was added from the dropping bottle under the guidance of the assistant. Finally, the assistant adjusted water to the marked line in the volumetric flask, and Ms. Amakawa performed mixing by inverting the flask.

◆ Observation of inclusion phenomenon

To prepare β-cyclodextrin solutions of different concentrations, a micropipette was used to dispense the phenolphthalein and β-cyclodextrin solutions into 50-mL volumetric flasks. The dispensing of the solutions whose volumes could not be handled by micropipettes as well as filling of volumetric flasks up to the required volume were performed by co-experimenters.

The prewashing of the absorbance cell was performed by filling it twice to the brim in a waste beaker, with the expectation that some solution will be spilled, and discarding the solution; the same procedure was employed in the "Water

Figure 1-6-3 ▶ Detection using a light probe

Quality Analysis." Dispensing solution into the cell was also performed in a waste beaker as a precise volume is not necessary in this case; instead, filling the cell with a sufficient amount of the solution was enough.

To compare the color intensity of each solution, flasks were initially placed in front of a white plate, similar to the "Water Quality Analysis," and their tones were checked by placing a light probe on the neck part of the flasks (Figure 1-6-3). Furthermore, the color tones were reconfirmed using a 1-cm absorbance cell with a constant length.

Co-experimenters performed experiments in which small amounts of α-cyclodextrin and 1-adamantanol were added as the host and guest molecules, respectively, and Ms. Amakawa measured absorbance using a UV–visible spectrophotometer.

Ms. Amakawa studied the button layout, and the screen display and switches of the UV–visible spectrophotometer were described to her prior to operating the spectrophotometer. Ms. Amakawa placed the absorbance cell into the spectrophotometer without any problem. Operating the device was easy to her because it beeped for each switch operation, and the assistant explained screen transitions for each operation (Figure 1-6-4).

The resulting spectrum was enlarged by 200% and displayed on the raised line drawing board; additionally, the measurement values were read out and recorded by co-experimenters, and then she prepared the respective graphs.

1 Basic Chemistry

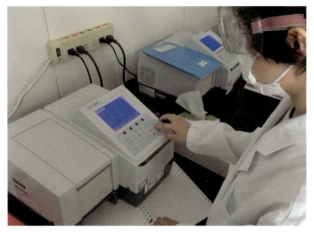

Figure 1-6-4 ▶ Operating the UV–visible spectrophotometer

In the experiment of replacing the host and guest molecules, there were two tasks. One was to check the change in pH and the other was to determine the change in the color tone. Among the two tasks, pH was reported by co-experimenters. Furthermore, the change in the color tone was determined by transferring the solution to an absorbance cell and comparing its color tone with the original solution's color tone (in the flask) using a light probe.

◆ **Energy calculations of the prepared inclusion complexes using quantum chemical calculations**

In the molecular modeling of phenolphthalein, the placement of molecules on the PC screen and setting of the calculation parameters were performed by co-experimenters. Changes in the molecular model before and after calculations were explained orally and confirmed using the tactile copies of the model on the screen before and after calculations.

To calculate the energies of inclusion complexes using the software, the co-experimenter operated the molecular model data file in the PC, entered the set values for distances between molecules, and set the calculation parameters. The calculation results were read out by the co-experimenter, and Ms. Amakawa recorded the values and prepared the graphs.

In addition, a method was implemented to enable her understanding of the inclusion state of phenolphthalein in β-cyclodextrin by touching a molecular

Figure 1-6-5 ▸ Checking the three-dimensional structure of the cyclodextrin model

model created using a 3D printer. While Ms. Amakawa could understand the relative positions of molecules, she seemed to have difficulty in grasping subtle 3D differences (Figure 1-6-5).

The following issues were raised regarding the experiment results.

- Absorbance obtained when 1 mL β-cyclodextrin was added was similar to that when 3 mL was added and was detected as low absorbance. The same trend was observed in the color tone analysis. This is probably because the micropipette sucked air when dispensing 5 mL phenolphthalein solution, resulting in a low actual volume. Because Ms. Amakawa could not check the filling status of the pipette, it is considered essential to have an assistant check the pipette when using micropipettes or Komagome pipettes.

(4) How to Confirm Understanding Level

The level of understanding was gauged based on the submitted report as usual. Two types of graphs were prepared using the Braille graph paper after completing the experiment, and she finished them in the same amount of time as other students. Subsequently, she started writing the report. The report was prepared in Word and was submitted by e-mail. She submitted it by the same deadline as other students.

(5) Comments

Overall, she conducted all experiments by sharing work with her co-experimenters. Improving the manual for absorbance measurement, which was performed by assistants in the "Water quality analysis," and providing instructions for each operations allowed her to grasp the entire experimental operations. In addition, assistants gave instructions to Ms. Amakawa regarding screen transitions so that she could perform measurements using instruments with a good understanding of them. Perhaps, because many operations involved in this experiment have been a review of the operations performed in "Water Quality Analysis," the experiment proceeded smoothly.

(Original text by Hattori, with some corrections by Umezawa)

1 – 7 Synthesis and Electrochemical Measurement of Ferrocene
(Basic Experiments in Science and Engineering 2B)

(1) Outline of Experiment

Ferrocene, an organometallic compound, was synthesized and purified via sublimation. The oxidation–reduction potential of the synthesized ferrocene was measured using cyclic voltammetry. Cyclic voltammetry was used to measure the oxidation–reduction potentials of ferrocene analogues with substituents on the cyclopentadienyl group and investigate the effect of these substituents on these potentials.

The second-year Basic Experiments in Science and Engineering 2B differs from the first-year Basic Experiments in Science and Engineering 1A/1B in that these experiments are designed for self-study and do not include a lecture at the beginning of the course. As experiments were conducted based on the flowchart created by each student and information in the textbook, it was important to organize experiments from the perspective of developing Ms. Amakawa's thinking skills.

(2) Advance Preparation

One week before the experiment, we made the following preparations with Ms. Hamada.

- Attachment of Braille labels to glassware.
- Arrangement of equipment to be used.
- Explanation of the experimental procedure (overview).
- Communication of precautions to be adopted during experiments (e.g., risk of burns, etc.).
- Explanation and exercises on items requiring calculations and pre-experiment.

| Basic Chemistry 131

(3) Observations on the Experiment Day

◆ Synthesis and sublimation purification of ferrocene

First, ferrocene ($Fe(C_5H_5)_2$), the main target of this experiment, was synthesized. Ferrocene is a compound with the so-called "sandwich structure," in which two cyclopentadienyl anions ($[C_5H_5]^-$) sandwich a divalent iron ion on both sides. To synthesize it, cyclopentadiene must initially be ionized via treatment with a base and then reacted with iron(II) chloride.

She weighed ~1.0 g potassium hydroxide on an electronic balance with a readout function and ground it to the powder form in a mortar. This powder was placed in a 50-mL Erlenmeyer flask with a stopper together with a stirrer, dissolved in 5 mL 1,2-dimethoxyethane, and then purged with nitrogen gas.

A total of 0.4 mL cyclopentadiene was added to this solution with a syringe and then stirred. The color of the solution gradually changed as ions were formed. Ferrocene yielded from this experiment exhibited orange color, but the solution underwent various color changes, such as yellow, ocher, and brown. Thus, Ms. Hamada who was assisting or students who were co-experimenters explained and recorded the color changes at each step of the synthesis.

Separately, 5 mL dimethyl sulfoxide was placed in a 50-mL sample tube and purged with nitrogen gas; further, 0.36 g iron(II) chloride tetrahydrate was added to it.

Ferrocene was synthesized by adding this iron chloride solution to the cyclopentadiene solution prepared previously under stirring; additionally, during stirring for 20 min, there was time to record observations and other results.

Once the required time had elapsed, reaction was stopped by adding hydrochloric acid and decreasing the temperature by cooling with ice, and the reaction solution was filtered via suction. The residue was then washed several times with pure water to obtain the desired solid substance. The solid substance was transferred to a large piece of a filter paper, pressed down on the table to allow the filter paper to absorb water, and then air dried.

The air-dried solid substance was sealed in a petri dish and heated using a hot stirrer to sublimate and purify the solid substance on the top lid. The solid substance was collected with a spatula to obtain pure ferrocene, and the yield was measured. Co-experimenters visually determined whether sublimation had completed or not.

◆ Cyclic voltammetry

Ferrocene derivatives in which a functional group is inserted at the cyclopentadienyl anion exhibit different electrical properties compared to the original ferrocene. In particular, cyclic voltammetry measurements were performed with derivatives containing electron-withdrawing or electron-donating groups at the cyclopentadienyl anion. Cyclic voltammetry is a widely used technique for measuring the oxidation–reduction potential of components dissolved in a solution. Note that ferrocene used for comparison was the product synthesized in the previous process.

First, a 0.1 mol/L tetra-*n*-butylammonium perchlorate solution (solvent: acetonitrile) was prepared. Next, three reagents—synthesized ferrocene, commercially available acetylferrocene, and commercially available 1,1-dimethylferrocene—were weighed separately into three 20-mL volumetric flasks to obtain a mass of 2 mmol. Because the amount to be weighed was extremely small and could not be handled by the available balance with a readout function, a precision balance was used in the laboratory, and Ms. Hamada and a co-experimenter assisted in weighing. After weighing, the tetra-*n*-butylammonium perchlorate solution was added to the 20-mL volumetric flask to make the volume constant. It was also difficult for Ms. Amakawa to check the marking on the flask, and assistance was required.

In the following measurement operations, including removing electrodes, fixing measuring instruments, and using a PC, Ms. Amakawa needed assistance in setting the parameters of the analysis software but performed the rest of the operations.

Ms. Hamada used a raised line drawing board to prepare the voltammograms obtained from measurements in such a way that their linearity could be checked, and the scale was supplemented with Braille labels.

◆ Reaction with 1,4-benzoquinone

The purpose of the experiment was to analyze the oxidation–reduction reaction between the three ferrocene derivatives and 1,4-benzoquinone via coloration; however, as the analysis was based on the color change, Ms. Hamada and co-experimenters reported color changes and recorded them.

◆ Cleaning

Ms. Amakawa cleaned experimental equipment.

Ⅰ　Basic Chemistry

(4) How to Confirm Understanding Level

The flowchart prepared before the experiment was created using a PC, received by e-mail, and printed out for review by TAs on the day of the class in the same manner as that for sighted students. Ms. Amakawa and other students took an oral examination that evaluates their understanding of the experiment, where they had to answer questions from the instructor regarding the experiment.

(5) Comments

Due to the COVID-19 pandemic, only a limited number of experiments were conducted in person, a situation different from previous years. However, knowledge she gained from the previous year's Basic Experiments in Science and Engineering 1A/1B was highly useful, and the staff could support her smoothly.

(Original text by Tsuzuki, with some additions by Umezawa)

1–8 Separation and Molecular Weight Measurement of Proteins
(Basic Experiments in Science and Engineering 2B)

(1) Outline of Experiment

An unknown sample containing a mixture of two proteins was separated via size-exclusion chromatography, and the resulting proteins were treated with various reagents and subjected to SDS–polyacrylamide gel electrophoresis. The molecular weight of proteins was determined based on the electrophoresis results.

In the first half of the experiment, proteins flowing out of the size-exclusion chromatography system were observed and collected using a UV monitor and a recorder. Determining how to check whether proteins are indeed flowing when the recorder could not be observed visually is important in this experiment. Because Ms. Amakawa already had experience in using micropipettes in Basic Experiments in Science and Engineering 1A/1B, we expected that there would be no problem in measuring and mixing reagents as she had done in previous experiments.

The latter half of the experiment involved setting samples on the electrophoresis gel, and she proceeded with the experiment with the help of co-experimenters for these detailed tasks.

(2) Advance Preparation

Prior to the day of the experiment, the following preparations were made with Ms. Hamada.

- Explanation regarding the arrangement of glassware and equipment used and an overview of the experiment.
- Confirmation of procedures and pre-experiments for size-exclusion chromatography, protein sample chemical treatment, gel preparation, and electrophoresis.

Ⅰ Basic Chemistry

(3) Observations on the Experiment Day

◆ Size-exclusion chromatography

In size-exclusion chromatography, a glass column is filled with a gel containing numerous pores, and as target molecules pass through these pores, they are separated according to their size. The laboratory was equipped with columns for each group, and the staff maintained them so that students only had to operate columns on the day of the experiment.

In this experiment, Ms. Amakawa was paired with a co-experimenter, and the table was the same as the one that was always set up in the laboratory.

Because Ms. Amakawa had touched and checked the appearance for the size-exclusion chromatography system in advance, she knew the locations of the column, UV monitors, recorders, and tubing. Instruction regarding the use of the sample inlet installed in the middle of the piping (e.g., direction of the cock) was given at each occasion, and the sample could be injected without any incident (Figure 1-8-1).

On injecting the sample, a peristaltic pump attached upstream of the column pumped the buffer solution along with the sample solution. The two proteins were separated as they passed through the column and then reached the UV monitor located downstream of the column. Some amino acids that make up proteins contain benzene ring structures, and when the protein of interest was irradiated with UV

Figure 1-8-1▶ Size-exclusion chromatography operation (sample injection)
Technical staff provided operational support.

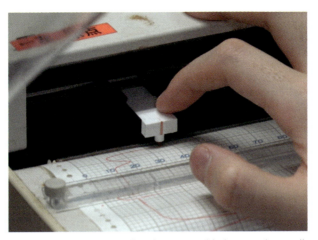

Figure 1-8-2▶ Protein detection via contact with the recorder needle
The needle movement was slowed down by a strong touch; therefore, it was necessary to touch it softly.

light, it absorbs a portion of the light. In other words, the UV absorbance information was transmitted to the recorder as an electrical signal, which could be read as the movement of the needle. In recent years, digital display recorders have become prominent; however, fortunately, the recorder used in the laboratory at that time was an analog recorder; therefore, she could understand the appearance of the peak tactilely by placing one hand on the needle without interfering its movement (Figure 1-8-2).

◆ **Preparation of gels for electrophoresis**

Because the timing (retention time) at which the protein efflux was expected to appear as a peak was ~15 and 40 min after sample injection, the gels to be used in the subsequent electrophoresis were prepared together with the co-experimenter before the retention time. Two types of gels had to be prepared: one for protein concentration and the other for separation, with each requiring the mixing of several reagents in small quantities. Ms. Amakawa had to use a micropipette because the reagent was liquid. However, it was not practical for the progress of the experiment that she had to adjust the scale of each reagent herself; therefore, Ms. Hamada assisted her in adjusting the scale of each individual micropipette.

◆ Trichloroacetic acid (TCA) precipitation method and preparation of sample solution

After eluting and subsequently securing the protein samples, the next step was to treat them with chemicals. In this process, the separated proteins were concentrated and broke down into their various 3D structures to form chains, thereby converting them into a state suitable for electrophoresis. Although these operations involved the delicate tasks of adding chemical solutions using micropipettes, this did not pose any particular inconvenience to Ms. Amakawa, who had used micropipettes numerous times in the past. The inside conditions of the colored samples and sample tubes were recorded by the co-experimenter and Ms. Hamada, who informed her as necessary.

◆ SDS–polyacrylamide gel electrophoresis

The co-experimenter was responsible for injecting the chemically treated protein samples into the prepared gel, while the subsequent connection to the power supply and setting of the electrophoresis conditions were done by Ms. Amakawa. This was the first half of the experiment, and they took a lunch break during electrophoresis, which took ~60–75 min.

After the lunch break, the experiment was resumed, and gels were removed from glass plates. The subsequent staining process was conducted with the co-experimenter.

The stained gel was photographed from above using a digital camera, and an A4-sized enlarged copy of the image was provided by the laboratory office. This copy was then transcribed using the raised line drawing board to determine the contour of the gel, boundary line between the concentrated and separated gels, position of migration completion, and band positions of the markers and protein samples (Figure 1-8-3).

Based on the numerical data obtained from the aforementioned electrophoresis results, correlation between the log (molecular weight) and relative mobility (R_f value) was plotted using the raised line drawing board. The scale was written in Braille on the ruled line, and the graph was plotted using pins (Figure 1-8-4).

Ms. Amakawa summarized the experimental results up to this point based on the reporting items specified in the textbook, and then participated in the oral examination (an examination in which students answer questions regarding experiments from the instructor) with other students.

Figure 1-8-3 ▶ Confirmation of electrophoresis results

Figure 1-8-4 ▶ Organization of electrophoresis results

◆ **Cleaning**

Ms. Amakawa cleaned experimental equipment.

(4) How to Confirm Understanding Level

The flowchart prepared before the experiment was created using the PC, received by e-mail, and printed out for review by TAs on the day of the class in the same manner as that for sighted students. Ms. Amakawa and other students took an oral examination that evaluates their understanding of the experiment, where they had to answer questions from the instructor regarding the experiment.

(5) Comments

Compared with synthesis experiments where reagents are added to a container and reacted or instrumental analysis experiments in which samples are filled into a glass cell or other apparatus and measured, we thought that the first part of this experiment might be difficult to imagine from the standpoint of a completely blind person. After placing the sample at the inlet, the peristaltic pump continued to run for several tens of minutes, and nothing happened until the recorder's needle moved. While a sighted person can see the entire apparatus and sense that something is going on, even if there is no movement, the lack of such information might be difficult for Ms. Amakawa. Therefore, during the experiment, explanations were given to supplement the visual information, such as, "The sample is now passing through this area, and separation should be progressing in the column." Furthermore, after obtaining the electrophoresis results, we did not have to offer any particular support other than printing materials because Ms. Amakawa did not seem to have much difficulty in processing and compiling the necessary numerical data, as had been the case in previous experiments.

(Original text by: Umezawa)

1 – 9 Synthesis of a Titanium Oxide Photocatalyst by the Sol-Gel Method and Scientific Information Search Using a PC (Basic Experiments in Science and Engineering 2B)

(1) Outline of Experiment

When titanium tetraisopropoxide (TTIP), a metal alkoxide, is hydrolyzed with pure water and hydrochloric acid in ethanol solvent, hydroxyl groups formed on titanium undergo dehydration condensation polymerization, forming continuous Ti–O–Ti bonds. By heat-treating it at a high temperature, a titanium dioxide photocatalyst can be synthesized. In the experiment, the diffuse reflectance spectrum of the synthesized titanium dioxide photocatalyst was measured and decomposition reaction of the dye was monitored to evaluate the physical properties and activity of the photocatalyst.

This experiment involved handling TTIP during synthesis and working with a high-temperature furnace; therefore, we had to be extra careful to avoid chemical and heat burns.

The experiment proceeded without any difficulty in numerical processing because the measured values of the physical properties and activity evaluation were provided by analyzers and other equipment.

(2) Advance Preparation

A trace experiment was conducted in advance with Ms. Hamada, and the following preparations were made.

- Ms. Amakawa would be responsible for basic operations.
- The approach adopted was that Ms. Amakawa would receive an explanation from a staff member regarding the use and operation of equipment she would be using and then proceed to the actual operation of equipment.
- Separate trays were prepared for chemicals to prevent them from tipping over.
- Micropipettes (1, 5, and 10 mL) and syringes (5 and 50 mL) were provided for collecting each solution, instead of graduated cylinder and Komagome pipette.

Ⅰ Basic Chemistry

(3) Observations on the Experiment Day

◆ Synthesis of titanium dioxide photocatalyst

According to the protocol provided in the laboratory textbook, ~6 mL TTIP should be dispensed into a 10-mL beaker and then 5 g should be weighed out from it using a balance. However, because TTIP is an unstable reagent that must be weighed quickly, in Ms. Amakawa's case, 5 mL TTIP was taken with a micropipette, placed in the synthesis beaker, and weighed. The weighed 5 mL TTIP corresponded to ~4.86 g, which was slightly less than the required amount; nevertheless, it was considered sufficient, given the amount used for measurement and amount lost in tactile observation. As the electronic balance with a readout function can read up to two decimal places, there was no problem with respect to weighing (Figure 1-9-1).

A total of 20 mL ethanol was injected into weighed TTIP using a plastic syringe with notches (Figure 1-9-2).

Hydrochloric acid is usually diluted in a meter glass, pipetted, and dripped with a Komagome pipette, but for Ms. Amakawa, it was decided that she would add hydrochloric acid using a plastic bottle (a container with a structure similar to eye drop containers). The solution was directly diluted in a plastic bottle, lidded and shaken, and then dropped into the reaction beaker by pushing once every 5 s. The number of drops was adjusted based on the verbal advice of the staff.

The prepared solution was stirred for 5 min after dropping the acid, 50 mL pure water was added to the reaction mixture, and the reaction mixture was allowed to stand for 1 min to facilitate the precipitation of the suspended solution. To obtain this precipitate, decantation (removal of supernatant by tilting) must be performed. While a sighted person can adjust the tilt to the point where supernatant is likely to flow out with a fine balance, this operation was very difficult for Ms. Amakawa. As a solution, two laboratory jacks were placed side by side to adjust the tilt of decantation, a beaker held in a hand was placed on one side and a plastic waste beaker was placed on the other side. We asked her to tilt the beaker in her hand slowly to pour some of the supernatant into the plastic beaker and to hold the beaker in the same position as she poured it in. By gradually lowering the jack on the side of the beaker for disposal, Ms. Hamada caused the beaker in her hand (with the outlet supported by it) to tilt further, slowly discarding the supernatant liquid. A staff member determined when to stop decanting and instructed her to do so (Figure 1-9-3). The remaining supernatant was filtered by suction, and the

Figure 1-9-1 ▶ TTIP weighing

Figure 1-9-2 ▶ Ethanol injection

powder was washed with 50 mL pure water.

The powder obtained via filtration was transferred to a crystallizing dish and heated to approximately 200°C using a hot stirrer until it solidified. Normally, heat-resistant gloves are worn during the entire heating process of the crystallizing dish; however, in the Ms. Amakawa's case, as operations relied on touch, wearing gloves made them difficult and dangerous. Therefore, operations were performed with bare hands as much as possible (during heating, the crystal dish bottom was

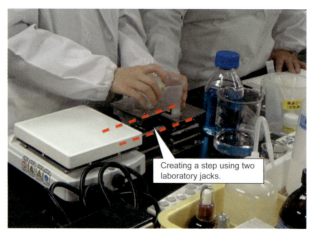

Figure 1-9-3 ▶ Decanting operation

Figure 1-9-4 ▶ Confirmation of solids after cooling

dangerous to touch, but the edges were cool enough to be touched by hand.)

　　The dried and solidified powder was transferred to a ceramic crucible and sintered in an electric furnace at 600°C for 30 min. Crucible tongs and heat-resistant gloves were used for removing the crucible from the electric furnace.

　　Ms. Amakawa touched the obtained solids after cooling to get an idea regarding their textures (Figure 1-9-4).

◆ Photocatalytic activity evaluation

Titanium dioxide photocatalysts oxidize and decompose organic matter when irradiated with UV light. In this experiment, the blue dye, methylene blue, was used as the organic material, and photocatalytic activity was evaluated by monitoring color fading as the prepared photocatalyst facilitates the oxidative decomposition of the dye.

Methylene blue solutions with and without the synthesized titanium dioxide were prepared. Further, each solution was set in a darkroom with a UV lamp. Sampling was conducted periodically while checking the passage of time with a timer.

Normally, in this sampling process, the cell used for measurement should be prewashed; however, if Ms. Amakawa was to do so, more sample solution would be required, and the overall solution loss would reach a non-negligible level. Therefore, prewashing was not performed to avoid the loss of the solution. Instead, we prepared dry absorption cells and filled them directly with the solution. In addition, we instructed her to suck the sample solution with a syringe and then put a 0.45-μm syringe filter (made of cellulose acetate) on the syringe before putting the solution into the absorption cell. (This was the opposite of what sighted students were instructed to do. Though if they put on the syringe filter and then sucked the solution, pores on the syringe filter would become clogged and sucking could not be performed properly, but Ms. Amakawa would not be able to grasp this aspect). Although 3 mL was to be sucked up and transferred to the absorption cell (about 80% of the cell capacity) because the filter itself absorbed the liquid the first time, we instructed her to suck 4 mL (Figure 1-9-5).

The solution in the cell was analyzed using the UV–visible spectrophotometer. This was not the first time Ms. Amakawa is using this device as it is exactly the same type used in Basic Experiments in Science and Engineering 1A and 1B. The operation proceeded according to the manual, and the measurement data were obtained. The measured data were entered as absorbance values in the Excel file used normally in face-to-face classes (i.e., values were read out by the staff and entered by Ms. Amakawa). Two graphs (one with absorbance on the vertical axis and the other with $\ln[A]/[A_0]$ on the vertical axis) were displayed based on the input values, which were then printed out in a large size and copied in 3D. In addition, the staff read out the slope of the latter graph (displayed in the graph).

Regarding dye absorption by the filter during sampling for photocatalytic activity evaluation, the absorbance of the sample solution at $t = 0$ was lower than the

1　Basic Chemistry

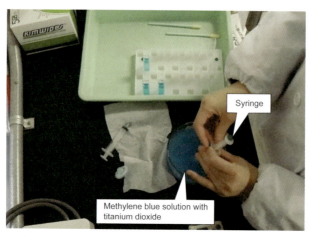

Figure 1-9-5 ▸ Sampling for evaluating photocatalytic activity

usual experimental value, and at t = 10, absorbance was higher than that at t = 0. Because this was a common result obtained in several trace experiments conducted using the method by Ms. Amakawa, we suspected dye absorption by the filter as the cause for the aforementioned result because that was the part of the operation different from the usual experiment. The difference between the normal experiment and Ms. Amakawa's experiment was the prewashing of the sample. The amount of solution collected was 3 mL for Ms. Amakawa (4 mL for the first time with a filter) compared with 6 mL per time in the normal experiment. We therefore conducted a simple check as follows.

Using the remaining 4 mg/L methylene blue solution prepared by Ms. Amakawa, 4 mL was taken using a new filter and another 3 mL was taken, and absorbance was measured for both cases. Absorbance was 0.599 for the former and 0.867 for the latter, suggesting that the filter absorbs the dye. Further, when the filter saturates, it will not further absorb the dye, increasing absorbance in the next sample. This is thought to be the reason for the decrease in absorbance observed at t = 0. Because such a result was due to the Ms. Amakawa's unique circumstances, we explained the situation to her and suggested, and although it was based on a simple investigation (due to time constraints), to provisionally substitute the latter value of 0.867 for t = 0 and conduct further confirmation separately from the original results.

While the Excel file used by sighted students was given to Ms. Amakawa in advance for the evaluation of photocatalytic activity, she may not have been aware of the existence of other tables and figures (two graphs and one table of $\ln[A]/[A_0]$ automatically calculated based on the input values) due to insufficient explanation regarding tables in the Excel file.

◆ Diffuse reflectance spectrum measurement

The diffuse reflectance spectrum was measured to determine the band gap energy by placing the synthesized titanium dioxide in a powder cell and measuring the spectrum using the UV–visible spectrophotometer equipped with an integrating sphere for diffuse reflection. Because the measurement data were printed as a spectral diagram, the absorption edge wavelengths, which are necessary data, were obtained by drawing a slope with a ruler along the contours of the tactile copy of the spectrum made in the laboratory. Values were read out by staff.

◆ Cleaning

Ms. Amakawa cleaned experimental equipment.

(4) How to Confirm Understanding Level

The flowchart prepared before the experiment was created using the PC and received by e-mail. Moreover, she brought back the result of the in-person experiment, and the level of her understanding was evaluated through the report she submitted by the designated date.

(5) Comments

This experiment was conducted amidst restrictions on educational and research activities at the university due to the global COVID-19 pandemic. Sighted students who took the course at the same time did not conduct this experiment in person but were assessed through the on-demand submission of assignments. In Ms. Amakawa's case, however, the experiment was conducted in person because we felt that visual materials on demand would not be sufficient to achieve the results. We keenly felt the significance of conducting experiments in person and difficulty in conducting experiments with limited human resources in an environment where behavior was restricted.

(Original text by Matsubara, with some additions by Umezawa)

1 – 10
Synthesis of Polystyrene by Suspension Polymerization and Its Recycling
(Basic Experiments in Science and Engineering 2B)

(1) Outline of Experiment

Polystyrene was selected as a representative example of a polymer compound, and polystyrene beads were synthesized from styrene and divinylbenzene through suspension polymerization. In addition, a polystyrene film was fabricated by dissolving recycled polystyrene in an organic solvent, and styrene foam was prepared by gelling it. Furthermore, polystyrene was heated and depolymerized to obtain a distillate, which was then analyzed via gas chromatography.

Normally, for preparing polystyrene beads and performing depolymerization reactions, the reaction apparatus is assembled by connecting glassware. Because the inside of the glassware is hot and inaccessible during the reaction, we were concerned about how well we could communicate to her the status of the reactants. We believed that her previous practical experience would be sufficient for the measurement of basic reagents, confirmation of the obtained sample texture, and processing of numerical data.

(2) Advance Preparation

A trace experiment was conducted in advance with Ms. Hamada, and the following preparations were made.

- Preparation of a Komagome pipette connected to a syringe for measuring liquid reagents.
- Installation of a silicone tube near the inlet of the gas chromatography analyzer (to guide the sample to the inlet and prevent burns).
- Preparation of the electronic balance with a readout function.
- Preparation of plastic trays for holding beakers.

(3) Observations on the Experiment Day

◆ Synthesis of polystyrene beads through suspension polymerization

To synthesize polystyrene, styrene monomer and divinylbenzene were collected. In this task, liquid was collected using an instrument comprising connected Komagome pipette and syringe, which had been prepared in advance (Figure 1-10-1). In general, the styrene and divinylbenzene reagents contain a polymerization inhibitor to prevent spontaneous polymerization. To remove it, the sodium hydroxide solution was added and stirred with a glass rod. The washing took ~2 min, during which the polymerization inhibitor reacted with the sodium hydroxide solution and turned it into a bright red or orange-brown color. This color change was communicated to Ms. Amakawa. When the sample was allowed to stand, it separated into an organic phase and an aqueous phase, and the unwanted aqueous phase was removed using the prepared Komagome pipette utilized in the weighing process. A plastic tray was employed for holding the beaker when a 50–100-mL beaker was stirred with a glass rod and the lower layer was aspirated (to prevent the beaker from tipping over and to check its position).

As anhydrous magnesium sulfate was used to remove trace amounts of water in the organic phase, the powder was also weighed. The electronic balance with a readout function was utilized for this purpose. A weighing dish (a commercially available disposable plastic dish, with a dimension of approximately 80 × 80 mm) was placed on the balance, and the powder was added using a medicine spoon or another weighing dish while constantly checking the position of the weighing dish

Figure 1-10-1 ▶ Komagome pipette with connected syringe

| Basic Chemistry

Figure 1-10-2 ▸ Checking the produced polystyrene film

with a finger.

A polyvinyl alcohol aqueous solution, a stirrer, previously prepared azobisisobutyronitrile, purified styrene, and divinylbenzene were added to an eggplant-shaped flask. Subsequently, the apparatus was set. Ms. Amakawa assembled the polymerization apparatus with the help of the assistant, Ms. Hamada.

Because the size of beads inside could not be visually confirmed, Ms. Hamada and the staff checked and adjusted heating and stirring, as required. After 20 min of heating, beads were successfully prepared.

◆ Preparation of the polystyrene film

The polystyrene film was prepared by dissolving ~0.5 g polystyrene for recycling in 10 mL ethyl acetate and volatilizing ethyl acetate on a petri dish. Weighing polystyrene was not difficult because an electronic balance with a read-out function was used. Weighing ethyl acetate (using the aforementioned Komagome pipette connected to a syringe) was also not challenging.

After production, the film was removed from the petri dish, and she checked its texture by touching it directly (Figure 1-10-2).

◆ Production of styrene foam

Polystyrene was gelatinized by adding ~2.5 g recycled polystyrene to a 200-mL beaker along with a small amount of acetone. When gelled, polystyrene was

Figure 1-10-3▶ Pretreatment for making styrene foam
(in the photo, the plastic bottle is on the left)

rolled up, filled into a tea strainer, and heated; further, it expanded to yield polystyrene foam. For this occasion, a separate plastic bottle was prepared for acetone drops (Figure 1-10-3). The required amount of acetone (~3 mL) was filled in advance, and acetone was dropped by lightly squeezing the bottle. This allowed Ms. Amakawa to avoid the failure of the experiment owing to the excess addition of acetone.

◆ **Polystyrene depolymerization**

As an experiment opposite to synthesis, the depolymerization of polystyrene by heating was conducted. Approximately 5 g polystyrene was weighed for depolymerization. The weighed polystyrene was placed in an Erlenmeyer flask and was heated and mixed with a hot stirrer. The assembly of the depolymerization apparatus was completed in cooperation with Ms. Hamada, as was the case with bead making (Figure 1-10-4). A thermometer with a readout function was installed in the depolymerization unit to monitor the distillate temperature.

The distilled liquid was analyzed using gas chromatography for comparison with purified styrene prepared during bead production. For this purpose, a guide was implemented for the sample inlet of gas chromatography, which was prepared in advance (a silicon tube with an inner diameter of 6 mm, an outer diameter of 9 mm, and a length of ~10 mm functioned satisfactorily). The sample inlet was hot;

| Basic Chemistry 151

Figure 1-10-4 ▸ Assembly of the depolymerization apparatus

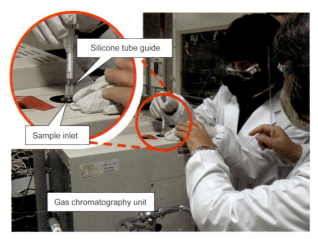

Figure 1-10-5 ▸ Gas chromatography operation

therefore, there was a risk of burn if touched directly with fingers. Thus, the installed guide could serve as a safety cover and a guide (Figure 1-10-5).

◆ Size distribution measurement of polystyrene beads

In this experiment, polystyrene beads synthesized at the beginning were observed under a stereomicroscope, and their radii were measured to determine their distribution. However, it was assumed that the visual confirmation of this work was difficult; therefore, a staff member performed this operation on behalf of Ms. Amakawa and read out the measured values. Though Ms. Amakawa tried to record the data, her personal PC did not open the Excel file we had prepared, so we lent her a PC in the laboratory to type the data.

◆ Cleaning

Ms. Amakawa cleaned experimental equipment.

(4) How to Confirm Understanding Level

The flowchart prepared before the experiment was created using the PC and received by e-mail. Moreover, she brought back the result of the in-person experiment, and the level of her understanding was evaluated through the report she submitted by the designated date.

(5) Comments

No major problems occurred throughout the experiment. Although there was some spillage from the medicine spoon during powder weighing (possibly due to static electricity), the required amount of powder was generally weighed. In addition, as we asked Ms. Amakawa to check the initial position of the reagent bottles while replacing them in the reagent box for each experiment, she could avoid the problem of accidentally knocking over reagent bottles, which had occurred occasionally in earlier experiments.

As it was in the midst of COVID-19 pandemic and to prevent burns, Ms. Amakawa had to wear protective nitrile gloves while working for a long period of time. We wondered how she felt about this compared to working with bare hands (it may have been an experiment with a different sensation than usual).

(Original text by Uchida, Umezawa)

2

Basic Physics

2-1 Making a Lens
(Basic Experiments in Science and Engineering 1A)

(1) Outline of Experiment

The goal of this experiment is to learn the physical properties of light, especially the fundamentals of geometrical optics. In Experiment 1, the refraction of light in a medium is investigated using a prism and a lens. Although this is also a review of high school physics, by actually drawing and measuring, students understand how light is refracted at the boundary of a medium and the principle of image formation using a spherical lens.

Next, in Experiment 2, an aspherical lens is fabricated using a machine tool. One of the objectives of the experiment is to experience crafting. Another objective is to confirm the advantages of aspherical lenses, which are now widely used, by demonstrating the fact that the aberration of a fabricated lens is smaller than that of a spherical lens. The actual measured value of the lens magnification is compared to the calculated value.

(2) Advance Preparation

Ms. Amakawa verified the setting of the angle of incidence of the laser light incident on semi-circular lens and reading of the refraction angle (conducted by the co-experimenter during the experiment), measured the magnification of an aspherical lens (using a sample) using a magnification-measuring instrument (conducted by the TA during the experiment), and practiced reading measurements to two decimal places using a Braille caliper (conducted by the co-experimenter and TA during the experiment). Finally, the lens-cutting device was checked.

(3) Observations on the Experiment Day

◆ Light refraction using a semicircular lens (acrylic) (Experiment 1-1)

The co-experimenter set the angle of incidence of the laser light incident on the diameter side of the semicircular lens and read the measured refraction angle. Ms. Amakawa performed trigonometric calculations to obtain the refraction angle

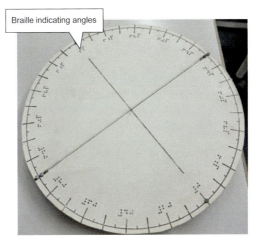

Figure 2-1-1 ▸ Rotating table with Braille letters attached to angle numbers on which a semicircular lens is placed (Experiment 1-2)

using the BrailleSense and recorded the data.

◆ Focal length measurement with an aberrated lens (cylindrical lens) (Experiment 1-2)

Ms. Amakawa moved the laser diode on the rail up or down by 5 mm simultaneously and measured the focal length at each incident position by shining light onto the cylindrical lens. She performed this operation using a braille ruler attached to the side of the rail (Figure 2-1-1). The co-experimenter recorded the focal length readings, and the refractive index was calculated by Ms. Amakawa using the BrailleSense (Figure 2-1-2).

◆ Fabrication of aspherical lens (Experiment 2)

Because she practiced the mounting and dismounting of the blade and material using a plastic blade (mock-up) in advance, she performed the operation smoothly. When operating the up/down handle of the machine, it was difficult for her to know whether the handle would not move any further as it has turned all the way to the upper or lower limit or whether it is the friction of turning the handle that is making it difficult to move. Thus, the TA checked and informed Ms. Amakawa of the situation. Ms. Amakawa and Ms. Hamada attached a felt sticker

Figure 2-1-2 ▶ Reading and recording the angle of refraction (Experiment 1-2)

to the blade handle of the milling machine to indicate the operating range, and by targeting the position of the sticker, she operated the machine normally. When setting up the milling machine, the power outlet was unplugged to prevent unintentional contact with the start switch. As Ms. Amakawa had a good grasp of the machine, this measure was not really necessary.

By relying on the cutting sound of the material and resistance applied to the handle during cutting, she performed the entire process of lens machining by herself (Figure 2-1-3). As she did not perform the actual processing during preparation, she was sometimes bewildered by the high noise and strong vibration caused by the sudden contact between the blade and material during processing; therefore, the TA checked the situation as needed, and she continued to work without any problems.

The polishing powder used for polishing, which is the final process, was divided into small bags so that the required amount could be used at her own table. It was difficult for her to apply the polishing powder on the cloth covering the bowl without spilling it. As this amount was not strictly fixed, we only told Ms. Amakawa when it overflowed. Further, the cloth was sprayed with water to make it wet. Ms. Amakawa performed polishing by touching the lens surface with her fingertips to check the degree of polishing (Figure 2-1-4). The staff checked polish

Figure 2-1-3 ▶ Fixing the material (left) and lens cutting by operating the handle (right)

Figure 2-1-4 ▶ Polishing a cut lens with a cloth coated with the polishing powder

and found that the entire lens surface was polished without any problem. Ms. Amakawa used a vacuum cleaner and paper towels provided on her table to clean the polishing powder and chips; nevertheless, the TAs helped her because she could not see where the dirt was. Ms. Amakawa also cleaned the bowls and cloth used in lens polishing.

The TA measured the magnification of the manufactured lens using a magnification-measuring instrument, instead of her. When measuring the thickness of the manufactured lens with calipers, it was difficult to hold the object in mid-air, so the TA assisted her in the measurement. After Ms. Amakawa had read the thickness of the lens to one decimal place with a Braille caliper, the TA used a normal caliper to confirm the measurements and shared the two decimal readings with her.

(4) How to Confirm Understanding Level

BrailleSense was used for recording values and other information during the experiment. Normally, the staff checks the data at the end of the experiment; however, as there was no written record for the staff to check, the data were checked verbally on the day of the experiment. The data and a summary of the experiment were to be sent by e-mail at a later date.

(5) Comments

Although there were some unfamiliar operations as "making a lens" involved many repetitive steps, these became easier to perform as she became more familiar with the layout of the tools used to cut the lens (Figure 2-1-3). Each operation took the same amount of time as other students. It would have been better to prepare a tray to prevent the polishing powder from spilling over during polishing work.

When a mistake was made in the calculation, it took a little longer for her to recalculate while looking for the mistake in BrailleSense, but the calculation was done without problems. Although the experiment was completed in the same amount of time as other students, it took some time to summarize the contents of the experiment using BrailleSense to check the data. When reviewing issues during the data check, she tried to calculate the principle of cutting an aspherical lens. However, because some diagrams and information required to visualize hyperbolic surfaces were omitted from the text, she found it difficult to understand and gave up the task halfway through the calculation. She could understand the experimental content and process calculations better than other students and obtained sufficient learning effects.

(Original text by: Nishi, Sakata)

2-2 Simulation of Physical Phenomena
(Basic Experiments in Science and Engineering 1A)

(1) Outline of Experiment

To perform the simulations of physical phenomena, in Experiment 1, students learn how to express the physical phenomena of free fall, oscillatory motion, and string vibration in terms of differential equations and how to solve them on a computer. In Experiment 2, the motion of masses and propagation of waves are simulated, and in Experiment 3, Brownian motion is simulated to learn how simulations can be used to understand and predict physical phenomena.

(2) Advance Preparation

Because there was a lot of data input in this experiment, we prepared an Excel sheet for simple input and confirmed the operation of the text-to-speech software (NVDA). We shared the manual and other materials with Ms. Amakawa in advance.

(3) Observations on the Experiment Day

◆ Simulation of free fall, oscillatory motion, and string vibration (Experiment 1)

In Experiment 1-1 (simulation of free fall), she took some time to input the parameters necessary for simulation, but she completed the Excel sheet for Experiment 1-2 (simulation of oscillatory motion) and discussion. While her progress in Experiment 1-3 (simulation of string vibration) was delayed, she could complete it in the same time as other groups with the help of the TA.

Ms. Hamada converted the output graphs to tactile graphs using the raised line drawing board and added titles and other information in Braille labels. Ms. Amakawa then confirmed the shape of the graph. In addition, as she understood the formulas to be entered, she could input them smoothly while checking with the text-to-speech software (Figure 2-2-1). In the simulation in which the calculation time was divided into 100 or more steps of 1–10 s to improve calculation ac-

Figure 2-2-1 ▶ Data processing in progress

curacy, the increased number of steps meant that input took a long time.

◆ Simulation of 1D and 2D waves (Experiment 2)

In the process of checking waveforms on the PC screen, the TA held Ms. Amakawa's finger and traced the waveforms together, which enabled her to understand how vibrations were occurring. The TA assisted her in compiling the simulation results on a sheet and checking the location of the answer columns; further, she proceeded to fill in the content in the same manner as other students.

To understand the vibration of the string whose linear density changes along the way in one-dimensional wave simulation, Ms. Amakawa not only traced waveform on the PC monitor with her finger but also repeatedly touched three-dimensional waveform on the raised line drawing board to check it and deepen her understanding. Because it was impossible for her to use the keyboard to measure the amplitude and period of the vibration waveform (sine wave) by placing the mouse pointer anywhere on the waveform, we asked the TA to do it for her. Ms. Hamada and the TA assisted in the simulation of a two-dimensional wave to confirm the Snell's law (the law of refraction of light) by drawing perpendicular lines and other auxiliary lines on waveform in the output diagram and reading the refraction angle with a protractor.

◆ Particles in water, simulation of Brownian motion using random numbers (Experiment 3)

In the Brownian motion simulation using a high-spec PC, Ms. Amakawa copied files, but there was a lot of mouse clicking on the screen, which required assistance from the TA. Regarding the movement of Brownian particles at different temperatures, Ms. Hamada made charts of particle trajectories for each 20-frame period at high and low temperatures. By comparing the two charts, Ms. Amakawa considered the difference in the Brownian motion due to the variation in temperature. In the simulation of the Brownian motion using a random function in Excel, five tables with 20 × 30 (rows × columns) were created. To reduce the amount of work, an Excel sheet that can be created by entering only the X direction (the X and Y directions are the same) was used. The process of searching for input errors in a 20 × 30 table using the text-to-speech software was time consuming. The simulation result was a movie of 100 frames; however, two frames were extracted from the result and converted to three dimensional images by Ms. Hamada using the raised line drawing board. Although the number of frames was small, some random motion of particles was confirmed.

(4) How to Confirm Understanding Level

The data were checked and tested by staff.

(5) Comments

The text-to-speech software (NVDA) was sometimes interrupted when arrow keys on the keyboard were pressed, so we asked the TA to read the text out loud. (Hovering the mouse pointer over a cell allows reading without interruption, but because Ms. Amakawa could not see where the mouse pointer was, we did not use that method this time). Tables utilized in Word were not suitable for cursor movement using arrow keys on the keyboard in the text-to-speech software; however, by recreating them in an Excel sheet, reading by cursor movement was possible without any problems. We felt that we needed to be creative in the way we communicated to Ms. Amakawa about this experiment and thus used illustrations and simulation-like videos. Because of time required to input the data into the PC, the staff checked the experimental notes only at the end of the class; nevertheless, she could complete all work within the class time. Additionally, she prepared the necessary documents and sheets for compiling her laboratory notes as well as of other students.

(Original text by: Sakata)

2 -3 Estimation of Measurement Uncertainty
(Basic Experiments in Science and Engineering 1A)

(1) Outline of Experiment

In this experiment, students learn the concept of uncertainty required to show the experimental results and basics of methods used for evaluating uncertainty based on the guide to the expression of uncertainty in measurement (GUM), an internationally standardized method for evaluating uncertainty. The period of a rigid pendulum is measured several times, and its uncertainty is evaluated. In addition to directly measuring the target quantity, there are also quantities that can be obtained indirectly by measuring the length and width of a rectangle and multiplying them together, for example, the area of a rectangle. To evaluate the uncertainty of a measurement of a quantity that can be calculated from multiple measurements, the propagation of uncertainty is also studied. In preparation for the experiment, students learn and practice the evaluation of uncertainty. In Experiment 1, the period of the pendulum is directly measured visually. The length of the pendulum is changed, and the period is measured for each length. In Experiment 2, the period data measured in Experiment 1 are organized using the spreadsheet software to determine the variation in the measured values. In Experiment 3, the combined uncertainty of indirect measurements is obtained. In Experiment 4, the propagation of the uncertainty of indirect measurements is obtained.

(2) Advance Preparation

Ms. Amakawa practiced to read measured values after the decimal point using a ruler to measure the length of the pendulum rod and read two decimal places using a vernier caliper to estimate the disk diameter. She also attached a scale reading tape (Figure 2-3-1) to identify the position of the axis of rotation and center of the disk, practiced pressing a stopwatch to measure the period of the pendulum only through voice while the light probe was turned off, practiced assembling a rigid pendulum, and wrote error bars (magnitude of uncertainty) on graphs. Finally, she checked the operation of the stopwatch, which produced a sound when a button was pressed.

166   Part 3   Record of Technical Support in Laboratory Education

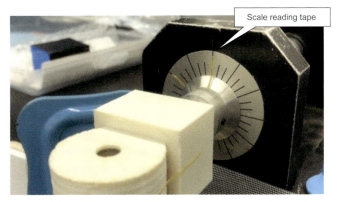

Figure 2-3-1 ▶ Reading tape attached to the scale on the axis of rotation of a rigid pendulum

(3) Observations on the Experiment Day

◆ Preparation before experiment

The text of the explanatory material was transcribed into Word. The text-to-speech software was used to confirm the contents of the material that contained only exercise assignments, and then BrailleSense was utilized to summarize and calculate the results. An assistant read aloud complicated formulas presented in the Word document, and the formula numbers in the text were given to Ms. Amakawa so that she could understand the content. Instead of checking the laboratory notes, answers were given orally to the staff. As with other students, she showed her PC screen to the staff and had her data checked.

◆ Measurement of pendulum parameters and preparation of equipment (Experiment 3)

To save time before measuring the period of the pendulum, we started with Experiment 3 first. The technical staff explained the points to be noted, or the TA read the manual aloud. On the day of the experiment, she did not refer to the manual in detail, and seemed to know the experimental procedure in advance. She weighed the pendulum disks herself using a balance with a readout function. Using a Braille ruler, the length of the pendulum rod was measured in approximately 5 mm increments. The TA then took measurements using an ordinary ruler and shared the measurement values with decimal points with the co-experimenter.

Measurements were recorded by Ms. Amakawa on BrailleSense and on a regular data sheet by Ms. Hamada and the TA. The disk diameter was measured to one decimal place using a Braille caliper. The TA then took measurements with a normal caliper and shared measurement values to two decimal places. The assembly of the experimental apparatus was completed smoothly because it had been done once during preparation the day before (Figure 2-3-2). Ms. Amakawa set the distance between the pendulum's axis of rotation and center of the disk at 30 cm by holding the metal rod of the pendulum horizontal to the ground and applying a Braille ruler. The measurement uncertainty of the distance was ~1 mm.

◆ 100 measurements, analysis, and indirect measurement of period (Experiments 1, 2, and 4)

The time it takes for a pendulum to swing through two periods after it has passed its lowest point is measured visually with a stopwatch. Ms. Amakawa,

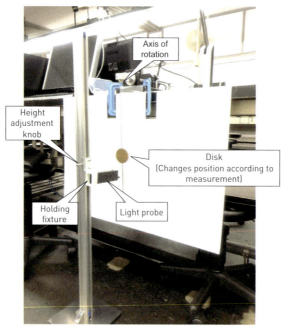

Figure 2-3-2 ▶ Experimental apparatus for the period measurement of a rigid pendulum using a light probe

however, determined whether the pendulum had passed its lowest point by the change in sound made by the light probe. The light probe was mounted on a device prepared in the laboratory, and its position was adjusted by Ms. Amakawa with the help of Ms. Hamada. The height of the photosensor was also adjusted by Ms. Amakawa while checking the change in sound by touching it with her hand (Figure 2-3-3).

Under Ms. Hamada's direction, the pendulum was released after the TA counted down "2, 1, 0," and measurement was started using a stopwatch at the moment the sound of the light probe changed, i.e., when the pendulum reached its lowest point (Figure 2-3-4). Measurement was stopped at the moment the sound changed, indicating two periods, and Ms. Hamada read out measured values and recorded all data. Ms. Hamada recorded the data, the TA read them out loud, and Ms. Amakawa entered all data into Excel. Moreover, the TA read through the manual while she entered formulas and other data into Excel to analyze the experimental data. For tasks such as visually counting the number of data in a range, the TA instructed Ms. Amakawa to enter Excel functions so that she could perform such tasks. Finally, Ms. Hamada provided a printed and enlarged copy of the histogram (frequency distribution) of one period of the pendulum in a form that

Figure 2-3-3 ▶ Adjusting the position of the light probe

Figure 2-3-4 ▶ Measuring the period of the pendulum with a stopwatch

could be touched using a simple raised line drawing board.

◆ 8 × 10 measurements and analyses (Experiments 1, 2, and 4)

In this experiment, the distance between the axis of the rotation of the pendulum and center of the disk was changed in the range of 5–40 cm, and two periods were measured. This experiment was conducted using the same procedure as for 100 measurements. Because the period was short at small distances and understanding the sound change was difficult, measurements were made at gradually decreasing distances, starting at 40 cm, to become accustomed to the sound change before taking measurements. Ms. Amakawa set the distance between the axis of the rotation of the pendulum and center of the disk in the same way as that for 100 measurements, and as the Braille ruler has a length of 30 cm, only the distance of 40 cm was set using a foldable ruler brought in by Ms. Hamada. It took some time because Ms. Amakawa was not accustomed to using the ruler. As in 100 measurements, the height of the light probe was adjusted by herself, and all data were acquired smoothly. The TA then read out cell numbers on the Excel sheet, and Ms. Amakawa entered the data. Ms. Hamada made graphs using the Braille graph paper and felt stickers. In this experiment, it was necessary to indicate the uncertainty of measured values with error bars at the top and bottom of the measurement data plots. Because it was impossible to write error bars, we instructed her to verbally explain the "values indicated by the error bars" to the staff when checking the data.

◆ Summary of experiment

Five questions provided at the end of the Excel sheet for evaluation were answered using a PC. As she had to check each sentence she entered, it took some time, but she could create and print the datasheet in an Excel sheet in exactly the same way as required. The handwritten data sheets were recorded by the TA and Ms. Hamada, the graphs were submitted without error bars, and the Excel sheet printouts were submitted as required for data checking. Because the staff member in charge at that day was checking data for each group, it was done one-on-one with the staff member. She completed the experiment in about the same amount of time as other students. After the experiment, while cleaning up, she spent approximately 20 min talking with the TA, who gave her advice on performing analysis.

(4) How to Confirm Understanding Level

The staff checked the measured data and asked her questions regarding the analysis of data.

(5) Comments

Although she was unfamiliar with the concept of "uncertainty," her understanding of the experiment was very deep, and she actively engaged in discussions with the staff regarding data analysis. Additionally, the experimental procedure went smoothly, thanks to prior confirmation. She was highly motivated to learn from start to finish, and even after completing the experiment, she went to the TA to ask for advice on improving her analysis.

(Original text by: Ueyama, Sakata)

2-4 Electric Guitar
(Basic Experiments in Science and Engineering 1A)

(1) Outline of Experiment

In this experiment, an electric guitar is used to make sounds, and its physical phenomena are investigated. To produce sound with an electric guitar, various physical phenomena related to vibration, waves, dynamics, electromagnetism, electric circuits, etc. are used. Through this experiment, students realize how one device utilizes various physical phenomena.

Specifically, students learn the following.

(1) Understand the vibration modes of strings (waves).
(2) Understand the relationship between the string tension, string length, wire density, and frequency (mechanics).
(3) Understand the principle of pickup using the phenomenon of electro-magnetic induction (electromagnetism).
(4) Understand that waveforms comprise fundamental waves and harmonics by analyzing the frequency of sound signal waveforms picked up by pickups (wave motion).
(5) Understand signal amplification, waveform deformation, and associated tonal changes (Electric circuit, wave motion).
(6) Understand a noise cancellation technology used in pickups (electrical circuits).

For the observation of string vibration modes (Experiment 1), the vibration modes of a string vibrated by an exciter are observed, drawn, and recorded. For determining the relationship between the string tension, string length, wire density, and frequency (Experiment 2), the fundamental frequency of a string is measured while varying tension, length, and linear density. Pickup assembly and operation check (Experiment 3) involve assembling and checking the operation of a pickup that detects string vibrations. In the observation of waveforms and frequency analysis (Experiment 4), the string is plucked with a finger, vibration waveform of the string is measured with an oscilloscope, and frequency components contained in vibration are analyzed. The effect on the frequency components of vibration owing to changes in the way the string is plucked and position at which it is plucked is observed. At the same time, students understand the principles of the noise cancellation technology.

(2) Advance Preparation

Because it was impossible for Ms. Amakawa to prepare a sketch of string vibration when observing the vibration modes of the string (Experiment 1), she practiced recording the distance from the end of the string to the knot. She learned the structure of a guitar by touching it with the hand to check the position and shape of the strings, pickup coils, and other components. The TA was to fill in the data sheet the data acquired in the experiment on behalf of Ms. Amakawa. The TA operated the oscilloscope that measured the vibration frequency of the strings on her behalf.

(3) Observations on the Experiment Day

◆ Observation of string vibration modes (Experiment 1)

The experiment proceeded with the co-experimenter and TA reading the experiment manual. As she had confirmed the location and operation of the equipment during preparation the day before and had placed felt stickers at necessary locations, she could operate the equipment almost by herself. When recording the readings of the digital multimeter (voltage, current, and resistance measuring instrument), the co-experimenter read out the readings, and Ms. Amakawa set string tension (Ms. Amakawa turned the pegs, and the co-experimenter read out the tension values). Ms. Amakawa confirmed the vibrations of the strings by actually touching the middle, knots, and other parts of the strings with her fingers. The direction of string vibration was difficult to determine even by touching the string with a finger. However, this task was also difficult to do visually; therefore, it took time for the co-experimenter to confirm the results. Observation of string vibration Although she could not sketch the vibration mode, she confirmed the vibration mode by placing a Braille ruler on the scale and measuring the distance from the end of the string to the knot. At first, the division of roles between the co-experimenter and Ms. Amakawa was unclear, but once the roles were voluntarily established, with the co-experimenter setting the frequency of the multimeter and Ms.

2   Basic Physics   173

Amakawa checking the vibration of the strings, the experiment progressed smoothly.

◆ Estimation of the relationship between the string tension, string length, linear density, and frequency (Experiment 2)

As in Experiment 1, the TA and co-experimenter read out the experimental conditions, etc., and Ms. Amakawa conducted the experiment. Moreover, the division of roles between the co-experimenter and Ms. Amakawa was the same as in Experiment 1. In Experiment 2, it was necessary to set the frets (ridges that hold the guitar strings in place with the fingers) in a specified position, and she set them roughly by checking the position of the frets with a special ruler attached to the scale. The co-experimenter then made fine adjustments. The experiment was conducted smoothly, with the co-experimenter visually checking the vibration of the strings that Ms. Amakawa had confirmed by touching them and fine-tuning the frequency at which the amplitude of the strings reached the maximum value. When measuring the diameter of the strings, it was decided in advance that it would be difficult to use a micrometer, but she performed all measurements, and the TA read out the measurements. Although the experiment duration extended slightly as she could not clamp the strings properly and the staff had to check on her, measurement was completed.

◆ Lunch break

Because the co-experimenter prepared the graph during the lunch break, there was a difference in experimental progress between Ms. Amakawa and the co-experimenter.

◆ Pickup assembly and operation check (Experiment 3)

Ms. Amakawa touched the pickup (coil), and the co-experimenter visually checked it, installed it in the designated position, and confirmed its operation.

◆ Waveform observation and frequency analysis (Experiment 4)

Ms. Amakawa plucked the guitar strings, and the co-experimenter operated the oscilloscope (Figure 2-4-1). The staff member in charge checked the images obtained using the oscilloscope. Normally, the staff would check the data when all data were ready; however, as the tactile and Braille conversion was going on simultaneously, a quick decision was necessary for each sheet, so the staff checked

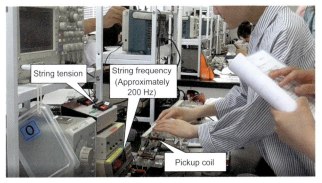

Figure 2-4-1 ▸ Checking the type of guitar strings (top) and plucking the strings (bottom)

the data as needed. The plan was that Ms. Hamada would print out each waveform image of the string on an A4 paper and then convert it into a tactile diagram and Braille for Ms. Amakawa to check; however, at Ms. Amakawa's request, the progress of the experiment was given priority, so the first printout was made once seven waveform images had been acquired, and the second printout was made once seven spectral images (vibration components) had been acquired. While Ms. Hamada was working on tactile and Braille conversion, the co-experimenter prepared an Excel sheet, printed two copies, including one for Ms. Amakawa, and had them checked by the staff. These sheets were attached to the report, and she kept the obtained images, which were processed in tactile diagrams and Braille, for her own use.

◆ Data organization

Ms. Hamada converted the waveform images to tactile diagrams and Braille at the next table simultaneously, while Ms. Amakawa and her co-experimenter calculated linear densities for Experiment 2 for data check. The calculation results of Ms. Amakawa did not match those of her co-experimenter, and a lot of time was expended to discover errors in her calculations. With the help of her co-experimenters and the TA, she worked on correcting the calculation errors. Nevertheless, Ms. Amakawa said that it was difficult to detect the errors quickly because all data recording, referencing, and calculations were done on BrailleSense. Although the graphs were not yet prepared completely, her experimental progress differed greatly from the co-experimenter at this point, so the data were checked using the data sheet (including the calculation results) prepared by the TA and Excel sheet printed by the co-experimenter. The data check was supposed to include the calculation process; however, as there was no time to transcribe data into a Word file, only the calculation results were checked.

◆ Graph preparation and report submission format confirmation

They created graphs that had not yet been created. The prepared graphs were photocopied and kept with the report, and the originals were returned to Ms. Amakawa. At that time, we also gave Ms. Amakawa a copy of the data sheet prepared by the TA and instructed her to have someone read it out loud if she needed to check the data.

As the report had to be submitted in the data format, which was different from the usual format, the experiment was completed after confirming the necessary items again.

(4) How to Confirm Understanding Level

As this experiment required a written report, the faculty member in charge of grading the reports evaluated the submitted data sheets and report.

(5) Comments

Initially, Ms. Amakawa seemed uncomfortable with her co-experimenter, but over the course of the experiment, they seemed to gradually become comfortable with each other. In Experiment 2, the co-experimenter sometimes read out the displayed values before measurements had stabilized, and whenever a correction was made, she had to rush to find the relevant part on BrailleSense, which was not always easy. Therefore, we felt that it was necessary to take some measures such as having the staff talk to the co-experimenter.

The TA actively tried to improve the level of understanding by, for instance, spontaneously asking questions to Ms. Amakawa and her co-experimenter. Because this TA was also in charge of "Estimation of Measurement Uncertainty," the experiment proceeded smoothly. As the waveform images had to be converted to tactile diagrams and Braille, the workload of Ms. Hamada increased considerably, and she could not keep up with it (she asked the TA to help with some of the work).

(Original text by: Tsuzuki, Sakata)

2 -5 Capacitor Design and Radio Reception
(Basic Experiments in Science and Engineering 1A)

(1) Outline of Experiment

This experiment focused on learning about the principles and applications of capacitors, in addition to understanding the physical properties of a parallel-plate capacitor and listening to an AM radio by utilizing its properties using an LC resonance circuit. When two metal plates (pole plates) are placed in parallel and connected to a battery, positive and negative charges are accumulated on the pole plates (parallel-plate capacitor). These charges are retained even when the plates are disconnected from the battery. An electrical component that stores electric charge in this way is called a capacitor. There are numerous different types of capacitors, which are designed for various applications (electronic equipment). Capacitors are one of the most basic and important electrical components. In the first part, to determine the relationship between the distance between electrode plates, area, dielectric, and electric capacitance (Experiments 1-1 to 1-4), students measure the electric capacitance of a parallel-plate capacitor when a dielectric is inserted while changing the distance between the electrode plates and area of the capacitor. In the second part, students design a variable-capacitance capacitor and confirm a frequency filter using an LC parallel resonance circuit (Experiments 2-1 to 2-3). Finally, students select a radio station and listen to the radio.

(2) Advance Preparation

◆ Preparation for the course

The following three items were sent to Ms. Amakawa as text data for basic understanding in advance: the slides prepared for the experiment, materials on the Waseda University Learning Management System (supplementary materials), and a comprehension check sheet (Ms. Amakawa was asked to prepare the Braille notes of the measurement results, have the TA write them down, and to write down comments pointed out by the staff on the spot in Braille). It was decided that if there is a request to translate materials to Braille, we would do so as much as possible.

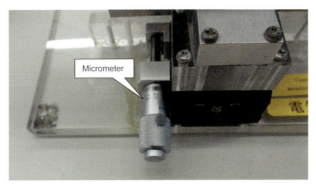

Figure 2-5-1 ▸ Position markers when the distance between the pole plates is zero (Experiment 1-1)

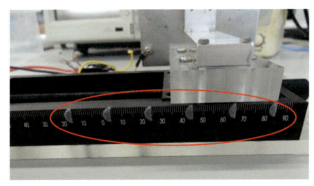

Figure 2-5-2 ▸ Scale for checking the amount of movement when shifting the pole plate laterally (markers at 20-mm intervals (Experiment 1-2))

◆ Preparations for the relationship between the distance between the pole plates, area, dielectric, and capacitance (Experiments 1-1 to 1-4)

By marking the position when the distance between the pole plates of the capacitor is zero, we asked Ms. Amakawa to confirm the correspondence between the number of the micrometer revolutions and movement distance (Figure 2-5-1). We explained the methods used to check the 20-mm spacing markings on the pole-plate area adjustment knob and to move the pole plate (Figure 2-5-2).

For the data to be entered into Excel, the TA was asked to read the entered calculated values by the co-experimenter.

Figure 2-5-3 ▶ Checking the wiring contact

◆ Preparation for design of a variable-capacitance capacitor and confirmation of a frequency filter using an LC parallel resonance circuit (Experiments 2-1 to 2-3)

On the day of the experiment, Ms. Amakawa was responsible for selecting stations by adjusting the micrometer while listening to the sound, and the co-experimenter was responsible for reading the frequency of the selected signal using an oscilloscope. The oscilloscope images to be acquired on the day of the experiment were to be checked by Ms. Amakawa on the spot using the textured graph prepared in advance.

◆ Overall preparation

Even if the LCR meter was to be operated by the co-experimenter, Ms. Amakawa was invited to experience the operation to deepen her understanding of it (Figure 2-5-3). The devices operated by Ms. Amakawa were marked with stickers and whether they could be read or not was verified, and they could be operated without any problem. We explained to her the actual accuracy of operation due to the large size of the markings. We also explained that although the reading uncertainty would be large, it would not affect the final result. Waveform signals to be obtained (printed) in the experiment were prepared in advance, and a large printout of the signals was given to Ms. Hamada for the Braille conversion work.

(3) Observations on the Experiment Day

◆ Relationship between the distance and area of the pole plates, dielectric, and capacitance (Experiments 1-1 to 1-4)

Ms. Amakawa submitted her preliminary work by e-mail and prepared for the day of the experiment.

Ms. Amakawa and her co-experimenter discussed the division of roles for performing the experiment. The TA read out the experimental operation manual. Ms. Amakawa operated the capacitor following the markings made on the previous day, and the co-experimenter (or TA) read the capacitance values for the distance and area of the plates and recorded them in a notebook. Ms. Amakawa wrote separately in BrailleSense. In Experiment 1-1, a special graphing sheet was used to create the handwritten graphs of the acquired data (the co-experimenter's graphs were submitted and used in the final test). The stray capacitance (electrical capacitance not associated with the capacitor) was read from the slope of the approximate straight line drawn on the handwritten graph. Because the reading accuracy of Ms. Amakawa's special graph was low, we decided to calculate stray capacitance by referring to the graph of the co-experimenter. The acquired data were entered into BrailleSense by Ms. Amakawa. Ms. Hamada printed out the Excel graph created based on the data, and Ms. Amakawa checked the shape of the Braile graph after it was processed into a Braille graph by Ms. Hamada.

◆ Design of a variable-capacitance capacitor and confirmation of a frequency filter using an LC parallel resonance circuits (Experiments 2-1 to 2-3)

While Ms. Amakawa operated the capacitor (changing the capacitance) and listened to the sound, the co-experimenter or TA adjusted the spectrum analyzer (waveform analyzer). As in Experiment 1, Ms. Hamada transcribed the frequency images to Braille.

(4) How to Confirm Understanding Level

Handwritten graphs and acquired data were checked by the TA in the notebook of the co-experimenter. The co-experimenter submitted their own comprehension confirmation sheet, Ms. Amakawa read the sheet recorded in BrailleSense, and a question-and-answer session was held with the staff.

(5) Comments

Throughout the experiment, there were no major problems. The results were almost as expected. Ms. Amakawa did not give the impression that she encountered a particularly difficult time. We felt that this experiment was easier for Ms. Amakawa because she had practiced the operation of the micrometer, which requires the greatest precision, in advance, and the measurement uncertainty was within an acceptable range. The experiment went very smoothly, and her group was almost at the top of the class, thanks to her practice on the previous day and the fact that no major mistakes were made. Though Ms. Amakawa and her co-experimenter did not feel that the experiment was progressing smoothly, other groups were progressing more slowly than them, so we advised them to be careful and not to be in a hurry.

The experiment of listening to the radio sound seemed to be quite well received, and progress in Experiment 1 was considerably fast. However, Experiment 2 took more time due to the change of roles as well as time required for transcribing the acquired data to BrailleSense and writing the comprehension confirmation sheet, which slowed down the process. Because a large amount of time was devoted to reviewing the contents of the comprehension check sheets, the group was the last of all groups to finish. She seemed to be very comfortable with her co-experimenter and the TA and seemed to be enjoying the experiment. Ms. Amakawa and her co-experimenter were heard saying, "It was a very fulfilling experiment." She appeared to be enjoying the process of conducting the experiment very much. The experiment with sound was probably good because it was familiar to her.

(Original text by: Nishino, Sakata)

2 -6 Electromagnetic Induction
(Basic Experiments in Science and Engineering 1A)

(1) Outline of Experiment

The purpose of this experiment is to learn through experimentation regarding the basic characteristics of the electromagnetic induction phenomenon, which is the principle behind generators, motors, and transformers used everywhere in our daily lives. In this experiment, students examine the induced electromotive force (EMF) from two primary perspectives to confirm the Faraday's law and Lenz's law.

(1) Measure the time variation associated with the induced electromotive force generated when a magnet moves in a solenoid, and study its characteristics.
(2) When electric current flows in a solenoid due to the induced electromotive force, it generates a magnetic flux, which also affects the motion of a magnet. These effects are studied in this experiment.

Here, students estimate the magnetic flux density generated by a magnet (Experiment 1). For observing the electromagnetic induction phenomenon (Experiment 2), a magnet on a string is held in a hand and passed through a coil at an arbitrary speed to study the difference in the time waveform of the induced electromotive force. In the measurement of EMF (Experiment 3), a magnet is dropped freely from different heights, and the time waveform of the induced EMF when it passes through the coil is examined. In the comparison of the measured and calculated values (Experiment 4), the time waveform of the induced EMF in Experiment 3 is compared with the theoretical value. In the falling motion of a magnet inside a metal pipe (Experiment 5), a magnet is allowed to fall freely into two types of metal pipes, and the difference in the time waveform of the induced EMF is examined.

2 Basic Physics

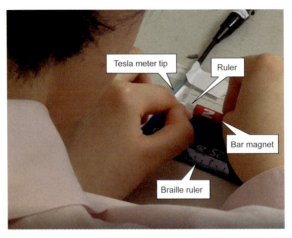

Figure 2-6-1 ▸ Determining the distance between the Tesla meter and tip of the bar magnet with a finger using a Braille ruler (Experiment 1)

(2) Advance Preparation

The readings of the tactile copies of both logarithmic graphs used in Experiment 1 and EMF graphs were checked, and the operation of the Tesla meter (a device for measuring magnetic field strength using the Hall element) was confirmed. Normally, measurements are performed by moving the probe of the Tesla meter, without moving the magnet; however, in the Ms. Amakawa's case, it was difficult to align the center of the probe's sensor with the magnet; therefore, the probe was fixed to the desk with a masking tape, and the magnet was moved (Figure 2-6-1). When attaching the probe to the desk, it was placed between the ordinary ruler and Braille ruler, creating rails that allowed the magnet to move parallel to the desk. The tip of the probe was fixed, and the bar magnet was moved along the rulers. The operation of the magnet drop system was checked, along with the positioning of the pickup coil.

Next, we confirmed that the data acquired in Experiment 3 could be read by enlarging the printout of the graph. Lastly, the reading recorded in the Excel sheet was checked, and the sheet was read without any problem. The software was improved so that the voltage–time waveform displayed on the PC could be printed, and the specifications were changed to display thicker lines for printing on a tactile copy machine.

(3) Observations on the Experiment Day

◆ Measurement of the magnetic flux density generated by a magnet (Experiment 1)

In the measurement of the magnetic field using the Tesla meter, the distance between the magnet and Tesla meter probe was measured using a Braille ruler. As in the preparation, a regular ruler and a Braille ruler were placed side by side and attached to the desk with a double-sided tape. During measurement, Ms. Amakawa determined the position of the magnet, and the co-experimenter read the readings from the Tesla meter (Figure 2-6-1). During measurement, the magnet was positioned by placing her nails on the Braille section of the ruler, resulting in a difference of ~2 mm between the actual scale and reading due to the thickness of the nails. Ms. Hamada pointed this out, and Ms. Amakawa re-conducted the experiment with her co-experimenter. Although the data obtained from the second try were more accurate, the data obtained by Ms. Amakawa were also sufficient to thoroughly investigate the objectives.

Because results and discussion of this experiment was to be presented the following week, we prepared an Excel sheet that could be read aloud automatically so that she could consider the result at home. Data were obtained with the co-experimenter and entered into the respective data sheets. Ms. Amakawa used a text-to-speech software (NVDA) to enter the data. The TA operated the Excel macro execution button, which did not work with the reading software. Because the Excel graphs contained three types of curves, they were enlarged so that one graph could fit on an A4-size sheet. Three sheets in total were printed so that each could be checked using a raised line drawing board. Because we assumed that Ms. Amakawa would have difficulty in recognizing the shape of a graph drawn as a double-logarithmic graph, we asked her to check whether she could recognize a double-logarithmic display and a normal display on the sample graph prepared using the tactile copy machine used during the preparation the previous day (she said that the narrower the line width of the graph and curves, the easier it was to understand).

◆ Observation of electromagnetic induction phenomena (Experiment 2)

In the experiment of electromagnetic induction using a magnet on a string, a magnet with a felt sticker attached to the north pole was prepared. The position of the pickup coil was set immediately nearby when the magnet on a string was

Figure 2-6-2 ▸ Position adjustment of the pickup coil in Experiment 2

inserted into the acrylic pipe, allowing the determination of the position where the coil has passed and speed at which the magnet is to be lowered for adjusted (Figure 2-6-2). The data obtained in Experiment 2 were plotted on a graph by drawing four different voltage–time waveforms with a raised line drawing board so that each waveform could be compared.

◆ Measurement of EMF (Experiment 3)

In EMF measurement using a falling bar magnet, Ms. Amakawa operated the apparatus, and her co-experimenter operated the PC. As with the magnet in Experiment 2, the polarity of the magnet was determined by placing a felt sticker on the N-pole end side. The magnet was attached to the base of a metal PC monitor arm because it rolled and stuck to metal products when placed on the tabletop, even though it could be installed in the device without any problem.

When determining the area (integral value) of the time waveform of the induced EMF voltage, the measured portion of the waveform was enlarged and copied onto a single A4 graph. Auxiliary lines were drawn from the apex to the vertical axis so that the position of the apex of the waveform could be determined with a raised line drawing board, and the area of the waveform was approximated by a triangle.

Figure 2-6-3 ▸ Sorting the data after the experiment using a text-to-speech software

Differences in waveforms due to the fall distance were summarized on a single A4 sheet depicting five different waveforms and plotted using a tactile copy machine. In addition, measurements derived from the waveform were read by writing the axis and shape on an enlarged copy of only the waveform section with a raised line drawing board. Enlarged copies were made on an A4 size paper. Handwritten graphs (linear functions) were plotted with felt stickers on a Braille graph paper. Ms. Hamada and the TA helped her to create the axis labels.

◆ Comparison of the measured and calculated values (Experiment 4)

When fitting the time waveforms of the experimental and calculated voltages, the input values were first set to deviate significantly from the experimental waveforms, and several graphs were printed, with the parameters changed in several places to identify which parameters affected the waveforms. The TA held Ms. Amakawa's finger and traced the screen, and the paper printout was then converted to a tactile diagram using a tactile copy machine. As the overlapping lines became thicker on the tactile copy machine, she could recognize the fitted area.

◆ Falling motion of a magnet inside a metal pipe (Experiment 5)

She studied the falling of the magnet through the copper and brass pipes based on the difference in the volume of the sound and time it took for the magnet to fall. Various materials were identified based on their different weights during the preparatory experiment in the previous day. The time waveforms of five differ-ent voltages at various drop distances (pickup coil positions) for the copper and brass pipes were compiled on a single sheet of an A4 size paper each, which were then printed using the tactile copy machine and compared. As in Experiment 3, handwritten graphs (linear functions) were plotted with felt stickers on a Braille graph paper. Ms. Hamada and the TA helped her to create the axis labels.

(4) How to Confirm Understanding Level

During the oral examination in the following week, the students presented explanations and discussions regarding this experiment based on their experimen-tal notes and had a question-and-answer session with the instructor.

(5) Comments

In Experiment 1, when Ms. Amakawa fixed the tip of the Tesla meter and moved the bar magnet to measure the magnetic field strength, the reading distance was off by few millimeters due to the thickness of her fingernail. She was con-cerned that she did not notice it. Ms. Hamada consoled her by saying, "An experi-ment includes such things that you may not have noticed". In Experiment 3, it seemed difficult for her to read the detailed numerical values on the graph, but she managed to accomplish it with the assistance of the TA. The overall volume of data employed in this experiment was large, so there were some errors in calcula-tions. In Experiment 4, she actively attached and detached magnets to and from the dropping device, showing the results of tracing on the previous day.

(Original text by: Nishi, Sakata)

2-7 Oral Examination
(Basic Experiments in Science and Engineering 1A)

This class comprises an oral examination on the subject of the "Electromagnetic Induction" experiment conducted the previous week. Each student is asked regarding the content of the experiment, and evaluation is made based on their answers. The purpose of this class is to deepen the students' understanding of experimental concepts, learn how to fill out laboratory notebooks, and acquire skills with respect to explaining concepts to others. On the day of the examination, Ms. Amakawa actively discussed the content of the experiment with her co-experimenter. She printed out materials compiled as homework and had the data sheets, handwritten graphs, and tactile graphs prepared during the electromagnetic induction experiment, which were checked by the TA. During the examination, she explained the experiment while projecting data sheets, handwritten graphs, and tactile copies of the graphs prepared during the electromagnetic induction experiment onto a document camera (a camera that projects the material at hand). Ms. Amakawa used BrailleSense instead of referring to her notes (Figure 2-7-1). The graphs corresponding to the experiment were projected using a document camera, but when the graph was placed on the document camera stand, the position and orientation of the graph were not clear to her; therefore, a staff member (Figure 2-7-1) operated the document camera.

(Original text by: Nishi, Sakata)

Figure 2-7-1 ▶ Presentation of the experimental results

2 -8 Brownian Motion
(Basic Experiments in Science and Engineering 1B)

(1) Outline of Experiment

Learn regarding the history of the Brownian motion discovery. Through the observation of the Brownian motion of microparticles using an optical microscope and analysis of the coordinates of microparticles using a PC, students experience the existence of invisible atoms and molecules and calculate the Avogadro constant from the measurement results using the Einstein–Stokes equation. Additionally, students observe and analyze the Brownian motion of particles of different sizes. Through these observations, students learn that there is regularity behind phenomena that appear irregular. Additionally, they gain a deeper understanding of the uncertainty of measured values and their averages.

(2) Advance Preparation

Ms. Amakawa practiced the use of a micropipette for preparing samples for the observation of Brownian particles and operation of holding a cover glass with tweezers. It was decided that the TA would be asked to check for air bubbles in the sample. Ms. Amakawa was to be the timekeeper when measuring the motion trajectory of Brownian particles. The macro of the data sheet for recording and analysis was modified to position the cursor in the top left input cell, irrespective of which sheet is selected, and the operation method was explained to her. Lastly, we gave her data sheets so that she could study them in advance, assuming that she would proceed with analysis sheets as usual with her co-experimenter.

(3) Observations on the Experiment Day

◆ Uncertainty in magnification and position measurements (Experiment 1)

The co-experimenter measured the grid size for magnification calibration using a microscope, and Ms. Amakawa entered the measurement values into an Excel data sheet on a PC. The magnification of the microscope was checked on

Figure 2-8-1 ▸ OPP sheet on a PC screen

the PC screen. Ms. Hamada converted the histogram of the measurement results into a tactile diagram using a raised line drawing board, and Ms. Amakawa confirmed the results.

◆ Measurement of Brownian motion (Experiment 2-1)

Ms. Amakawa took a specified amount of liquid from the container containing Brownian particles with a micropipette, dropped a specified amount onto a glass slide, and gently placed a cover glass on top of them using tweezers. The TA confirmed that there were no air bubbles between the slide and cover glass before taking measurements. Ms. Amakawa measured the time using a stopwatch on a PC, and the co-experimenter was responsible for measuring the motion of particles. The co-experimenter used a magic marker to mark the center of a Brownian particle on an OPP sheet attached to a PC screen every 30 s up to 300 s (5 min) for each particle (Figure 2-8-1).

◆ Measurement of Brownian particle trajectories and their analysis and estimation of the Avogadro constant (Experiment 2-2)

With the Excel sheet used for Brownian motion analysis open on the PC screen, the positions of particles were recorded at each time point by placing the mouse pointer over the points recorded on the OPP sheet pasted on the PC screen and clicking them in the order in which they were measured. This task was performed by the co-experimenter. Ms. Hamada used a raised line drawing board to create a tactile graph of the Brownian particle's two-dimensional coordinates over time, and Ms. Amakawa actually read the coordinates. However, this reading took time.

◆ Observation of Brownian motion (Experiment 3)

The motions of Brownian particles with diameters of 0.8 and 1.5 μm were measured five times for each particle (in Experiment 2, only particle with a diameter of 1.5 μm was measured once). The analysis work in Excel requires inputting formulas, so the co-experimenter took the lead. Ms. Hamada made copies of the histograms and graphs displayed in Excel using a raised line drawing board, and Ms. Amakawa pasted them into her lab notebook.

◆ Data analysis

The answers were entered on a PC using a comprehension check sheet formatted for the text-to-speech software. The TA helped her to enter the input. When creating the particle distribution (histogram) on the Excel sheet for analysis, the TA assisted in the mouse operation of the PC, and Ms. Amakawa operated the keyboard to create the histogram. It was time-consuming to create a comprehension check sheet using an unfamiliar PC input method.

(4) How to Confirm Understanding Level

Ms. Amakawa was evaluated by the staff using the comprehension check sheet.

(5) Comments

Ms. Amakawa operated the micropipette and measured the time using the stopwatch on the PC smoothly. Meanwhile, the process of creating the comprehension check sheet was time consuming because she had to think carefully regarding the issues to be considered. By tracing the trajectory of the Brownian motion with her finger, she confirmed the random motion of particles, and she also seemed to understand that they followed a certain distribution over time. We believe that the advance preparation was sufficient to handle this experiment.

(Original text by: Ueyama, Sakata)

2-9 The Physics of Air Hockey
(Basic Experiments in Science and Engineering 1B)

(1) Outline of Experiment

In this experiment, students study various motions of disks used in air hockey, including the translational motion of disks on the runway, collisions between disks, rotational motion of disks, and collisions and bounces between disks and the wall. Through concrete examples, students learn the basic laws of mechanics by examining with their own hands and eyes forces acting on disks in each motion, quantities conserved in each process, and relationships that exist between these quantities. In the confirmation of the law of inertia and friction force (Experiment 1), students determine the coefficient of kinetic friction when friction is present and confirm the law of inertia when friction is very low. In the conservation of the momentum and law of action and reaction (collision without rotation) (Experiment 2), students confirm whether the law of conservation of momentum and law of action and reaction hold true in the translational motion. In the conservation of angular momentum (Experiment 3), the disk is rotated in place to check whether the law of conservation of angular momentum holds. In the collision between the disk and wall (Experiment 4), the disk is made to collide with the wall of the air hockey table from the front or from an angle to study the degree to which the law of conservation of momentum is valid. Students also collide a rotating disk with a wall to examine how the laws of the conservation of momentum and conservation of angular momentum apply compared to when the disk is not rotating. In the bouncing of a disk and a rubber string (Experiment 5), a rubber string is stretched across the air hockey table, and the disk is collided with the rubber string to investigate the laws of the conservation of energy and conservation of momentum.

(2) Advance Preparation

The staff explained how to use Excel to analyze the data obtained in the experiments. Because of the analysis macro that automatically processes the measured data, it was impossible to change the form of the Excel table, so an

Figure 2-9-1 ▸ Throwing a disk from the edge of the air hockey table (Experiment 1)

explanation was given using only a form that shows the parts to be filled in. Given the size of the table and amount of data, the explanation was limited to Experiment 1 and Experiment 2. She practiced throwing the disk (air hockey puck) in each experiment. The practice was conducted in such a way that Ms. Amakawa could check whether the puck was thrown straight or not by touching the position of the puck as it bounced back after colliding with the wall or another puck. Later, she received the pre-assignment by e-mail.

(3) Observations on the Experiment Day

◆ **Confirmation of the law of inertia and frictional force (Experiment 1) and the conservation of momentum and law of action and reaction (collision without rotation) (Experiment 2)**

Ms. Amakawa was in charge of throwing the puck (Figure 2-9-1), and the co-experimenter analyzed the motion of the disk and edited the video on a PC. In Experiment 1, a disk was thrown on the air hockey table without airflow, the position of the center coordinate of the disk was analyzed at different times, and a graph was made showing the velocity of the disk on the vertical axis and the time on the horizontal axis. The coefficient of friction was calculated from the slope of the graph and equation of motion. Next, the disk was thrown with the airflow on the air hockey table, and the same analysis was performed to verify if the law of inertia holds. However, while it was possible to judge whether or not disks were thrown straight by observing whether or not they bounced straight back from the wall, it was difficult to tell whether or not disks collided with each other on their central axes, making it difficult to correct the throwing position (Experiment 2).

The distance and direction of the movement of disks in the video that was edited after the recording were simply confirmed by tracing them on the PC monitor with a finger with the help from the TA, and then the center position of the disk was copied onto an OPP (transparent) sheet and a felt sticker was attached to identify the center position of the disk by touch. Because editing and analysis would have taken time if videos were prepared in the order of acquisition, editing, and analysis, the videos of all experiments were obtained first, and then editing and analysis were performed separately. Additionally, as it took time to prepare four graphs for Experiments 1 and 2, she worked on them for approximately 15 min during her lunch break.

◆ Conservation of angular momentum (Experiment 3), Collision of the disk with the wall (Experiment 4), Bouncing of the disk with a rubber string (Experiment 5)

In Experiments 3–5, she seemed to be more accustomed to throwing disks than in the morning experiments and seemed to enjoy it. In some experiments, the co-experimenter re-acquired the data alone during the lunch break. In others, the co-experimenter re-acquired the data they had failed to acquire during the morning video acquisition together, and the co-experimenter edited the videos. The analysis work using Excel was done separately for each person because the input points were complicated and completing the process was difficult for her without support. The TA helped her to confirm the input position in Excel, for instance, by helping her to find where the input boxes were located. After confirming with Ms. Amakawa which data were needed in cells that required calculations, the TA read out the data in the corresponding cells, and Ms. Amakawa entered the contents of the cells. All graphs displayed in Excel were printed using the tactile copy machine, and shared with her. In the final examination, she answered the questions based on the data sheet, graphs she had prepared, and printed graphs. The

Figure 2-9-2 ▸ Rotating the disk at the center of the field hockey stand (Experiment 3)

examination was completed smoothly and without problems. However, due to the speed at which the Excel work progressed, her examination and the examination of the co-experimenter were conducted separately.

(4) How to Confirm Understanding Level

Ms. Amakawa submitted the pre-assignment and underwent a data check and examination by the staff.

(5) Comments

She could throw the hockey puck with good accuracy, thanks to her prior practice. Although she had a hard time analyzing the large amount of data in Excel, she seemed to enjoy the experiment from start to finish.

(Original text by: Nishi, Sakata)

2-10 Electronic Circuit Workshop
(Basic Experiments in Science and Engineering 1B)

(1) Outline of Experiment

In this experiment, students build an oscillation circuit called an astable multivibrator using electronic components commonly used in electronic circuits, such as resistors, capacitors, light-emitting diodes, and transistors, and verify its operation. The purpose of this experiment is to learn the basic knowledge of electronic components and their handling as well as to acquire skills to actually design and fabricate simple electronic circuits. In the measurement of the static characteristics of a diode (Experiment 1), the relationship between the forward current and voltage of the diode (static characteristics) is measured. The characteristics of a transistor amplifier circuit are measured in the Experiment 2. In the determination of the resistance of the astable multivibrator circuit (Experiment 3), the resistance of the circuit that will be built in Experiment 4 is calculated to determine the resistor to be used. In Experiment 4, students solder components to a circuit board to create a multivibrator circuit and measure the base and collector voltages of the circuit with an oscilloscope.

(2) Advance Preparation

After checking the actual apparatus with Ms. Amakawa, we found that it was difficult for her to construct a circuit using a soldering iron, so we created a system in which a circuit could be constructed by inserting and removing components with lead (wire) legs onto a breadboard that could form a circuit in a grid pattern (Figures 2-10-1 and 2-10-2). The horizontal socket terminals on the breadboard were connected on the back and could be used as common terminals, so the structure was designed to insert components vertically (or to short-circuit with conductors). The output LED (light-emitting diode) flashed when the electric motor was powered, and rotational vibrations indicated successful operation.

198   Part 3   Record of Technical Support in Laboratory Education

Figure 2-10-1 ▸ Checking the insertion of electrical components the day before the experiment

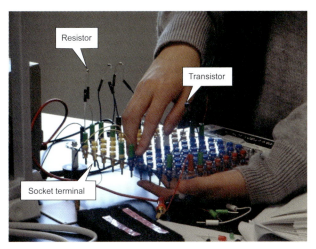

Figure 2-10-2 ▸ Ms. Amakawa checking electrical components on the bread board circuit by hand

2　Basic Physics

Figure 2-10-3 ▸ Measurements being recorded (Experiment 2)

(3) Observations on the Experiment Day

The measurement of the static characteristics of diodes (Experiment 1), measurement of the characteristics of transistor amplifier circuits (Experiment 2), and determination of the resistance of the astable multivibrator circuit (Experiment 3) were conducted in the morning. With the assistance of the TA, the measured values were recorded numerically in BrailleSense (Figure 2-10-3). In Experiment 4 in the afternoon, as it was impossible for her to fabricate the circuit while looking directly at the circuit diagram, she was asked to construct the circuit on a breadboard after gaining a good understanding and memorizing the circuit and its operation in advance. Although the circuit was properly assembled on the breadboard, it did not work initially due to insufficient contact in some areas. In fact, the staff was also not familiar with connection circuits on a breadboard, so they had to think about it (Figure 2-10-4). Subsequently, she repeated the continuity check using a tester and found the defective part of the connection and ensured that the device was working properly. All experiments were completed, and the data were checked by the staff.

Figure 2-10-4 ▶ Checking the contact of parts

(4) How to Confirm Understanding Level

For Experiments 1–4, the staff checked the data, verified the operation of circuits, and examined the results of experiments.

(5) Comments

The breadboard circuit we made in the laboratory received extremely positive remark from Ms. Hamada. Furthermore, Ms. Amakawa seemed to be enjoying the task as if she was solving a puzzle.

(Original text by: Nishino, Sakata)

2 –11 Light and Waves
(Basic Experiments in Science and Engineering 1B)

(1) Outline of Experiment

In this experiment, students learn the properties of visible light as waves (diffraction and interference), principle and characteristics of wavelength filters, and principle of the white light spectroscopy using a diffraction grating. In the white light spectroscopy using a wavelength filter and diffraction grating (Experiment 1), experiments are conducted using a white LED light, an interference filter, and a diffraction grating. Reflected and transmitted light from six different filters are observed and recorded. Diffracted white light is observed and recorded using a transmission-type diffraction grating (film type). The distance between the zero-order and first-order light and that between the diffraction grating and screen are measured, and the wavelength of the light corresponding to the observed color is calculated using the theoretical equation. In the diffraction and interference of laser light (Experiment 2), the diffraction and interference of laser light, a slit, and a diffraction grating are observed, and the distance between dark and bright spots is measured. The slit width and lattice constant are calculated using theoretical formulas and compared with the slit width and lattice spacing measured using a microscope.

(2) Advance Preparation

Because there were no particularly dangerous devices, we decided that she should check devices by touching them with her bare hands. Because grease adhered to the wavelength filter surface when touched with a finger, another spare filter was substituted when checking the shape by touch, and all other devices were checked by touch. The part of the continuous spectrum of white light in Experiment 1 that can be confirmed graphically was copied to a tactile format. By clarifying the wavelength band at this time, it is possible to relate it to the reflection and transmission bands of the filter in subsequent experiments. The wavelength band observed due to the filter was to be expressed as numerical values.

◆ Characteristics of wavelength filters (Experiment 1-1)

By marking wavelength filters, Ms. Amakawa distinguished six types of filters. The color readings of transmitted and reflected light were performed by the co-experimenter and entered on the data sheet. Ms. Amakawa replaced the filters, while the co-experimenter took the pictures as it was possible for her to replace filters in the experimental operation. The base on which the filter was set was prone to movement and likely needed to be fixed in a place. If this would be necessary, we decided to fix it to the table with a double-sided tape.

◆ White light spectroscopy using diffraction grating (Experiment 1-2)

Ms. Amakawa marked rails on which the instruments were mounted so that she could set them herself, and the co-experimenter was responsible for adjusting the optical axis. As in Experiment 1, the color was checked by the co-experimenter, and Ms. Amakawa set up the filter. The position of the dispersed light was checked by tracing it on the screen with a finger and with a light probe.

◆ Diffraction and interference of laser light (Experiment 2) and data organization

As in Experiment 1-2, Ms. Amakawa set up the apparatus. Reading of the measurement results was done by the co-experimenter, while Ms. Amakawa checked the laser spacing using, for instance, a fingernail. When working on a PC, the slit was confirmed by tracing on the screen because the text-to-speech software was not compatible with the microscope. Tables and graphs were created using the text-to-speech software. Pasting of photographs was done by the co-experimenter, who joined in the preparation of the graphs of the experimental data as soon as the pasting was completed.

(3) Observations on the Experiment Day

◆ White light spectroscopy using a wavelength filter and diffraction grating (Experiment 1)

In Experiment 1-1, the co-experimenter checked the color of the transmitted and reflected light of the wavelength filter and took pictures with a camera. The TA explained the colors to Ms. Amakawa, and she recorded them. In Experiments 1-2, Ms. Amakawa set up and adjusted lenses, support stands, and other equipment in place. The position of the dispersed white light on the glass screen was

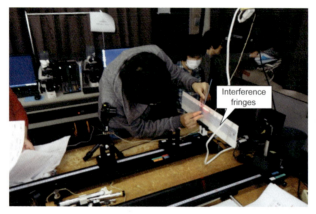

Figure 2-11-1 ▸ Reading dark spot intervals and recording numerical values (Experiment 2)

adjusted by the co-experimenter and recorded by Ms. Amakawa. The co-experimenter took the spectrographs.

◆ Diffraction and interference of laser light (Experiment 2)

In Experiment 2, the height and horizontal position of the laser beam were adjusted by the co-experimenter, while Ms. Amakawa adjusted the position of the slit folder. The co-experimenter read and photographed the diffraction and interference intervals on the screen, and Ms. Amakawa recorded the readings (Figure 2-11-1). Finally, the slit spacing was measured using a microscope by the co-experimenter and recorded by Ms. Amakawa. After the completion of Experiment 2, they moved to another room, where the co-experimenter pasted and cropped the photos on a PC, while Ms. Amakawa performed calculations. The slit width was incorrectly measured using the microscope, so the co-experimenter measured it again. It took time to organize the data because of the large amount of calculations involved in analyzing the experimental data. The data were checked by the staff, and then the experiment was completed.

◆ Measures taken on the day of the experiment

Initially, the plan was to read the first-order white light diffracted on the screen by placing a light probe on it; however, the intensity of light was so low that the light probe did not react. Therefore, the diffraction grating was irradiated

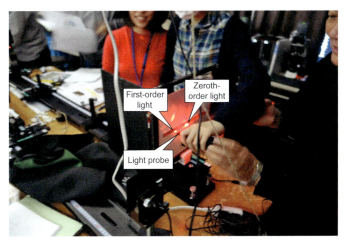

Figure 2-11-2 ▸ Confirmation of light diffraction by a diffraction grating using a light probe (sound) (Experiment 2)

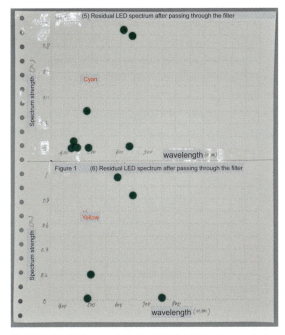

Figure 2-11-3 ▸ Spectral diagram of light after transmission through the wavelength filter made with felt stickers (Experiment 1)

with a high-intensity red-wavelength laser beam, the photosensor was placed at a position where light passes through without diffracting (zeroth-order light) and with diffraction (first-order light), and the diffraction of light was confirmed based on the presence or absence of sound (Figure 2-11-2). Ms. Amakawa was pleased to be able to confirm the diffraction of light by sound. After the experiment, the data (e.g., Figure 2-11-3) were submitted to the laboratory, along with a report.

(4) How to Confirm Understanding Level

This experiment required a report, so the teaching staff in charge of grading the reports evaluated the content of the experimental data and students' considerations regarding the points to be considered.

(5) Comments

Ms. Amakawa had taken a class using lasers in high school, so she already had a good understanding of the characteristics of lasers and was fully aware of what was happening in the experiment. While there was a situation in which the light probe did not respond to the diffraction of white light due to insufficient light intensity, using a laser light with high light intensity instead, we confirmed the actual diffraction of light by checking the sound of the light probe depending on the position, which made Ms. Amakawa happy, and it left an impression on us. The method of recognizing one signal by converting it into another is a very powerful observation tool in science, so we think the experiment was meaningful for Ms. Amakawa.

(Original text by: Nishi, Sakata)

2 –12 Measuring Devices
(Basic Experiments in Science and Engineering 1B)

(1) Outline of Experiment

In this experiment, students learn the basic operations of a tester for measuring voltage and resistance, an oscilloscope for plotting electrical signals in two dimensions, and a function generator (arbitrary waveform oscillator) for oscillating voltage signals with an arbitrarily set frequency and amplitude, such as sine waves and square waves. Students have to think about how to measure the induced Electro Motive Force (EMF) and set up wiring and measuring instruments by themselves. Students recognize the importance of thinking about what to use and how to use various equipment to obtain necessary measurements. In other experimental subjects, there were many opportunities to prioritize the type of measurements, and students have operated according to the staff's instructions and manuals. The purpose of this experiment is to understand the operation of measuring instruments and to become familiar with their operation through trial and error. In the resistance measurement (Experiment 1), a tester is used to measure the resistance value. In the observation and measurement of voltage (Experiment 2), the voltage of a dry cell battery is measured using a tester and an oscilloscope. Next, the voltage of the sine wave from the function generator is measured with an oscilloscope. In the observation and measurement of circuit voltages (Experiment 3), sine-wave voltages applied to a resistor circuit and a resistor–condenser circuit are measured with the oscilloscope. In the observation and measurement of physical phenomena (Experiment 4), sound waveforms and time waveforms of the induced EMF of a magnet are measured using the oscilloscope.

(2) Advance Preparation

The staff thoroughly explained to Ms. Amakawa the mechanism and principle of measuring instruments. Particular emphasis was placed on the operating principles and usage of the oscilloscope trigger and function generator. For the tester (voltage/resistance measuring instrument), a tape was used to mark the positions corresponding to necessary modes in advance so that it can be operated.

2 Basic Physics

Figure 2-12-1 ▶ Dropping a magnet (Experiment 4)

Components such as resistors and capacitors were also marked in the same way.

(3) Observations on the Experiment Day

With the assistance of the co-experimenter and TA, the measurement of resistance (Experiment 1), observation and measurement of voltage (Experiment 2), and observation and measurement of circuit voltage (Experiment 3) proceeded without problems, thanks also to the preparation on the previous day. In the observation and measurement of physical phenomena (Experiment 4), the actual oscilloscope image data were graphed using a raised line drawing board so that the time waveform of voltage caused by electromagnetic induction when a magnet was dropped (Figure 2-12-1) and sound signal data collected by a microphone could be traced with a finger. Although it was rather difficult for her to understand the trigger for setting the threshold and acquiring the data, she understood the content of the experiment.

In the second half of Experiment 4, sound waveforms were measured with the oscilloscope. The participants were asked to vocalize the sound of "C" as a reference tone (Figure 2-12-2). Generally, in this experiment male students were

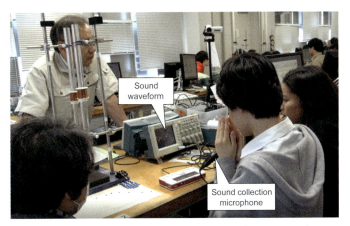

Figure 2-12-2 ▸ Vocalization of the " C" sound (Experiment 4)

asked to sing at 131 Hz and female students at 262 Hz, an octave higher, plus 523 Hz, an octave higher. Ms. Amakawa's result deviated by only 1 or 2 Hz, indicating that she had the best sense of pitch among students enrolled in the course. Ms. Amakawa, who also studied vocal music, even produced a sound one octave higher at 1047 Hz.

(4) How to Confirm Understanding Level

Students selected one of the five assignments, and then took a practical test on the selected assignment in front of a TA. Ms. Amakawa selected the assignment of connecting an oscilloscope to a microphone, capturing her own voice and measuring the period and amplitude of the voice. The time scale of the horizontal axis was estimated from the frequency (period) of the audio signal. As she understood the magnitude of the signal in the prior experiment, she completed the task without any problems by having the TA set the trigger points and other settings.

(5) Comments

Ms. Amakawa operated the oscilloscope with a thorough understanding regarding how to use it and measured the target period and amplitude, giving the impression that she had a deep understanding of the experiment and was enjoying it immensely.

(Original text by: Nishino, Sakata)

2 -13 Heat and Motion of Gas Molecules
(Basic Experiments in Science and Engineering 1B)

(1) Outline of Experiment

A gas is a group of microscopic molecules, which reach thermal equilibrium by repeatedly colliding with each other. Here, the macroscopic state of a gas is described by physical quantities such as temperature, pressure, and volume. In this class, student first investigate the Boyle–Charles law, which describes a relation between these physical quantities, through experiments of isobaric and isothermal changes. Next, an experiment demonstrating an adiabatic change (rapid compression/expansion) is conducted to verify the "conservation law" between heat, work, and energy, known as the first law of thermodynamics. Furthermore, by replacing air with argon, students examine how the microscopic characteristics of molecules are reflected in their macroscopic properties.

Thermodynamics, like mechanics and electromagnetism, is a fundamental field of classical physics. While mechanics and electromagnetism are most basic theories for understanding nature by precisely describing the position and velocity of particles and spatial variables of electromagnetic fields as a function of time, thermodynamics is more concerned with interactions between macroscopic physical quantities (temperature, volume, pressure, etc.) that describe the average properties of objects (equilibrium state) rather than temporal causality, thereby connecting the understanding of mechanics and electromagnetics with the world of everyday experience, and is therefore very different from the methods and ideas used to describe nature in mechanics and electromagnetics. Note that "thermodynamics of non-equilibrium states" deals with the time variation, but this experiment does not deal with it.

Through these experiments, students will not only familiarize themselves with thermodynamic descriptions and ideas, but will also understand phenomenological results from a microscopic perspective based on the motion of gas molecules ("condensed matter" perspective). This is important in learning the methodology of treating matter as a collection of many atoms and molecules. Specifically, the class includes the following experiments.

2　Basic Physics

(1) Confirmation of the characteristics of ideal gases (air and argon), such as the Boyle–Charles law
(2) Adiabatic change and specific heat ratio of air
(3) Adiabatic change and specific heat ratio of argon gas.

In Experiment 1, students verify the Boyle–Charles law and absolute zero. In Experiment 2, students determine the gas constant R from the change in the volume of the piston-sealed gas. Because this experiment is optional, it is selected by groups that had completed all experiments. In Experiment 3, students observe the process of heat transfer in air and measure the specific heat ratio. In Experiment 4, students observe a thermal cycle (an inverse Otto cycle) involving adiabatic processes in air and argon.

(2) Advance Preparation

Felt stickers were attached to markers on each stop cock of the apparatus used in Experiment 1, and a Braille sticker was attached to the volume reading scale. In Experiment 2, notches were cut into the syringe piston so that its volume could be determined when it was used. Ms. Amakawa practiced reading pressure gauges (TA operated the gauges). She read the values displayed on the panels of the temperature controller and electronic balance and set up the data loggers (running on a PC) (operated by the TA). We added line breaks in the Excel file (for data sheets and analysis) and confirmed that formulas, units, etc. in each file can be read aloud. The graphs to be obtained in the experiment were to be copied in tactile form as needed.

(3) Observations on the Experiment Day

◆ Boyle's law (Experiment 1-1)

The co-experimenter operated the heater to control the temperature and pushed the syringe piston, and Ms. Amakawa recorded the value of the pressure gauge, as read by the co-experimenter.

◆ Charles' law (Experiments 1-2)

Ms. Amakawa operated the heater, as instructed by the staff for this experiment and per preparation for Experiment 3 (setting up the data logger). The TA

Figure 2-13-1 ▸ Pushing the piston with both hands to acquire data (Experiment 3)

checked the readings displayed on the heater and confirmed that the pressure remained constant.

◆ Observation of the adiabatic process and measurement of the specific heat ratio (air) (Experiment 3-1, 3-2)

Ms. Amakawa pushed the adiabatic compression piston (Figure 2-13-1), and her co-experimenter performed analysis. At Ms. Amakawa's request, the staff provided support, and she analyzed some data herself using a special Excel program.

◆ Observation of the adiabatic process and measurement of the specific heat ratio (air) (Experiment 3-3)

The piston was pushed slowly to compress air, and this was performed as in Experiments 3-1 and 3-2. There were no major delays up to this point, and the group proceeded to Experiment 4 earlier than other groups.

◆ Observation and comparison of an inverse Otto cycle and adiabatic processes for air and argon (Experiment 4)

Here, Ms. Amakawa not only pushed the piston in but also pulled it out. As experiments were to be presented at the "Presentation and Discussions" session the following week, she was especially careful when conducting them. The TA and co-experimenter checked the acquired data, which were displayed in real time on the PC, until they had acquired enough data for discussion.

◆ Data analysis, organization, and data checking

The group continued the analysis, and each data were organized individually. Transcribing handwritten data sheets filled out by the TA into Excel data sheets was time consuming. Therefore, the TA proposed to check the data of the co-experimenter first. As a result of the data check, the staff instructed them to re-acquire the data for Experiment 3-2.

◆ Re-experiment, data check

Experiment 3-2 was conducted again. While the co-experimenter was analyzing the data, Ms. Amakawa worked on the Excel file and checked the data, together with the co-experimenter for the second time, with the above-mentioned difference in the working speed being resolved.

◆ After the experiment

Ms. Amakawa proactively discussed with her co-experimenter the division of labor for the following week and date and time of the work. The staff members advised her on how to proceed when she seemed reluctant to bring up something (e.g., difficulty in making slides on her own). Because there was enough time, the TA and Ms. Amakawa conducted Experiment 2 (determination of the number of moles of gas and gas constant) in preparation for the "Presentation and Discussions" session in the following week, although this experiment was not necessary for presentation. In Experiment 2, a syringe (the same as that used in "Extraction of Caffeine") with notches cut in advance was used after carefully checking the position to which the piston should be pulled (Figure 2-13-2). The weight of the air-filled syringe was measured on an electronic balance; the value was read by the TA, and Ms. Amakawa recorded it. After completing all experiments, she checked the flow of the presentation prepared for the "Presentation and Discussions" session the following week, and materials to be submitted.

Figure 2-13-2 ▸ Checking the position of notches on the syringe piston in Experiment 2

(4) How to Confirm the Understanding Level

As this experiment was an assignment for the following week's "Presentation and Discussions" session, it was evaluated by the supervising faculty member during the session.

(5) Comments

The total number of graphs obtained during the experiment was about 40, and it was necessary to devise axes, scales, markers, and the thickness and density of lines to make their tactile copies, making the amount of work to be done enormous. Moreover, the compatibility of a tactile copy paper and printers/copy machines was poor, and printing was often impossible due to errors or paper jams, making it difficult to keep up with the work. Therefore, printing should have been checked in advance.

(Original text by: Tsuzuki, Nakagawa, Sakata)

2-14 Presentation and Discussion
(Basic Experiments in Science and Engineering 1B)

In the "Presentation and Discussion" session, students make oral presentations and hold discussions based on the results of the previous week's experiment on "Heat and the Motion of Gas Molecules." The goal of this class is to present the results of your experiments in a way that is easy for others to understand, to understand and answer questions appropriately, to extract useful information from others' presentations, and to express your doubts and opinions regarding the content of others' presentations.

On the day of the presentation, Ms. Amakawa brought a Braille text, BrailleSense, and her own PC to review and work with her co-experimenter; additionally, she had a rehearsal with the co-experimenter. The co-experimenter was in charge of the first half of the presentation, and Ms. Amakawa was responsible for the second half, i.e., from the discussion onward. The presentation proceeded in the following manner: Ms. Amakawa read out loud the text typed in BrailleSense, and the co-experimenter pointed to the corresponding part on the slide (Figure 2-14-1).

After presentations, we received positive comments from other students and faculty members in charge of examinations, saying, "It looked like they had practiced a lot." She shared the responsibility for the Q&A session with her co-experimenter, and with the cooperation of the faculty members in charge, she was given equal opportunities to speak up with other students. We got the impression that she understood the content well and engaged in lively discussions. She did not take many notes during the presentations of other groups but concentrated on listening to the presentations. Ms. Amakawa commented, "I was too focused on finishing in time."

(Original text by: Nishi, Sakata)

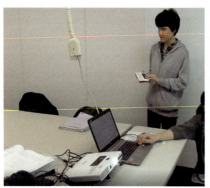

Figure 2-14-1 ▶
Ms. Amakawa creating her presentation

3

Basic Life Science

3 –1 Microscopic Observation of Cells
(Basic Experiments in Science and Engineering 1A)

(1) Outline of Experiment

In this experiment, students observe plant and animal cells using a bright-field microscope and various other microscopes to understand the structure of cells, including organelles, and learn about the characteristics of microscopes.

In this experiment, students deepen their understanding by observing and sketching the structure and characteristics of cells through plasmolysis and staining organelles.

Initially, each student operates a bright-field microscope and uses plant cells as samples to observe plasmolysis and somatic cell division by staining with acetocarmine, then sketches them on a paper, and submits it for evaluation.

Next, human oral epithelial cells as animal cells are observed under a bright-field microscope after Giemsa staining and a phase-contrast microscope and sketched. In addition, the real-time images of oral epithelial cells stained with fluorescent dyes are observed under differential interference contrast and fluorescence microscopes operated by the staff to understand differences in the appearance of these cells (Table 3-1-1).

In this experiment, the basic steps are to prepare a sample for observation on a glass slide, focus the microscope, select the subject to be observed, and then sketch it.

As it would have been difficult for a completely blind person to operate a microscope and make sketches, in this experiment, Ms. Amakawa prepared specimens for observation and checked the structure of the microscope used; further, she understood the characteristics of cell organelles and microscopes by tracing the provided tactile copies of the observed images with her finger or by other means.

(2) Advance Preparation

Because experiment is based on visual information, such as microscopic observations and sketches, it was extremely difficult for Ms. Amakawa to conduct

Table 3-1-1 ▸ Microscopes that was used, observation items, pretreatment, etc.

Microscope	Observation items	Pretreatment, etc.
Bright-field microscope	Plasmolysis of an Anacharis (*Egeria densa*)	Addition of sucrose solution
	Somatic division of spring onion cells	Fixation, hydrochloric acid treatment, acetocarmine staining
	Observation of animal cells	Giemsa staining
Phase-contrast microscope (inverted type)	Observation of animal cells	—
Differential interference contrast microscope	Observation of animal cells	—
Fluorescence microscope	Observation of animal cells	Fluorescent dye

the experiment. However, the preparation of samples for observation was performed in principle by Ms. Amakawa, as described in the text, to gain an understanding of pretreatment such as staining. Meanwhile, the observations were explained based on the real-time images as well as separately prepared and processed images so that she could learn what she needed to understand this experiment as a whole.

Only the following changes were made to the sample preparation procedures based on knowledge gained from chemistry experiments, which we believed she can perform by following the contents of the textbook.

- Using a jig made of wire or button for the treatment of spring onion roots with a fixing solution or a hydrochloric acid solution (Figure 3-1-1).
- Using plastic drip bottles instead of pipette bottles for sucrose and staining solutions.
- Providing the necessary quantities of the fixing and hydrochloric acid solutions in containers in advance. In this case, the container used should be larger than usual, with a capacity of 50 mL.
- The cutting of a large-flowered waterweed and the root ends of spring onion as well as placement of specimens on glass slides are to be performed by an assistant. A highly water-repellent, printed slide glass with slight unevenness was used so that the placement position can be identified (Figure 3-1-2).

For microscopic images and sketches, a microscope with a CCD camera was used to magnify microscopic images so that the real-time images could be viewed

3   Basic Life Science

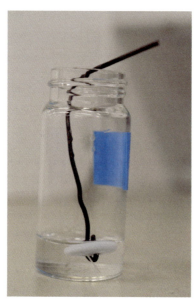

Figure 3-1-1 ▶ Jig for fixing spring onion roots and vial bottle containing solution

on a PC (Figure 3-1-2). Because it was difficult for her to make sketches, we decided to use the tactile copies of sketches made by past students and microscopic images taken in advance to explain the images to her.

However, there were issues, such as the shape of these images was too complex when copied in tactile form and was difficult to recognize due to continuous changes. Thus, complex figures were traced from sketches and microscope images using Adobe Illustrator, converted into simple lines and patterns, and the thickness of each line was increased to 1 mm or more. The edited images were printed as tactile copies. For complex images, contrast was enhanced, and the simplified tactile copies of the images were also made (Figure 3-1-3 and Figure 3-1-4).

Similarly, as images of somatic cell division and other diagrams in the text were necessary for understanding, they were enlarged, simplified, and copied in tactile form to aid in understanding.

In addition, students were asked to calculate the size of a cell using an ocular micrometer and magnification and then to correctly indicate the scale bar on a sketch based on that size. Ms. Amakawa was asked to calculate the cell size from

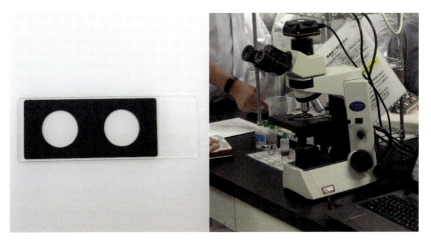

Figure 3-1-2 ▶ A highly water-repellent, printed glass slide (left), a drop container, and a microscope with a CCD camera (right)

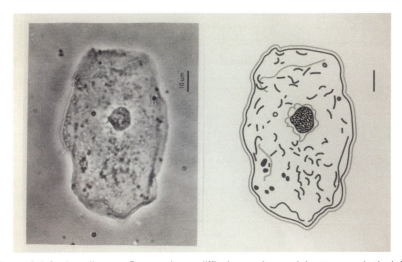

Figure 3-1-3 ▶ A tactile copy. Because it was difficult to understand the structure in the left figure, a schematic was created (on the right)

the scale bar on the tactile copy rather than the observed image, although this was the opposite of what was done by sighted students.

(3) Observations on the Experiment Day

On the day of the experiment, the assistant first explained the structure of the microscope, while Ms. Amakawa touched the actual device and then confirmed how to move the stage up and down, change lenses, and move samples using two types of microscopes.

◆ Observation of plasmolysis in an Anacharis

The protoplasm of plant cells generated from Anacharis was prepared in much the same way as that for a sighted student. The assistant cut the leaf ends of the plant to the appropriate size and placed them on a glass slide, to which Ms. Amakawa added drops of water or sucrose solution. While she smoothly placed the cover glass on the glass slide, it was difficult to check for air bubbles remaining under the cover glass, so the assistant removed air bubbles and made minor positional adjustments.

Additionally, she set up specimens on the microscope, operated the stage, and adjusted the focus. The assistant communicated the position of the sample and focus status while looking at the screen, and Ms. Amakawa moved the dials to adjust them so that the sample could be observed. Then, she traced the real-time image on the PC screen with her finger to confirm the characteristic shapes. In addition, a tactile copy of the sketch was shown to deepen her understanding of the approach required for the sketch and cellular changes, and the size of cells was calculated with a Braille ruler using the scale bar on the sketch (Figure 3-1-4).

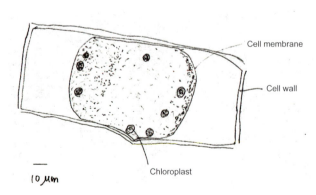

Figure 3-1-4 ▶ Sketch with contrast enhancement for preparing a tactile copy

◆ Observation of the somatic cell division of spring onion cells

Furthermore, she performed staining operation on the spring onion root tip cells. The spring onion root was placed on a simple jig made of a button and wire and hooked to the edge of a vial bottle containing the fixing and hydrochloric acid solutions so that the root tip was immersed in the solutions. Heating the vial bottle in a water bath and collection from the bath were also performed by herself. Meanwhile, it was difficult for her to recognize the point from which water was coming out of the tip of the washing bottle when she washed the spring onion root to remove the solutions, and she had a somewhat difficult time doing so.

After that, the assistant removed the spring onion root from the jig, cut the root tip with a scalpel, and placed it on the glass slide, but she stained the root tip placed on a glass slide by herself by dropping acetocarmine on them. She also smoothly dispersed cells by lightly tapping them with a metal rod after placing a cover glass and lightly pressing them with a layer of filter paper, with the assistant checking the situation and instructing her.

She operated the microscope herself, as she had done for Anacharis, and the assistant provided detailed information regarding the microscope screen to obtain the best images for observation. She traced the real-time image with her finger to confirm the image and confirmed the schematic and sketch diagrams of somatic cell division on a tactile copy.

Although many students took time to find a cell during somatic division among many cells and to obtain an optimal image, she completed operation in about the same time as other students with the help of the assistant and completed the experiment up to this point in a short time because she did not make any sketches.

◆ Observation of animal cells

For the observation of animal cells (human oral epithelial cells), she collected her oral epithelial cells with cotton swabs, applied them to glass slides, dropped Giemsa reagent, and placed cover glasses on the slides to prepare samples for observation. However, the assistant had to check whether the required amount of the Giemsa reagent was dropped to cover the entire cell because she could not determine it.

The washing of the remaining Giemsa reagent after staining on a glass-slide using washing bottle was a difficult task because one had to be careful not to wash away cells. However, with a prior explanation of the position of the flowing water

3 Basic Life Science

and the assistant's observation of the situation, she prepared a specimen that was sufficient for photographing. It was not easy for her to get a sense of how much the washing bottle must be pressed and how much must be released, so she had to be careful in this respect.

Similarly, the microscopic images of animal cells could be obtained with the help of the assistant checking the screen.

Regarding the characteristic images obtained from the phase-contrast microscope, differential interference microscope, and fluorescence microscope, she traced real-time images with her finger, and the assistant provided the details to deepen her understanding (Figure 3-1-5). Moreover, a tactile copy of the real image was prepared after image processing to aid in her understanding, and a comparison was made. However, even with image processing, it appeared that it was not easy to accurately grasp differences in the detailed shading of the real image from the tactile copy.

(4) How to Confirm the Understanding Level

Understanding regarding this experiment was confirmed through an oral examination based on the recorded data sheets. Her examination was conducted together with sighted students. Because examination for sighted students was conducted by showing images, we evaluated her comprehension by asking her

Figure 3-1-5 ▸ Explanation of the image on the screen by the assistant

questions related to the theory. She answered the questions clearly, confirming that she had a good understanding of the subject matter.

Experiment was completed earlier than other students because she did not make any sketches, and she completed the calculation process faster.

(5) Comments

This experiment was based on visual information, namely, observation with a microscope, and it was thought that there would be many problems for a visually impaired person to take the course. Therefore, it was necessary to change the method, but we secured enough time for her to examine each step, and we believed she has a good understanding of the objectives of the experiment. Meanwhile, pretreatment for sample preparation was conducted without major changes based on our knowledge from chemistry experiments.

Although Ms. Amakawa seemed to have some difficulty in understanding life science, she fully understood the tasks and objectives of the course and was able to deepen her understanding of the structure and functions of the equipment through hands-on experience.

(Original text by: Hattori)

3-2 Extraction and PCR Amplification of DNA
(Basic Experiments in Science and Engineering 1B)

(1) Outline of Experiment

DNA was extracted from human oral epithelial cells using the alkaline heat extraction method and was observed. Specific regions of the DNA sequence were amplified using polymerase chain reaction (PCR), and the length of the amplified product was confirmed via agarose gel electrophoresis. The purposes of these experiments are to gain an understanding of the structure and characteristics of DNA as well as principles and applications of PCR.

In the first half, DNA was extracted by adding several reagents to the collected oral epithelial cells and heating the cells. In general, there were many operations that are common to chemical experiments.

The second half of the experiment involved much more detailed work, even compared with other experiments, such as handling minute amounts of chemicals of few μL and introducing PCR products into an agarose gel with a width of approximately 1 mm.

In addition, because the results of agarose gel electrophoresis were obtained as ultraviolet (UV) fluorescent photographs, it was necessary to consider the need for analysis based on the photographs.

(2) Advance Preparation

Although experiment involved the use of many small equipment, such as micropipettes and tubes, most procedures were the same as those performed in chemistry experiments; therefore, it was decided that Ms. Amakawa would be able to conduct experiment as usual. However, we switched to alternative methods for the following items.

- The micropipette values were set by the assistant or co-experimenter. The assistant checked whether the solution was properly obtained.
- Felt stickers were used instead of writing the sample names on tubes, etc.
- DNA precipitation was checked based on an explanation by the assistant and

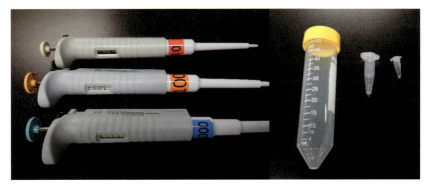

Figure 3-2-1 ▸ Micropipette (left) and various tubes (right)

by actually touching the recovered DNA.
- Black and white inversion and the contrast enhancement of the electrophoresis photographs were performed with an image processing software (Adobe Photoshop); subsequently, a tactile copy was made.
- Some operations were shared with the co-experimenter (sighted students also shared the workload in the same way: heating in a water bath, preparation of the agarose gel, and preparation of the PCR reaction solution).

(3) Observations on the Experiment Day

◆ DNA extraction from biological samples

Although micropipettes were used extensively in this experiment, she already had experience in using them in chemistry experiments and could use them in the same basic manner. Therefore, she only needed little additional training and used them smoothly.

The task of inserting the tip into a small microtube placed on the table and extracting the solution sometimes took little time, but she held the 1.5 or 50 mL tubes in her hands and performed the operation smoothly.

DNA extracted from saliva containing oral epithelial cells via alkaline heat extraction. Extraction was not particularly difficult because the process was similar to that employed in chemistry experiments, including the addition of several reaction solutions and heating in a hot water bath. The co-experimenter was responsible for placing the samples in the bath. However, DNA recovery is a delicate and careful process that requires two layers of ethanol gently being layered on top of the water layer. Nevertheless, by confirming in advance how the solution comes out of the washing bottle and the operation involved and by working carefully while the assistant checked the state of the solution, the mixing of the boundary surface was avoided and operation was conducted without any problems (Figure 3-2-2). Furthermore, because DNA was collected from the boundary between the two layers, namely the water and ethanol layers, using a bamboo skewer, the visual inspection of the floating DNA was essential; however, Ms. Amakawa was able to do this with the help of the assistant who held her hand and assisted her in the operation (Figure 3-2-3).

We expected that she would be able to confirm viscosity, which is one of the properties of DNA (being a polymer), by touching the recovered DNA; however, it was difficult to clearly confirm viscosity because the amount of recovered DNA was very small. Subsequently, DNA was dissolved in a TE buffer solution to make a DNA solution.

◆ DNA amplification from trace amounts of biological samples using PCR

The preparation of the PCR reaction solution was extremely comprehensive as she had to deal with the solution in units of microlitres in a 0.2-mL tube with a height of about 1 cm and diameter of 5 mm. She shared the work with her co-experimenter and performed the necessary operations without any problems. The task of handling few microliters of solution, which was particularly small in volume, was the responsibility of the co-experimenter as it was necessary to visually check whether the solution was in the tip of the micropipette; however, the mixing of the solution by tapping (finger flicking) was performed by Ms. Amakawa.

Although the co-experimenter was in charge of the separation of the PCR reaction solution into 0.2-mL tubes, she tried to put her own DNA solution (5 μL) into the reaction solution, and she was able to do so without any problem (Figure 3-2-4). After that, the staff set 0.2-mL tubes with the prepared PCR reaction solution for all students in a thermal cycler and started PCR.

◆ Confirmation of the PCR product via agarose gel electrophoresis

The introduction of the PCR product into the agarose gel was expected to be difficult because the process required precise operation with respect to placing the tip of a micropipette precisely into a gap that was about 1-mm wide, 1-cm long,

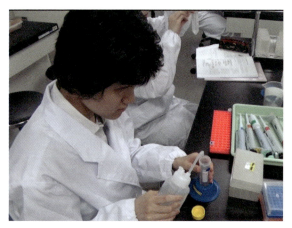

Figure 3-2-2 ▶ Ethanol layering for DNA precipitation

Figure 3-2-3 ▶ DNA recovery operation

and 5-mm depth.

The co-experimenter was responsible for mixing the dye solution and five PCR products on the film, staining DNA, and adjusting specific gravity;

Figure 3-2-4 ▶ Feeding the solution into the 0.2-mL tube

nevertheless, Ms. Amakawa also performed the operation of introducing the mixture of dye solution and PCR products into the gel. The assistant helped with precise positioning and confirmed that the height was appropriate, and although it took some time, she performed adjustment accurately (Figure 3-2-5). The structure of the electrophoresis apparatus was checked in advance, and electrophoresis start-up operation was performed while the co-experimenter explained it to Ms. Amakawa.

The assistant explained the post-electrophoresis process and observation of the DNA images (bands) detected on the gel by the UV camera in the presence of Ms. Amakawa. In addition, the location of the bands was indicated with a finger using the photographed image to give her an overview, and a tactile copy of the photographed image was employed to confirm the details (Figure 3-2-6). Comparing multiple fine lines in a small area, checking lines that were close in length, and accurately understanding them were more difficult than initially anticipated; however, by collaborating and exchanging ideas with her co-experimenter, she arrived at a correct solution.

The responsibility for the disposal and replenishment of supplies was also shared with the co-experimenter, and some of the work was done by Ms. Amakawa.

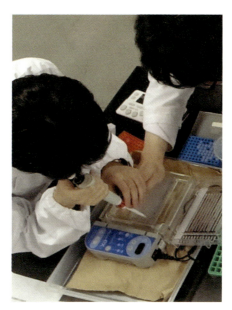

Figure 3-2-5 ▶ Introducing the mixture of dye solution and PCR products into agarose gel

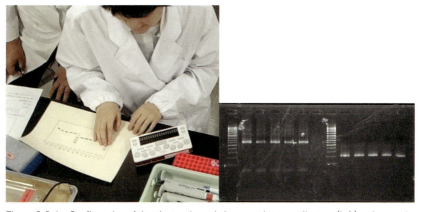

Figure 3-2-6 ▶ Confirmation of the electrophoresis image using a tactile copy (left) and example of an electrophoresis image (right)

(4) How to Confirm the Understanding Level

Comprehension regarding this experiment was evaluated through an oral examination. Examination was conducted by a faculty member, who engaged in a lively discussion. Some tasks required illustrations, and it would have been difficult for her to accurately follow the answers of other students. Therefore, she was asked other questions to confirm her understanding of the experiment. In particular, she could explain the theory satisfactorily, and we believed that the objectives of this experiment were achieved.

(5) Comments

While Ms. Amakawa commented that she felt less comfortable with life science as the requirement of imaging is difficult to perform, this experiment dealt with small molecules that even sighted students were not able to observe in real life, and we think she understood it well enough. Because this was a group experiment, work was shared with the co-experimenter, and although Ms. Amakawa performed fewer operations than in the previous experiments, she conducted difficult operations that were the core of this experiment and generally understood the objectives of the experiment. It was significant that other students naturally shared and assisted in the work, providing an opportunity for communication among students.

(Original text by: Hattori)

4

Basic Engineering

4-1 Elasticity and Viscoelasticity
(Basic Experiments in Science and Engineering 2B)

(1) Outline of Experiment

In this experiment, a specimen (stainless steel) to which a strain gauge was affixed, was supported at both ends on a test stand and a single-point load was applied at the center or the specimen was mounted on a universal testing machine (autograph) and strain was measured when a tensile load was applied to obtain the Young's modulus (ratio of stress to strain) and Poisson's ratio (ratio of lateral strain to longitudinal strain) from the stress–strain relationship. Stress is generated when an external force is applied to an elastic body and tension or pressure arises within the object attempting to restore it from the deformed state. Stress is not the same as an external force causing deformation in an elastic body but is something induced in the elastic body via deformation caused by the external force.

Experiment was conducted using a viscoelastic test specimen (polyvinyl chloride) to record changes in stress (tension) from the point at which a sudden tensile load was applied to the specimen until stress reached an equilibrium value, and the relaxation time was calculated from the measurement results.

When using an autograph as an experimental device, even sighted students were instructed to be careful of safety when handling it. In the case of Ms. Amakawa, who is visually impaired, we focused on how to prevent her from getting hurt and how to prevent unexpected accidents from occurring during the experiment. During pre-experiment, we were especially careful to ascertain the extent to which Ms. Amakawa was able to manipulate the device.

(2) Advance Preparation

Ms. Amakawa's Excel data sheet used for recording the experimental data contained several tables on one sheet, and we felt that it would be difficult for her to use the sheet as it was. Therefore, as in the "Resonant Circuits and Vibration Systems" experiment, we prepared a datasheet in which all tables were separated, and only one table could be entered on one datasheet.

Part 3　Record of Technical Support in Laboratory Education

Figure 4-1-1 ▶ Stainless steel specimen used for bending test

Figure 4-1-2 ▶ Stainless steel specimen used for tensile test

Figure 4-1-3 ▶ Viscoelastic specimen (polyvinyl chloride)

(3) Pre-experiment

Ms. Hamada, Ms. Amakawa, teaching assistant (TA), and technical staff members conducted pre-experiment. Ms. Amakawa touched and operated specimens with strain gauges, switch boxes, static strain measuring devices, and autographs. We witnessed her checking the shape and size of the device by touching it with her hands and saw that she took enough time to check the shape of the autograph, which is a large device. As the strain gauge attached to a specimen cannot be directly touched by hand, we explained to her that the resistance value of the strain gauge attached to the specimen changes when an external force is applied, which is measured as strain by a static strain meter.

The operation of attaching a specimen to the autograph and tightening the gripper and operation of removing the specimen from the gripper were the most important operations from a safety point of view, but it appeared that she was able to confirm that she could perform these operations in cooperation with the TA. In addition, the TA was to read values from the static strain meter and set the conditions of the autograph. After consulting with Ms. Hamada, she decided to prepare Braille graphs and submit them separately from the main text.

Table 4-1-1 ▶ Datasheet for use by sighted students

Elastic and Viscoelastic Data Sheet

This sheet may not be attached to the report unless specific instructions are provided.   Date of experiment: __Year Month Day__   Group :____ Unit :____

Table 1.1 Dimensions of bending specimens, distance between fulcrums

Width b(m)	Thickness h(m)	Cross-section coefficient Z(m³)	ℓ(m)	x'(m)

Table 1.5 Comparison of Young's modulus obtained and literature values

Material	Tensile test experimental values (Pa)	Bending test experimental values (Pa)	Literature values (Pa)

Table 1.2 Stress-strain relationship from bending test

Load (kgw)	Force P (N)	Stress σ(Pa)	ε Upper right	ε Upper left	ε Lower right	ε Lower left
0.0						
0.2						
0.4						
0.6						
0.8						
1.0						

Table 1.6 Comparison of the obtained Poisson's ratio with literature values

Substance	Experimental value	Literature values

Table 1.7 Cross-sectional area and length of the specimen (polyvinyl chloride) before and after the test

Width	Thickness b(m)	Cross-sectional area A(m²)	Length before test L1(m)	Length after the test L2(m)

Table 1.3 Dimensions and cross-sectional area of tensile specimens

Width b(m)	Thickness b(m)	Cross-sectional area A(m²)

Note $1Kgw=9.81N$ $P=9N\cdot m^2$

Table 1.8 Relationship between time variation and stress in the test specimen (polyvinyl chloride)

Elapsed time t(s)	Voltage (mV)	Force P(N)	Stress σ(Pa)	$(\sigma-\gamma_0\sigma_0)$(Pa)	$\ln[\sigma-\gamma_0\sigma_0]$
0.0					
3.0					
6.0					
9.0					
12					
15					
18					
21					
24					
27					
30					
33					
36					
39					
42					
45					

Table 1.4 Relationship between stress and strain from tensile test

Load (kgw)	Force P (N)	Stress σ(Pa)	Strain ε	Strain ε'
0				
(20)				
(40)				
(60)				
(80)				
(100)				
(120)				
(140)				
(160)				
(180)				
(200)				

*Fill in the measured values for load.

Table 4-1-2 ▶ Example of an Excel sheet (Table 1.1) for use by Ms. Amakawa

The column to be entered is labeled as "input column" to distinguish it from blank columns.

Table 1.1 Dimention of bending specimens, distance between fulcrums   [The columns to the right of this row are blank.]

Width b(m)	Thickness h(m)	Cross Section Coefficient Z(m³)	ℓ(m)	x'(m)	[The column to the right of this line is blank]
Input column	Input column	Input column	Input column	Input column	Input ends here
All columns below this line are blank	No more entries in this column	No more entries in this column	No more entries in this column	Input ends here	

Table 4-1-3 ▶ Example of an Excel sheet (Table 1.2) for use by Ms. Amakawa

The column to be entered is labeled as "input column" to distinguish it from blank columns.

Table 1.2 Stress- strain relationships from bending tests   [The columns to the right of this row are blank.]

Load(kgw)	Force P(N)	Stress σ(Pa)	ε Upper right	ε Upper left	ε Lower right	ε Lower left	[The columns to the right of this line are blank]
0	Input column	Input column	Input column	Input column	Input column	Input column	End of input for this row
0.200	Input column	Input column	Input column	Input column	Input column	Input column	End of input for this row
0.400	Input column	Input column	Input column	Input column	Input column	Input column	End of input for this row
0.600	Input column	Input column	Input column	Input column	Input column	Input column	End of input for this row
0.800	Input column	Input column	Input column	Input column	Input column	Input column	End of input for this row
1.00	Input column	Input column	Input column	Input column	Input column	Input column	End of input for this row
All columns below this row are blank						Input ends here	

End of input for this column

Table 4-1-4 ▶ Example of an Excel sheet (Table 1.4) for use by Ms. Amakawa

The column to be entered is labeled as "input column" to distinguish it from blank columns.

Table 1.4 Stress- strain relationships from tensile tests   [The columns to the right of this row are blank.]

Load (kgw)	Force P(N)	Stress σ(Pa)	Strain ε	Strain ε'	[The columns to the right of this line are blank]
Input column	Input column	Input column	Input column	Input column	End of input for this row
Input column	Input column	Input column	Input column	Input column	End of input for this row
Input column	Input column	Input column	Input column	Input column	End of input for this row
Input column	Input column	Input column	Input column	Input column	End of input for this row
Input column	Input column	Input column	Input column	Input column	End of input for this row
Input column	Input column	Input column	Input column	Input column	End of input for this row
Input column	Input column	Input column	Input column	Input column	End of input for this row
Input column	Input column	Input column	Input column	Input column	End of input for this row
Input column	Input column	Input column	Input column	Input column	End of input for this row
Input column	Input column	Input column	Input column	Input column	End of input for this row
Input column	Input column	Input column	Input column	Input column	End of input for this row
Input column	Input column	Input column	Input column	Input column	End of input for this row
Any rows below this are blank	End of input for this column	End of input for this column	End of input for this column	Input ends here	

Table 4-1-5 ▸ Example of an Excel sheet (Table 1.8) for use by Ms. Amakawa
The column to be entered is labeled as "input column" to distinguish it from blank columns.

Table 1.8 Relationship between time variation and stress in the test specimen (polyvinyl chloride)

The columns to the right of this row are blank.

Elapsed time t (s)	Voltage (mV)	Force F (N)	Stress σ (Pa)	$(\sigma-\gamma_a Q_a)$ (Pa)	$N(\sigma-\gamma_a Q_a)$	The columns to the right of this line are blank
0	Input column	Input column	Input column	Input column	Input column	End of input for this row
3	Input column	Input column	Input column	Input column	Input column	End of input for this row
6	Input column	Input column	Input column	Input column	Input column	End of input for this row
9	Input column	Input column	Input column	Input column	Input column	End of input for this row
12	Input column	Input column	Input column	Input column	Input column	End of input for this row
15	Input column	Input column	Input column	Input column	Input column	End of input for this row
18	Input column	Input column	Input column	Input column	Input column	End of input for this row
21	Input column	Input column	Input column	Input column	Input column	End of input for this row
24	Input column	Input column	Input column	Input column	Input column	End of input for this row
27	Input column	Input column	Input column	Input column	Input column	End of input for this row
30	Input column	Input column	Input column	Input column	Input column	End of input for this row
33	Input column	Input column	Input column	Input column	Input column	End of input for this row
36	Input column	Input column	Input column	Input column	Input column	End of input for this row
39	Input column	Input column	Input column	Input column	Input column	End of input for this row
42	Input column	Input column	Input column	Input column	Input column	End of input for this row
45	Input column	Input column	Input column	Input column	Input column	End of input for this row
Any rows below this are blank	End of input for this column	End of input for this column	End of input for this column	End of input for this column	Input ends here	

(4) Observations on the Experiment Day

◆ Stainless steel bending test

In the bending test, a stainless steel specimen with four strain gauges attached to it, two on the top and two on the bottom, was used to measure the strain value when a load was applied by a weight to the center of the specimen on the test stand. Except reading the values displayed on the static strain meter, Ms. Amakawa did most of the work.

◆ Tensile test of stainless steel using an autograph

She performed experimental operations as much as she was able to do. The operation of switching the switches in the switch box could be performed by ex-plaining the position of the switches in advance, provided that she knew where the strain gauge lead wires were attached.

Although it seemed difficult to attach the test specimen to the autograph without being able to see, she operated it almost as well as sighted students fol-lowing the TA's instructions. When mounting and dismounting test specimens, the TA helped her to avoid injury from hitting her hands. The operation to apply load (pressing the button switch) was also performed by Ms. Amakawa by checking the position of the button first, and when the required load was added, the TA called out "stop." The instrument values were read by the TA, and she recorded the readings.

4　Basic Engineering

◆ Experiment using a viscoelastic material (polyvinyl chloride)

The polyvinyl chloride test could be performed in the same manner as the stainless steel tensile test, except for different autograph conditions; therefore, the installation work was not problematic. The difference was that the operating procedure of the recorder was somewhat complicated when reading the data stored in the graphic recorder, and the data reading work was done by the TA. As a result, she proceeded with the experiment with the help of the TA.

◆ Experiment to observe the change in tension when rubber is heated

In the case of sighted students, a staff member demonstrated how tension changes when rubber is stretched and its temperature is increased (heated with a hair dryer). In Ms. Amakawa's case, she wanted to have as much opportunities as possible to handle the device, so we asked her to check the state (temperature) of rubber when heated with a hair dryer by touching it with her hands.

The results were almost identical to the data obtained by sighted students. Data entry was done by Ms. Amakawa, with the support of the TA. She created a Braille graph to observe the shape of the graph. She obtained the experimental results necessary for the report, such as Young's modulus and Poisson's ratio.

Figure 4-1-4 ▶ Ms. Amakawa checking the condition of rubber in an experiment in which tension changes when rubber is stretched and its temperature is increased (heated with a hair dryer)

(5) How to Confirm the Understanding Level

According to Ms. Amakawa, it was difficult to paste tables created in Excel into a Word document; therefore, we asked her to submit tables and graphs of measurement results separately from the main body of the report. Tables were submitted as Excel files, and graphs were submitted to the office as Braille graphs, which were scanned in the laboratory and graded by a faculty member.

(6) Comments

In strain measurement experiments, Ms. Amakawa performed almost the same procedures as sighted students because she was able to confirm the shape of specimens by touching them with her hands. However, basic tasks such as measuring the dimensions of the specimens with a caliper and reading strain values with a measuring instrument required support from the TA. Moreover, importing

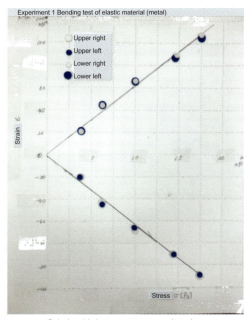

Relationship between stress σ and strain ε

Figure 4-1-5 ▶ Experiment 1 Graph of the bending test of an elastic material (stainless steel)

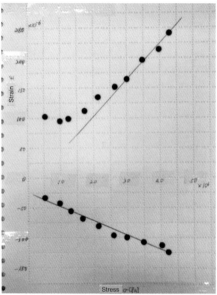

Relationship between stress σ and strain ε

Figure 4-1-6 ▶ Experiment 2 Graph of the tensile test of an elastic material (stainless steel)

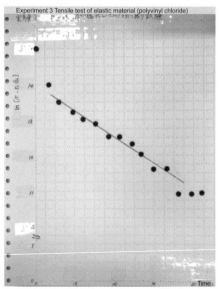

Relationship between stress σ and time t

Figure 4-1-7 ▶ Experiment 3 Graph of the experimental measurement of stress relaxation in a viscoelastic material (polyvinyl chloride)

tables from an Excel sheet prepared in advance into a Word report seemed to be a difficult task for her, and she had to submit the table data in a separate file from the main text. We felt that the way tables were written and their format should be made easier for her to study.

(Original text by: Tanaka)

4-2 Resonant Circuits and Vibration Systems
(Basic Experiments in Science and Engineering 2B)

(1) Outline of Experiment

Generally, when an external voltage close to the system's natural frequency is applied to an electric circuit, oscillations with an amplitude larger than the input amplitude can occur in the system. This phenomenon is called resonance.

In this experiment, an electric circuit comprising a coil, a resistor, and a capacitor connected in series was used to measure the frequency response characteristics (frequency dependence of the amplitude ratio and phase difference of the input and output voltages) when the frequency of the AC input voltage was changed. Another purpose of this experiment was to deepen the understanding of resonance phenomena by measuring the response characteristics (step input response characteristics) when a step input signal was used.

(2) Advance Preparation

The experiment could be broadly divided into two parts: (1) frequency response and (2) step input response. The data entry sheet used by sighted students had multiple tables mixed on a single sheet of paper, with extra margins, which we felt would be difficult for Ms. Amakawa to use. Hence, we prepared a separate Excel sheet for Ms. Amakawa to input data. In principle, only one table per sheet was to be created, and columns for input were marked as "input column" to distinguish them from blank columns so that the text-to-speech software could identify the cell to which the data must be inputted. As a result, 12 Excel sheets were created.

Moreover, sighted students were to draw four different curves on a graph paper sheet when plotting the frequency response.

For the report, we decided to use Braille graphs, but found it would be difficult for her to create four graphs on a single graph paper with Braille graphs. Therefore, we decided to use an Excel macro that was rewritten in the laboratory for printing so that only one line is printed per graph. The final output was a graph printed in the experiment and copied using the tactile copy machine.

Table 4-2-1 ▶ Data entry sheet used by sighted students (frequency response)

Basic Experiments in Science and Engineering 2B   Resonant Circuits and Vibration System

Date of experiment: Year Month Day   Group : _____ Team _____

Frequency Characteristics Data Sheet

Experiment 1
Resonant Frequency f_0 = _____ [Hz]

ω/ω_0	Frequency f (Hz)	$R_1 = 20.0$ (Ω)			$R_2 = 100$ (Ω)			$R_3 = 200$ (Ω)			$R_4 = 400$ (Ω)		
		Output voltage E_{out} (V)	Voltage gain g (dB)	Phase ϕ (deg)	Output voltage E_{out} (V)	Voltage gain g (dB)	Phase ϕ (deg)	Output voltage E_{out} (V)	Voltage gain g (dB)	Phase ϕ (deg)	Output voltage E_{out} (V)	Voltage gain g (dB)	Phase ϕ (deg)
0.10													
0.20													
0.30													
0.40													
0.50													
0.70													
0.90													
0.95													
1.00													
1.05													
1.10													
1.20													
1.50													
2.00													
4.00													
10.00													

Table 4-2-2 ▶ Excel data entry sheet used by Ms. Amakawa (frequency response: R_1 = 20.0 Ω)

Resonant Circuits and Vibration System
Frequency Characteristics Data Sheet

Voltage gain g=20log$_{10}$E$_{out}$/E$_{in}$
(Note that the input voltage is 1.00V)

The value of resonant frequency f_0 is entered into the cell of the right side column ___ Input column ___ Hz

The columns to the right of this row are blank.

Table 1.1 Frequency Response Characteristics

ω/ω_0	Frequency f (Hz)	$R_1 = 20.0$ (Ω): Output voltage E_{out} (V)	$R_1 = 20.0$ (Ω): Voltage gain g (dB)	$R_1 = 20.0$ (Ω) : Phase ϕ (deg)
0.10	Input column	Input column	Input column	Input column
0.20	Input column	Input column	Input column	Input column
0.30	Input column	Input column	Input column	Input column
0.40	Input column	Input column	Input column	Input column
0.50	Input column	Input column	Input column	Input column
0.70	Input column	Input column	Input column	Input column
0.90	Input column	Input column	Input column	Input column
0.95	Input column	Input column	Input column	Input column
1.00	Input column	Input column	Input column	Input column
1.05	Input column	Input column	Input column	Input column
1.10	Input column	Input column	Input column	Input column
1.20	Input column	Input column	Input column	Input column
1.50	Input column	Input column	Input column	Input column
2.00	Input column	Input column	Input column	Input column
4.00	Input column	Input column	Input column	Input column
10.00	Input column	Input column	Input column	Input column

All columns below this row are blank   End of input for this column   End of input for this column   End of input for this column   End of input for this column

Five graphs (one input waveform and four response waveforms) were to be printed for the step input response characteristics as well. In the graphs for sighted students, the maximum scale of the horizontal axis of the four graphs of response waveforms differs from graph to graph.

4   Basic Engineering

Table 4-2-3 ▸ Data entry sheet used by sighted students (step input response characteristics)

Step Input Response Characteristics Data Sheet

Experiment 2

1) Input waveform

Input signal waveform	Period T (ms)	Amplitude $V_{p,p}$ (V)
Measurement		

2) Start-up time t_r

Resistance R (Ω)	Start-up time t_r (μs)
$R_1 = 20.0$	
$R_2 = 100$	
$R_3 = 200$	
$R_4 = 400$	

3) Measurement of voltage/period of each part of output waveform

(1) With Resistance R_1

	Voltage of each part				
	a_1 (V)	a_2 (V)	a_3 (V)	a_4 (V)	a_5 (V)
Measurement					

	Period of each part			
	T (μs)	T (μs)	T (μs)	T (μs)
Measurement				

(2) With Resistance R_2

	Voltage of each part		
	a_1 (V)	a_2 (V)	a_3 (V)
Measurement			

	Period of each part	
	T (μs)	T (μs)
Measurement		

(3) With Resistance R_3

	Voltage of each part		
	a_1 (V)	A_1 (V)	a_2 (V)
Measurement			

	Period of each part
	T (μs)
Measurement	

Note 1) Voltage an of R_1 to R_3 are maximum
Note 2) Voltage A_1 of R_3 is minimum

(4) With Resistance R_4

	Voltage of each part					
	a_0 (V)	a_1 (V)	a_2 (V)	a_3 (V)	a_4 (V)	a_5 (V)	a_6 (V)
Measurement						

Table 4-2-4 ▸ Excel sheet for inputting the period and amplitude of the input waveform used by Ms. Amakawa (step input response characteristics)

Resonant Circuits and Vibration System
Step Input Response Characteristics Data Sheet
Table 2.1 Frequency and amplitude of input waveform

Input waveform signal	Period T (ms)	Amplitude V_{p-p} (V)	
			The columns to the right of this row are blank.
Measurement	Input column	Input column	End of input for this row
All columns below this row are blank	End of input for this column	End of input for this column	

244   Part 3   Record of Technical Support in Laboratory Education

Table 4-2-5 ▶ Excel sheet for inputting the relationship between resistance R and rise time t_r used by Ms. Amakawa (step input response characteristics)

Resonant Circuits and Vibration System
Step Input Response Characteristics Data Sheet — The columns to the right of this row are blank
Table 2.2 Relationship between resistance R and start-up time t_r — The columns to the right of this row are blank

Resistance $R(\Omega)$	Start-up time t_r (μs)	The columns to the right of this row are blank
R_1= 20.0	Input column	End of input for this row
R_2= 100	Input column	End of input for this row
R_3= 200	Input column	End of input for this row
R_4= 400	Input column	End of input for this row
All columns below this row are blank	End of input for this column	

Table 4-2-6 ▶ Excel sheet for inputting the voltage measurements (resistance R_1) of each part of the output waveform used by Ms. Amakawa (step input response characteristics)

Resonant Circuits and Vibration SystemStep
Input Response Characteristics Data Sheet
Table 2.3 Measurement of voltage of each part of output waveform — Note) Voltage an is maximum — The columns to the right of this row are blank.

Period	a_1 (V)	a_2 (V)	a_3 (V)	a_4 (V)	a_5 (V)	
Measurement	Input column	Input column	Input column	Input column	Input column	End of input for this row
All columns below this row are blank	End of input for this column	End of input for this column				

End of input for this column

Table 4-2-7 ▶ Excel sheet for inputting the measurement of the period of each part of the output waveform (resistance R_1) used by Ms. Amakawa (step input response characteristics)

Resonant Circuits and Vibration System
Step Input Response Characteristics Data Sheet
Table 2.4 Measurement of frequency of each part of output waveform (Resistance R1) — The columns to the right of this row are blank.

Period	T (between a1 and a2) (μs)	T (between a2 and a3) (μs)	T (between a3 and a4) (μs)	T (between a4 and a5) (μs)	
Measurement	Input column	Input column	Input column	Input column	End of input for this row
All columns below this row are blank	End of input for this column				

End of input for this column

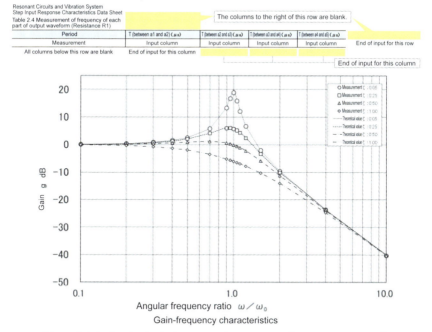

Figure 4-2-1 ▶ Graph of gain-frequency characteristics (for sighted students)

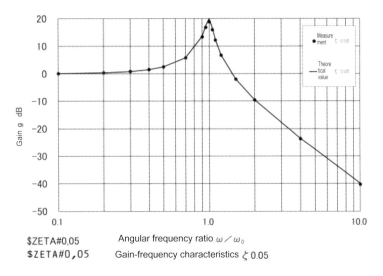

Figure 4-2-2 ▶ Graph of gain-frequency characteristics 1 (for Ms. Amakawa)

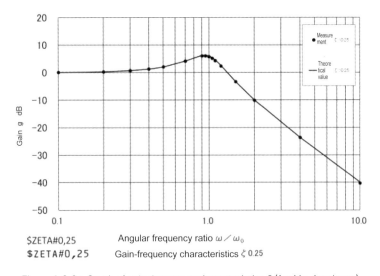

Figure 4-2-3 ▶ Graph of gain-frequency characteristics 2 (for Ms. Amakawa)

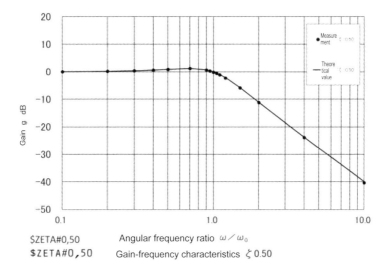

Figure 4-2-4 ▸ Graph of gain-frequency characteristics 3 (for Ms. Amakawa)

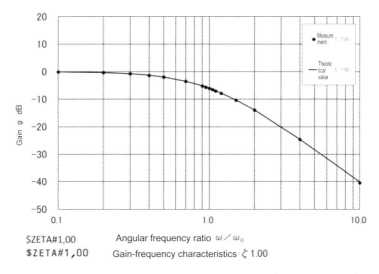

Figure 4-2-5 ▸ Graph of gain-frequency characteristics 4 (for Ms. Amakawa)

Graph 1: Horizontal axis maximum scale 1000 (μS)
Graph 2: Horizontal axis maximum scale 700 (μS)
Graph 3: Horizontal axis maximum scale 500 (μS)
Graph 4: Horizontal axis maximum scale 200 (μS)

We thought that it might be difficult to compare graphs printed using a tactile copy machine if the scales of the axes were different when touched by hand;

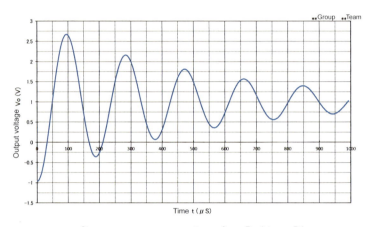

Step response measurement waveform_Resistance R1

Figure 4-2-6 ▶ Graph of step input response waveform 1 (for sighted students)

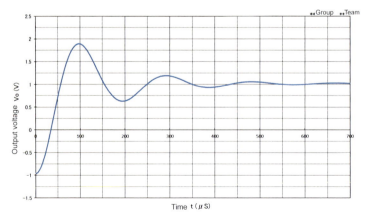

Step response measurement waveform_Resistance R2

Figure 4-2-7 ▶ Graph of step input response waveform 2 (for sighted students)

therefore, we printed graphs in which the maximum scale of the horizontal axis was 1000 (μS) for all four graphs of response waveforms.

In addition, a separate document (Word file) containing only textual information, excluding photographs and images, based on the operation manual for sighted students was prepared as an operation manual for Ms. Amakawa. It was decided not to provide a Braille translation, but to have her read and use it on her

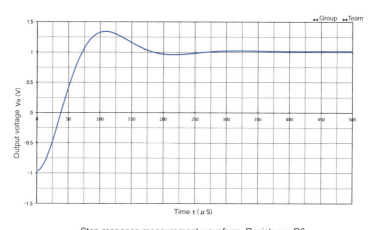

Step response measurement waveform_Resistance R3

Figure 4-2-8 ▶ Graph of step input response waveform 3 (for sighted students)

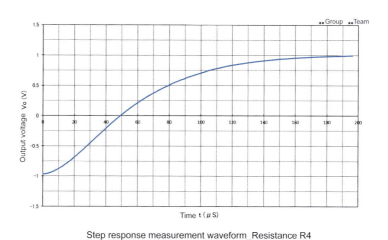

Step response measurement waveform_Resistance R4

Figure 4-2-9 ▶ Graph of step input response waveform 4 (for sighted students)

4 Basic Engineering

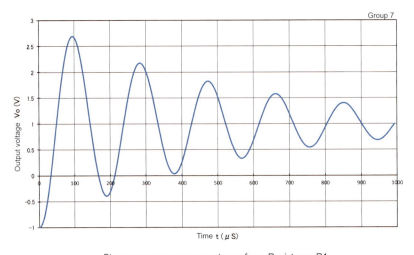

Step response measurement waveform_Resistance R1

Figure 4-2-10 ▶ Graph of step input response waveform 1 (for Ms. Amakawa)

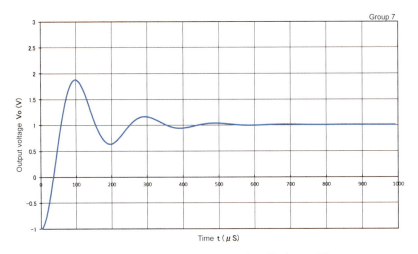

Step response measurement waveform_Resistance R2

Figure 4-2-11 ▶ Graph of step input response waveform 2 (for Ms. Amakawa)

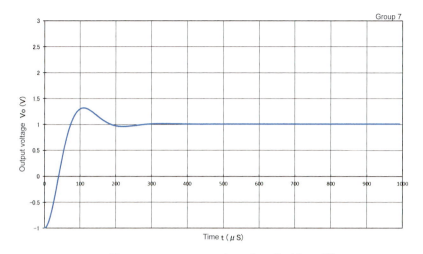

Step response measurement waveform_Resistance R3

Figure 4-2-12 ▶ Graph of step input response waveform 3 (for Ms. Amakawa)

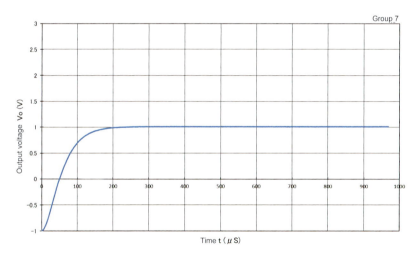

Step response measurement waveform_Resistance R4

Figure 4-2-13 ▶ Graph of step input response waveform 4 (for Ms. Amakawa)

PC for reference purposes as needed.

(3) Pre-experiment

Owing to Ms. Amakawa's study schedule, it was difficult to find time to conduct experiment in advance, so it was decided to start pre-experiment at 5:30 p.m., which was late. In Ms. Amakawa's case, as she conducted pre-experiments for all experiments, we felt that as her study progressed, it became increasingly difficult for her to coordinate her time with other classes. However, it was essential to conduct pre-experiment because problems that are not usually noticed when working with sighted students were often found in pre-experiments.

The basic operations of a resonance circuit experiment included setting the waveform (sine wave and square wave) and frequency of the function generator, setting the digital multimeter to read the input and output voltages, and setting the oscilloscope to measure the phase difference. The operating procedures were often repetitive. In the pre-experiment of the resonance circuit, we decided to limit it to only the necessary aspects and to focus on the rest on the day of the experiment. Lastly, she was asked to actually touch the graph she had prepared in advance, which was printed using the tactile copy machine, to see whether or not she could understand the image of the graph.

(4) Observations on the Experiment Day

◆ **Experiment on frequency response characteristics and step input response characteristics**

The operation of the function generator, amplifier, multimeter, and oscilloscope did not seem to pose much of a problem, but it was necessary for the TA to hold Ms. Amakawa's finger and have her trace the screen with her finger to understand the shape of the waveform displayed on the oscilloscope. For the entire experiment, we decided to have the TA read the measurement values displayed by instruments and have Ms. Amakawa enter the data into Excel.

(5) How to Confirm the Understanding Level

For the frequency response graph, the laboratory printed the equivalent of a single-logarithmic graph paper with axes, scales, etc., and Ms. Hamada labeled the paper in Braille so that the values of the scales on the graph could be recognized, which was given to Ms. Amakawa.

When creating a graph, the plot location was first identified by sticking pins into the graph paper. Theoretical value curves were prepared using pins on the graph paper as a guide and drawing lines with a flexible ruler. Lastly, felt stickers were placed in the place of plots at positions indicated by pins.

Graphs of the step input response characteristics (one input waveform and four response waveforms) were prepared by attaching Braille labels to graphs printed during experiment. Other graphs (relationship between the attenuation

Figure 4-2-14 ▶ Plotting (sticking pins) the experimental values of the gain-frequency characteristics

Figure 4-2-15 ▶ Drawing the theoretical curve of the gain-frequency characteristics

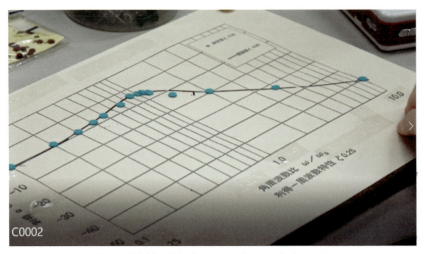

Figure 4-2-16 ▸ Gain-frequency characteristic graph

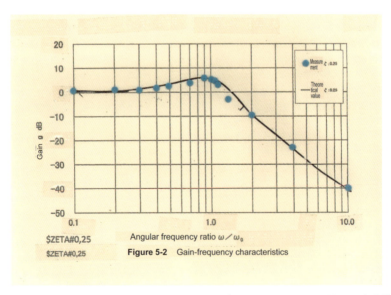

Figure 4-2-17 ▸ Gain-frequency characteristic graph (when attenuation coefficient ζ =0.25)
Blue plots denote measured values, and solid lines represent theoretical values

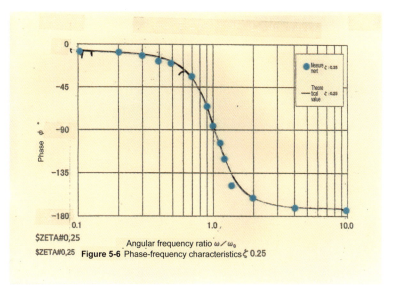

Figure 4-2-18 ▶ Phase-frequency characteristic graph (with attenuation coefficient ζ= 0.25)
Blue plots denote measured values, and solid lines represent theoretical values

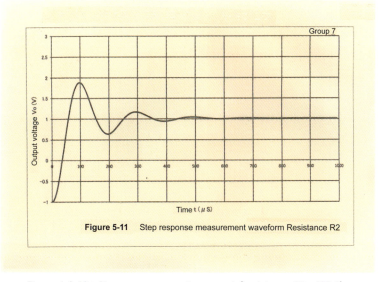

Figure 4-2-19 ▶ Step response waveform graph (resistance R2 = 100 Ω)

4　Basic Engineering

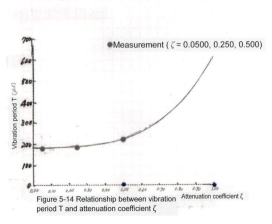

Figure 4-2-20 ▶ Graph depicting relationship between the attenuation coefficient ζ and vibration period T

coefficient ζ and vibration period T as well as that between the attenuation coefficient ζ and logarithmic decrement η, that between the attenuation coefficient ζ and overshoot Os, and that between the attenuation coefficient ζ and rise time t_r) were made by employing felt stickers instead of plots on the Braille graph paper.

(6) Comments

A total of 17 graphs were created: four graphs of gain-frequency characteristics, four graphs of phase-frequency characteristics, five graphs of step response characteristics, and four graphs showing the relationship with the attenuation coefficient ζ. Sighted students followed the same procedure of acquiring data and creating graph in the experiment with a resonance circuit. However, Ms. Amakawa had to create a larger number of graphs than sighted students, and we believed that her work load was much larger. It was impressive to see her working so hard on graphs.

(Original text by: Tanaka)

4 -3 Automatic Measurement Using a Computer
(Basic Experiments in Science and Engineering 2B)

(1) Outline of Experiment

In this experiment, students learn the basics of laboratory automation, which involves measuring the current and voltage characteristics of a diode and connecting measuring instruments, such as a function generator and a digital multimeter, to a computer to automate experiments. In the first half of the experiment, students manually measure a circuit comprising a diode, a resistor, and a function generator, and in the second half of the experiment, they work on automating manual measurements.

Through this practical experiment, students understand the principles of analog and digital signal conversion using electronic circuits and a computer-based automatic measuring device technology. They also experience the conversion of audio signals from analog to the digital format and changes in sound with variations in the bit resolution and sampling frequency.

Because most of the experiments with automation in this section were conducted in LabVIEW (a computer program) and relied heavily on visual information, we had to devise experimental methods for Ms. Amakawa to conduct experiments, such as having a TA read out numerical values and operate the PC on her behalf. In particular, for the operation of arranging block diagrams on the PC and creating a circuit (Figure 4-3-1), a significant change was made to the experimental method, in which the TA operated the PC based on a model constructed by Ms. Amakawa by hand.

(2) Advance Preparation

The content of slides was written down with additional explanations so that Ms. Amakawa could understand the content before the actual presentation. In addition, for Excel, which was used to create graphs, the auxiliary scale lines were hidden, and plots were changed from white to filled to allow the creation of tactile copies.

We prepared an Excel sheet for recording the results, with additional expla-

4 Basic Engineering

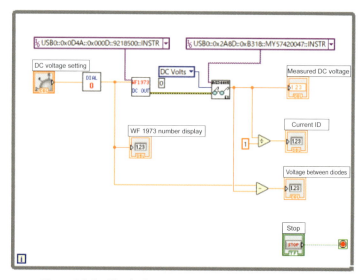

Figure 4-3-1 ▸ Circuit diagram created by a student on a PC

Table 1.1 Result of manual measurement of static characteristic of voltage-current of diodes	The columns to the right of this row are blank The columns to the right of this row are blank	
Applied DC current	Voltage at both ends of resistor E_R V	Current I_R mA
−2.0	0.00000200	0.00000200
−1.5	0.00000200	0.00000200
−1.0	0.00000200	0.00000200
−0.5	0.00000100	0.00000100
0.0	0.00000100	0.00000100
0.2	0.00020900	0.00020900
0.4	0.00947500	0.00947500
0.5	0.04018700	0.04018700
0.6	0.10300000	0.10300000
0.8	0.25570000	0.25570000
1.0	0.43060000	0.43060000
1.5	0.89730000	0.89730000
2.0	1.37880000	1.37880000
Every column of the rows below is blank	The end of input for this column	The end of input for this column

Figure 4-3-2 ▸ Excel sheet with additional explanation for Ms. Amakawa

nations added specifically for Ms. Amakawa (Figure 4-3-2).

Though we downloaded the text-to-speech software (NVDA) for PC operation, its compatibility with LabVIEW was poor, and it could not read the text aloud properly. Therefore, we concluded that it would be difficult for Ms. Amakawa to build the measurement circuit directly on the PC, so we decided to

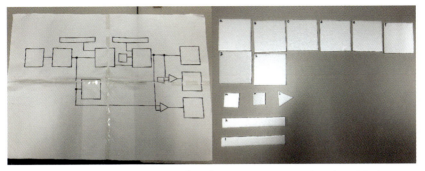

Figure 4-3-3 ▶ Complete circuit diagram (base)　　Figure 4-3-4 ▶ Styrofoam blocks

use a method in which Ms. Amakawa builds the model of the circuit diagram, and the TA operates the PC based on the model. For the circuit diagram model, we prepared styrofoam blocks (styrofoam was cut to resemble a block diagram), placed the blocks below paper on which the completed circuit diagram was printed (four sheets of A3 paper were used), and used kite strings to connect the blocks. The blocks were assigned symbols a through n, and a separate sheet of paper was prepared to summarize the information represented by each symbol.

　The size of each block was as follows:
Completed circuit diagram (base): 60 cm × 85 cm,
Square block (large): 8 cm × 8 cm,
Square block (small): 3.5 cm × 3.5 cm,
Rectangular block: 2.5 cm × 15.5 cm, and
Triangular block: 4 cm × 4 cm × 4 cm

(3) Pre-experiment

　Pre-experiment was conducted by Ms. Hamada, Ms. Amakawa, the TA, and the staff about a month before the actual experiment. In addition to reviewing how the entire experiment would proceed, we had Ms. Amakawa actually touch and feel the experimental equipment and circuit diagram model. Feedback on the circuit diagram model included the following: 1) blocks are too large, 2) the orientation of blocks is not clear, 3) blocks move around when placed on the paper, and 4) kite strings must be glued. Therefore, we (1) made the blocks smaller by

Figure 4-3-5 ▶ Magnetic block

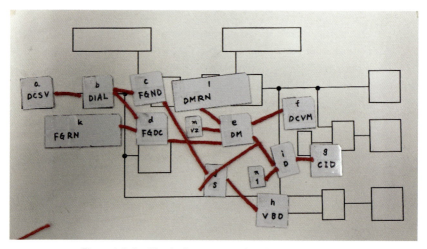

Figure 4-3-6 ▶ Circuit diagram completed by Ms. Amakawa

changing them to magnets (Figure 4-3-5) and cutting the upper right corner to indicate the direction, (2) changed the base from paper to a white board, and (3) changed kite strings to WiKKi STiX (adhesive strings provided by Ms. Hamada) for the actual experiment. Magnets used in the experiment and the completed circuit diagram model are shown in the figure (Figure 4-3-6).

The size of each component was as follows:

Whiteboard: 43.5 cm × 30 cm,

Square magnet: 3 cm × 3 cm,

Rectangular magnet (large one): 3 cm × 7 cm,

Rectangular magnet (middle size one): 3 cm × 2 cm, and Rectangular magnet (small one): 4 cm × 4 cm × 4 cm

(4) Observations on the Experiment Day

Normally, this experiment was conducted in groups of two or three students, but because the class was conducted online due to the impact of the COVID-19 pandemic, it was impossible to form experimental groups with other students. For this occasion, Ms. Amakawa formed a team of two with the TA to conduct the experiment.

Although most experimental procedures could be carried out as normal, innovative changes were made and alternative measures were taken for the following points.

- Ms. Amakawa mainly operated measuring instruments (function generators, digital multimeters, and oscilloscopes), and the TA assisted her.
- For electronic elements (diodes, fixed resistors, and lead wires), lead wires with banana plugs were connected, and a felt sticker was attached to one of the banana plugs so that Ms. Amakawa could handle it (Figure 4-3-7).
- Felt stickers were attached to the buffer amplifier and lead wires with banana plugs so that Ms. Amakawa could identify the position of the terminals by touching them.
- A breadboard was not normally used by students (a length of 8 cm and a width of 14.5 cm), but Ms. Amakawa employed one (Created in "Electronic Circuit Workshop").
- The TA read out the command string, and Ms. Amakawa directly entered the commands into the PC (Figure 4-3-8).
- Ms. Amakawa recorded the numerical values of the measurement results by entering those read out by the TA into Excel.
- The TA took Ms. Amakawa's hand and had her trace the graph of the measurement results on the PC screen to share the information (Figure 4-3-9). Moreover, after printing the resultant images on a paper for the tactile copy machine, the staff put them through the tactile copy machine to create a tactile chart.
- For creating a circuit by arranging block diagrams on a PC, Ms. Amakawa constructed a model of the circuit diagram, and the TA operated the PC based

Figure 4-3-7 ▶ Ms. Amakawa replacing a diode

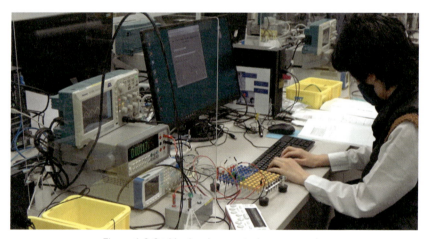

Figure 4-3-8 ▶ Ms. Amakawa entering commands

on the model.
- Ms. Hamada wrote the numbers on the graph with a pen and attached Braille stickers to the numbers on the graph axis and title of the graph.

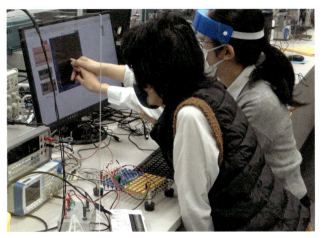

Figure 4-3-9 ▶ TA assisting Ms. Amakawa in checking the measurement results on the PC

(5) How to Confirm the Understanding Level

Normally, reports were submitted to the Waseda University's learning management system (Waseda Moodle), but Ms. Amakawa was asked to submit them to the laboratory as email attachments.

Tables and graphs of the measurement results were to be submitted separately from the main body of the report. Tables were submitted as Excel files and graphs as tactile copies to the office, and scanned data were evaluated by the faculty members in the laboratory (Figure 4-3-10).

Comments from the graders were usually made using the feedback comments in Waseda Moodle, but for comments to Ms. Amakawa, feedback was provided by sending a text file as an email attachment.

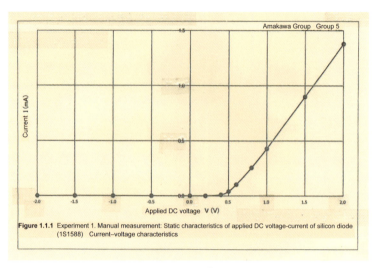

Figure 4-3-10 ▶ An example of the obtained graphs (a tactile copy with Braille labels attached)

(6) Comments

In this experiment, the text-to-speech software (NVDA) was downloaded to the PC, but because of its incompatibility with LabVIEW, Ms. Amakawa could not create the measurement circuit directly on the PC. Thus, there is room for improvement in this respect as visually impaired students can experience more practical measurement methods if the compatibility issue between the text-to-speech software and programming software can be addressed.

(Original text by: Yoshino)

4-4 Thermal Conduction and Diffusion
(Basic Experiments in Science and Engineering 2B)

(1) Outline of Experiment

In the first half of this experiment, Bakelite and stainless steel samples at different thicknesses were used to measure the thermal conductivity of each sample by estimating the temperature distribution of the rod (metal column) of the thermal conductivity measurement device that clamped the samples. In the second half of the experiment, the thermal diffusion coefficient was obtained by measuring the temperature distribution in the material over time when a resin heated to a constant temperature (80°C) was placed in a bath at a low temperature (0°C).

Figure 4-4-1 ▶ Thermal conductivity measurement device

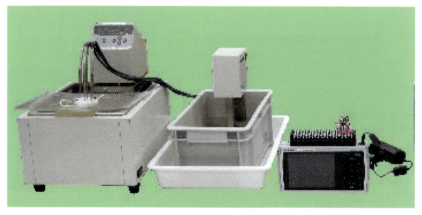

Figure 4-4-2 ▶ Experimental equipment for thermal diffusion

4 Basic Engineering

(2) Advance Preparation

While we prepared a separate Excel sheet in the lab for data entry, as in other experiments, Ms. Amakawa in the end could enter the data directly into the Excel input sheet used by sighted students (Figures 4-4-3 and 4-4-4). However, the output graphs (e.g., temperature distribution graphs for Bakelite and stainless steel samples) had four lines printed on one graph, and it was expected that distinguishing between them would be difficult for her. Therefore, as in the resonance circuit experiment, the Excel sheet was modified in the laboratory so that the final graphs would be printed as separate graphs (Figure 4-4-5 and 4-4-6). The final output was a graph printed in the experiment and copied using the tactile copy machine.

(3) Pre-experiment

In the thermal conductivity measurement experiment, before conducting experiment using Bakelite, the temperature distribution of the upper and lower rods in contact with each other was first measured without anything between them. Each rod had five thermocouples embedded at some intervals. The temperature distribution of the contact surface of the rod without any coating and with a layer of glycerin solution was measured and compared. Because the upper rod was heated by a plate heater up to a temperature of 80°C, we warned her not to touch the rod contact surface with her fingers when she applied glycerin solution with a brush. Ms. Amakawa, as she did in other experiments, initially touched the device with her hands to check its shape before conducting the experiment. Based on this impression, we could see that she was conducting the experiment while paying attention to where she should not touch. In fact, glycerin was applied without any problems.

The thermal conductivity measurement device used in this experiment (Figure 4-4-7) had a structure in which the sample was sandwiched between the upper and lower rods. If the upper rod is raised too far up until it touches the upper frame of the device, it cannot come down. It can be repaired by disassembling the device, but if this happens during the experiment, it will interfere with the experimental progress. In the case of sighted students, the problem can be avoided by warning them not to raise the upper rod too much during the experiment. However, during pre-experiment, it was found that Ms. Amakawa had a problem in that it was difficult to know how far she could raise the rod. When we consulted with Ms.

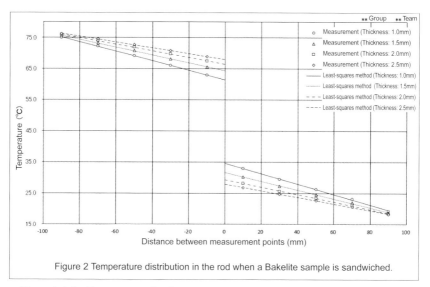

Figure 4-4-3 ▸ Temperature distribution of rods when a Bakelite sample is sandwiched between them (for sighted students)

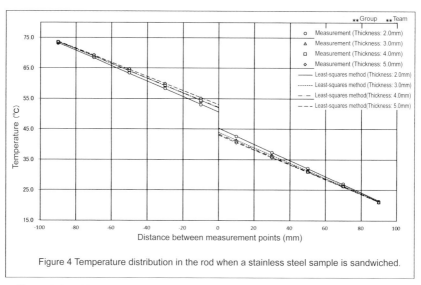

Figure 4-4-4 ▸ Temperature distribution of rods when a stainless steel sample is sandwiched between them (for sighted students)

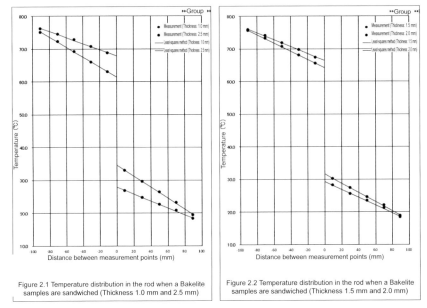

Figure 4-4-5 ▸ Graphs for Ms. Amakawa that show how the temperature distribution of rods differs depending on the thickness of the Bakelite sample (left: thickness of 1.0 and 2.5 mm and right: thickness of 1.5 and 2.0 mm)

Hamada, she suggested that we could avoid this problem by placing something narrow between the rod and frame while she raises the upper rod. Therefore, during the actual experiment, a 2-mm-thick sample (polyvinyl chloride) used in "Elasticity and Viscoelasticity" was inserted between the rod and frame when the rod was raised (Figure 4-4-8). When Ms. Amakawa actually operated the machine in this way, she could avoid the aforementioned problem by stopping the raising of the rod when the PVC sheet hit the frame of the device.

Thermal conductivity measuring experiment included the task of removing a resin cylinder (Delrin) from water heated to 80°C and transferring it to an ice water bath (Figure 4-4-9). In this experiment, we instructed her to be careful to avoid burns and to move the cylinder around by holding the string attached to the resin.

Reading the data recorded on the graphic recorder was performed by having the TA read the values displayed on the screen while she filled in the data.

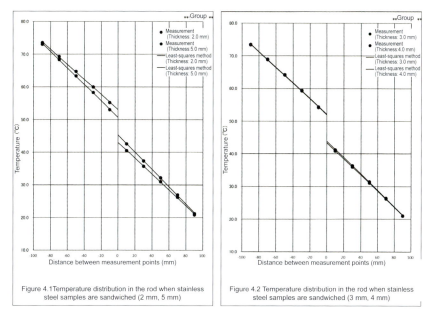

Figure 4-4-6 ▶ Graphs for Ms. Amakawa that show the difference in the temperature distribution in rods depending on the thickness of the stainless steel sample (left: thickness of 2 and 5 mm and right: thickness of 3 and 4 mm)

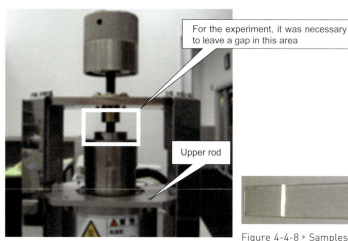

Figure 4-4-7 ▶ Thermal conductivity measurement device (upper rod)

Figure 4-4-8 ▶ Samples used in strain measurement with a resistance-wire strain gauge

4　Basic Engineering

Figure 4-4-9 ▸ Resin cylinder heated to 80°C

(4) Observations on the Experiment Day

◆ Thermal conductivity measurement experiment

Raising the rod of the device was made possible by placing a piece of a PVC sheet between the rod and frame. When inputting measurement data, the TA pointed out the input position (cell) on the Excel sheet used by sighted students, and Ms. Amakawa entered the measured values at the indicated position. For graphs, an Excel sheet prepared in advance was used.

◆ Thermal diffusion measurement experiment

There were safety concerns, such as burns, when removing the resin from water heated to 80°C and transferring it to an ice water bath; nevertheless, the experience gained during the pre-experiment stage allowed the work to proceed without problems.

She ran graphs printed in the experiment through the tactile copy machine to understand how they look like by touching them. She obtained the experimental values of the thermal conductivity of the test samples (Bakelite and stainless steel) and confirmed them. Moreover, when measuring thermal diffusion, the change in the temperature distribution within the material over time was measured using a graphic recorder, and the experimental value of the thermal diffusion coefficient was obtained from the read data and compared with the theoretical value.

(5) How to Confirm the Understanding Level

At the time, the assignment results for sighted students were to be submitted via the on-demand method, but in the Ms. Amakawa's case, the on-demand method, which focused on video clips, seemed difficult to implement because she could not actually touch the equipment. As a result, in the Ms. Amakawa's case, we decided to conduct the experiment similar to the usual in-person experiment and confirm the results on the spot.

In this experiment, when sighted students enter the measured values into an Excel sheet on the PC, the PC tentatively calculates the experimental values of thermal conductivity. The same method could have been used in the Ms. Amakawa's case, but we decided to have her calculate thermal conductivity using the equations given in the textbook. While a system in which a PC automatically performs calculations is indispensable for teaching a large group of students, we decided to conduct the experiment in such a way because there was sufficient time as Ms. Amakawa was the only one who was conducting the experiment.

(6) Comments

In the academic year 2020, when Ms. Amakawa took Basic Experiments in Science and Engineering 2B, the course was conducted in an on-demand format for sighted students, with the exception of some experiments. Because Ms. Amakawa has the handicap of being blind, all experiments were conducted in person. As a result, we believed that having the valuable opportunity to "touch the equipment" was beneficial, both for her and for the laboratory staff.

(Original text by: Tanaka)

4 –5 Laser and Holography Interference
(Basic Experiments in Science and Engineering 2B)

(1) Outline of Experiment

A hologram recording device was assembled by placing a 50-mW red He–Ne laser generator, a shutter, a half mirror, a plane mirror, lens, a film holder, an object stage, an object, etc. on a vibration isolation table of 900 mm × 1800 mm. The optical components were mounted on a magnetic stand so that they could be freely fixed in any desired position. The polarizing filter was adjusted to match the intensity of the object and reference light. The film used for hologram recording was loaded into a cassette in a simple darkroom with curtains drawn. The cassette was attached to the holder of the hologram recording device, shutter was opened, and laser light was emitted. After removing the exposed film and attaching it to a film clip, the film was developed by immersing it in a tray of developing solution, stopping solution, fixing solution, and tap water (for rinsing) sequentially. After drying the film with a hair dryer, it was irradiated with the reference light to observe a 3D image that emerges.

The basic approach for understanding experimental equipment was to touch and try it out. Because operation that requires visual observation was impossible for Ms. Amakawa, an assistant (TA) performed it and verbally described the observation. For precise optical-axis adjustment, Ms. Amakawa used the sound of the light probe as an indicator, instead of visual inspection, as the light probe can be used for positioning.

(2) Advance Preparation

The optical plane mirror, the main component of the hologram recording device, was a plane mirror made of glass, with a plane accuracy of λ /10 (one-tenth of the wavelength of light) and metallic aluminum vapor-deposited onto it, exposing a scratch-prone metal surface without protective coating. Therefore, Ms. Amakawa's primary means of observation, "freely touching it with her finger," would damage the mirror and render it unusable. Therefore, instead of using a plane mirror that cannot be touched, a mock plane mirror with a cardboard disk

Part 3　Record of Technical Support in Laboratory Education

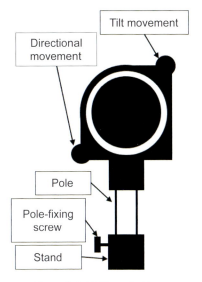

Figure 4-5-1 ▶ Mirror holder

Figure 4-5-2 ▶ Mock and plane mirrors

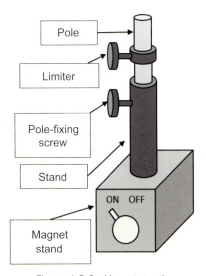

Figure 4-5-3 ▶ Magnet stand

Figure 4-5-4 ▶ Laser equipment and power supply

4　Basic Engineering

fitted into the mirror holder was prepared as a substitute (Figure 4-5-1 and Figure 4-5-2).

Laser generators and high-voltage power supplies, which cannot be touched while energized, were touched under safe conditions when power was off (Figure 4-5-4).

(3) Pre-experiment

Ms. Amakawa and the assistant checked devices that could and could not be touched, received an explanation regarding safety measures, traced the operation of devices, and confirmed the use of the light probe. Even if the assistant was familiar with the existing experimental equipment, there would be unexpected situations when a blind student has to operate it. In addition, the assistant was not familiar with any support devices such as the light probe. For this reason, we believed that pre-experiment was very meaningful for Ms. Amakawa and the assistant.

Items that may be touched freely include vibration isolators, optical equipment other than mirror surfaces, the laser generator that is turned off, He–Ne laser safety glasses (Figure 4-5-5), photographic films, shutters, the figurine to be photographed, and developing process kits.

Experimental equipment that cannot be freely touched include the energized laser generator and high-voltage power supply, the surfaces of the plane mirror

Figure 4-5-5 ▸ He–Ne laser safety glasses

and half-mirror.

During the actual experiment, several groups used the laser device simultaneously in the same laboratory. Although each experimental table was enclosed by light-shielding curtains, all students wore safety glasses because of the danger of inadvertent exposure to the laser beam, which could be hazardous to their health. These safety glasses look like pale-blue fit-over glasses, but they have a strong effect with respect to attenuating the intensity of light rays by approximately 1/100, limited to the wavelength of the He–Ne laser.

Unlike industrial laser equipment, which is equipped with interlocks and other safety devices to prevent the accidental leakage of laser light, in educational and research laser equipment, where users assemble their own optical system, operational errors can lead to the leakage of laser light. Students confirmed in advance precautions to take when using laser equipment in such an environment while being mindful of each other's safety. Because it was impossible for Ms. Amakawa to check the laser and optical equipment during the actual experiment, the assistant visually checked the safety of the laser and optical equipment and explained verbally what was going on.

(4) Observations on the Experiment Day

Ms. Amakawa was very skillful in darkroom operations that were difficult for sighted students, such as film loading. When selecting figures to photograph, she would identify and select the character names just by touching them, without any explanation. She was accustomed to handling fragile plane mirrors through the experience of arranging and operating the cardboard mock plane mirror, so there was no problem.

Meanwhile, tasks that require looking at light, such as placing optical components relative to the laser beam or introducing the laser beam into the unadjusted optical system, were difficult. A light probe, whose sound changes in proportion to variations in the light intensity, has a very small photosensitive area, making it excellent for tracking changes in minute areas. This allowed for the final fine-tuning of the experiment.

However, it was difficult to use the light probe for tasks such as determining the approximate position of an optical instrument or a laser beam path. Because the plane mirror used in the experiment could not be touched freely, the optical system was assembled primarily by the assistant who explained the situation

4　Basic Engineering

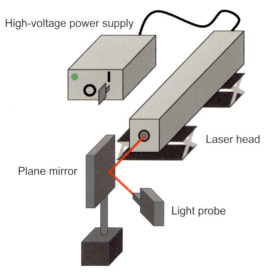

Figure 4-5-6 ▶ Laser and light probe

verbally.

Subsequently, the optical axis was adjusted. The optical path of the narrow laser before diffusion was adjusted as accurately as possible. The position of the light probe was adjusted to maximize the sound produced in response to the incoming laser light. When the optical path of the laser light was intentionally shifted slightly, the sound changed. From there, Ms. Amakawa turned the adjustment knob to maximize the sound.

When adjusting light intensity, Ms. Amakawa performed the same role as sighted students. She was in charge of adjusting the angle of the polarizer, while the TA read out the light meter values. Adjustment to align the intensity of the object light and reference light by rotating the polarizer went smoothly.

Once the intensity of the laser light became stable, the next step was to take pictures. From this process, Ms. Amakawa conducted the experiment herself. In preparation for shooting, the film was loaded in a darkroom with no lighting. This process was very difficult for sighted students, but she performed it quickly and without difficulty. A film cassette was placed in front of the object, and the shutter was operated to illuminate the object with laser light for several tens of seconds. The film was then developed in the darkroom, followed by drying. Up to this process, the operations had proceeded smoothly.

The final step in confirming the results of the experiment was to visually observe the hologram (stereoscopic image) that was taken. Unfortunately, it was not possible for Ms. Amakawa to observe the developed images, so the TA described the images verbally to her.

(5) How to Confirm the Understanding Level

Because the in-person experiment on laser and holography interference was to be assessed through submitted notebooks, there was only a brief oral examination at the end of the experiment and no report assignment, similar to sighted students participating in in-person experiments.

(6) Comments

It was unfortunate that Ms. Amakawa could not observe the images taken in the experiment that used the holography technique and holograms (stereoscopic photographs). However, we were surprised to find that while working with the holography lab equipment, she often demonstrated excellent skills in her role as an operator of the laser and optical equipment.

Through this experience of working in a place where experiments using lasers are conducted, we thought that she would apply this experience to her behavior and safety management in a place where lasers and optical instruments are handled after she advances to a research laboratory.

(Original text by: Harashima)

4-6 Optical and Electron Microscopes
(Basic Experiments in Science and Engineering 2B)

(1) Outline of Experiment

Experiment 1 involves visual observation and sketching using an optical microscope (OM). Experiment 2 involves photographing using an optical microscope equipped with a camera that can utilize various attachments, including transmitted illumination, incident illumination, bright-field observation, dark-field observation, polarized light, phase contrast, and differential interference contrast (Figure 4-6-1). Experiment 3 involves sample preparation and observation using a scanning electron microscope (SEM) (Figure 4-6-2). The visual observation plays a central role in all experimental operations, such as observation, sketching, and reading values.

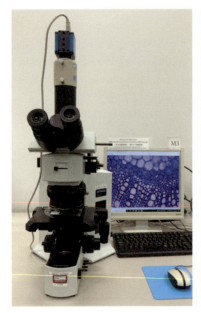

Figure 4-6-1 ▶ Optical microscope with a camera (BX51TRF)

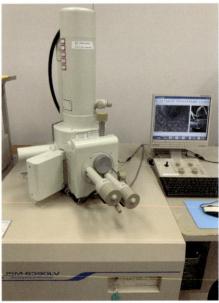

Figure 4-6-2 ▶ Scanning electron microscope (SEM) (JSM6390LV)

Because the task in Experiment 1 was to determine the magnification rate by making sketches based on visual observations and by reading the scale of the stage micrometer, we thought it would be difficult to conduct the experiment, even with some modifications. Therefore, the two key points of Experiment 1—the observation of the sample and confirmation of magnification—were incorporated into Experiment 2, which were supported by electronic equipment. For Experiments 2 and 3, we devised a method to replace "visual observation" with "confirmation by touch" using binarization with an image processing software and a tactile copy machine. In addition, in accordance with the policy of Ms. Hamada and the faculty members, we also ensured that Ms. Amakawa understood what she could do on her own in the field of microscopy, what she could do with reasonable support, and what she could not do even with the support.

(2) Advance Preparation

Ms. Hamada pointed out that observing samples through a microscope or reading the scale on the stage micrometer by a sighted person would not be a valid experiment, even if an assistant was present. Therefore, we considered substituting the observation of sample images with the tactile observation of their tactile copies printed out with a tactile copy machine.

A tactile copy machine that uses a special thermal paper that inflate in height when the black part of a document is heated is a simple and powerful support device that can be used as easily as a photocopier. However, its resolution is very poor and thin lines do not expand. To distinguish between two lines, the width of the lines and distance between them must be at least several millimeters. Its shortcomings include the fact that it can only represent two values: a convex state, which is inflated by applying heat, and a planar state, which is not heated. For this reason, if a full-color image is taken and then processed as in a tactile copy machine, the output will be completely unrecognizable. Therefore, the preprocessing of images is essential.

In preparation for this experiment, the GNU image processing program GIMP (GIMP official website https://www.gimp.org/) was selected for the preprocessing of tactile copies. GIMP has the following characteristics.

- It has functions such as grayscale conversion, tone curve, contour extraction, and noise reduction.

- Computers with various OSs, such as Windows, macOS, and Linux, are supported.
- The application can be used free of charge

Because of these characteristics, we selected GIMP as the support application for this experiment. Naturally, not only GIMP, but other commercial applications, such as Adobe Photoshop, which is well known for its extensive functionality and wide use, are also good candidates.

(3) Pre-experiment

A pre-experiment was conducted five days prior to the day of the experiment. We traced the steps involved, such as Ms. Amakawa operating the device by touch, the assistant (TA) operating it on her behalf, and another assistant (technical staff member) processing the captured images one by one to make tactile copies. Ms. Hamada helped us decide what to assign to the TAs and what to Mr. Amakawa and checked the staff's response and tactile copies of the sample images that we had prepared in advance.

(4) Observations on the Experiment Day

◆ Observation using an optical microscope (Experiment 1) and photography utilizing an optical microscope with a camera (Experiment 2)

In Experiments 1 and 2, the TA performed operations that required visual confirmation and verbally explained to Ms. Amakawa what is happening, such as sample selection; the approximate positioning of the sample stage; focusing, aperture, and illumination adjustments; and the observation of the sample shape and color. Technical staffs supplemented explanations in aspects where the TA was unfamiliar. Because the visual feedback of the operation was not available, Ms. Amakawa only simulated the main adjustment operations, such as the focusing knob and XY stage knob, by touching the moving parts. For SEM sample preparation, a small piece of tangerine peel was attached to the sample mounting table with a double-sided tape by Ms. Amakawa.

The visual observation of the experimental results was substituted by Ms. Amakawa after touching the tactile copies of the microscopic images created by

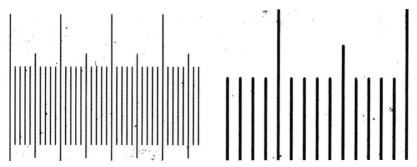

Figure 4-6-3 ▶ Stage micrometer (x20)   Figure 4-6-4 ▶ Stage micrometer (x50)

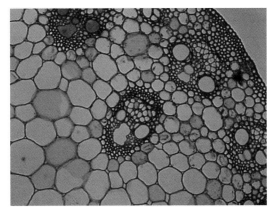

Figure 4-6-5 ▶ Cross section of a corn stalk

the staff. She confirmed that the scale interval of the stage micrometer changed in proportion to the variation in magnification by making A4-size tactile copies of the images taken with a 20x objective lens (Figure 4-6-3) and with a 50x objective lens (a scale of 1/100 mm at the smallest scale). In addition, the magnification ratio and sample size were checked by touch alongside sample images shown in Figure 4-6-5.

Because the objective micrometer has a simple shape and high contrast, we performed preprocessing required for tactile copying using a simple image processing function built into the imaging application IC Capture, which is equipped in the backside CMOS camera manufactured by Imaging Source (DFK 41AU02 https://www.theimaging source.com/).

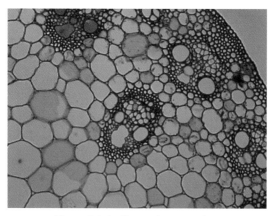

Figure 4-6-6 ▶ Grayscale conversion

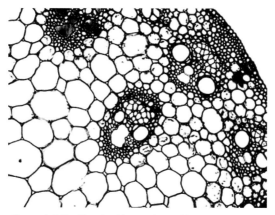

Figure 4-6-7 ▶ Binarized image for making a tactile copy

  Unlike an objective micrometer, herein, sample images were dyed, as shown in Figure 4-6-5, and were rich in color and gradation. When converted to grayscale using GIMP, the image was decolorized and became a grayscale image, as shown in Figure 4-6-6. Furthermore, image processing using the GIMP's tone curve function produced a black-and-white binarized image without the gray areas of intermediate colors, as shown in Figure 4-6-7.

  Let us explain the process of binarizing black and white using the GIMP's tone curve. Figure 4-6-8 shows a histogram of brightness (horizontal axis: brightness and vertical axis: pixel frequency) corresponding to the grayscale image in

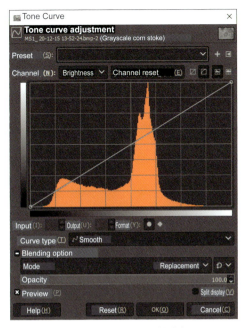

Figure 4-6-8 ▶ Histogram of brightness

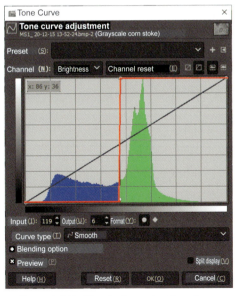

Figure 4-6-9 ▶ Binarization using Tone Curve

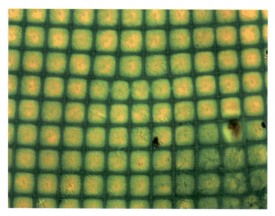

Figure 4-6-10 ▶ Compound eyes of a dragonfly

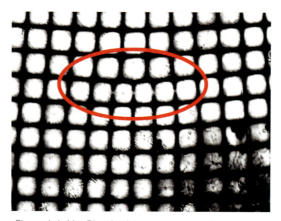

Figure 4-6-11 ▶ Binarized compound eyes of a dragonfly

Figure 4-6-6. Using the tone curve function shown by red line in Figure 4-6-9, the pixels corresponding to the blue portion of the histogram were assigned to black (brightness 0) and those corresponding to the green portion of the histogram were assigned to white (maximum brightness). As a result, a binarized image shown in Figure 4-6-7, which is suitable for tactile copying, was obtained.

When the image shown in Figure 4-6-7 was printed using a monochrome laser printer to the special paper, and it was heated by a tactile copy machine, the black part underwent foaming and expansion. This yielded a tactile copy that allowed to feel and understand the distribution of cell walls and vascular bundles.

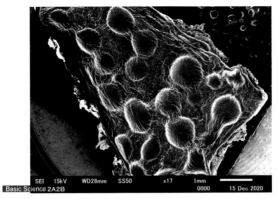

Figure 4-6-12 ▶ Tangerine peel (front side)

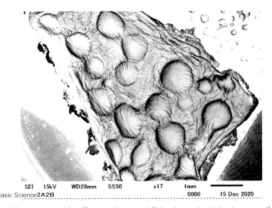

Figure 4-6-13 ▶ Tangerine peel (black-and-white inverted)

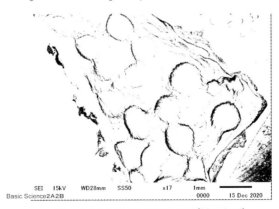

Figure 4-6-14 ▶ Tangerine peel (binarized)

The compound eye of a dragonfly (Figure 4-6-10) was observed as the second sample for the optical microscope. A tactile copy was prepared to feel and understand the structure with an arrangement similar to that of a lattice defect in the area indicated by red circle in Figure 4-6-11.

◆ Observation via a SEM (Experiment 3)

In Experiment 3, observation using a SEM was conducted. Ms. Amakawa attached the front side of a tangerine peel she had selected to the sample table and made it conductive via platinum sputtering. Because the text-to-speech software could not be installed, the TA operated the SEM to observe images, yielding a secondary electron image of the tangerine peel (front) (Figure 4-6-12). In this experiment, students could either collect samples from the campus courtyard during their lunch break on the day of the experiment or choose a sample of their choice from small objects around them for observation. Because of this experimental procedure, there was no prior information regarding the sample to be used for analyzing with the SEM during the trace experiment. The technical staff could not come up with a method that can be used to convert and process the sample image in Figure 4-6-12 (the secondary electron image of a tangerine peel) into a form suitable for tactile copying during the experiment and could not obtain a tactile copy that was easy to touch and understand. Therefore, the TA was obliged to verbally explain the displayed image.

During later verification, it was found that the binarized image in Figure 4-6-14, which is suitable for tactile copying, can be obtained by performing black and white inversion in GIMP (Figure 4-6-13) and then binarizing with a tone curve. If we had noticed this during the day of the experiment, we could have provided a tactile copy that would have allowed Ms. Amakawa to confirm the distribution of oil cells (skin grains) on the exocarp by touch.

(5) How to Confirm the Understanding Level

Because in-person experiments with optical and electron microscopes were to be assessed through the submitted notebooks, there was only a brief oral examination at the end of the experiment and no report assignment, as was the case with sighted students who participated in these experiments.

We assessed whether she had a good understanding of the principles of magnification and observation techniques.

Sighted students observed and studied what they could see and could not see through visual sketching. Because this could not be done by her through visual observation, she examined the characteristics of the observation method using an optical microscope by making a binarized tactile copy of the digital microscope image and observing it by touching the copy with her finger.

(6) Comments

Optical microscopes are widely used in science studies up to high school. However, because most observations rely on visual observation, we thought that it was difficult to experience what they are like without vision. A photograph that was left simply as it is was not suitable as an output material for a tactile copy machine because it is an image with rich gradations of the shades of colors. The image processing application GIMP, which uses tone curves to binarize images for experiments employing optical and electron microscopes, worked well with the tactile copy machine, so it was beneficial for obtaining images that could be checked by touching them.

(Original text by: Harashima)

5

Applied Physics

5 -1 X-ray Diffraction
(Experiments in Applied Physics A, Physical Properties)

(1) Outline of Experiment

In this experiment, students learn the basics of crystallography and X-ray structural analysis, which are important methods for structural analysis, by measuring powder samples and single-crystal samples using an X-ray diffractometer. Inorganic powder samples (Si or NaCl) were ground using a mortar and pestle, packed onto a glass sample plate, and each sample was measured using the X-ray diffractometer. The diffraction peaks were assigned from the diffraction pattern, and the diffraction peak list was obtained through a series of data analyses. At the same time, students worked on research assignments distributed separately. Similar to sighted students, in 2021, in response to the COVID-19 pandemic, Ms. Amakawa conducted data analysis based on distributed data for an experiment to track the phase transition of barium titanate ($BaTiO_3$) upon heating.

The main tasks in the first half of the experiment comprised grinding an NaCl sample and packing it onto a glass sample plate. Because the reagents used were not dangerous, we tried to have Ms. Amakawa perform the actual sample preparation work as much as possible. The second half of the experiment consisted primarily of data analysis and research assignments, including assistance with reading data from diffraction data that had been measured and tactile copied, entering the data into Excel, and analyzing them. We also provided support to her to work on research assignments that were distributed separately.

(2) Advance Preparation

A set of tactile copies of materials used to explain the experiment was prepared and organized in rings according to their purpose. A list of tactile copy materials was prepared and given to Ms. Amakawa in the Excel format on the day of the experiment. In addition, crystal structure models (body-centered cubic structure, diamond structure, NaCl structure, perovskite structure, etc.) were prepared to explain these structures (Figure 5-1-1). Small pieces of Si wafers were prepared in addition to measurement samples. All other laboratory equipment were pre-

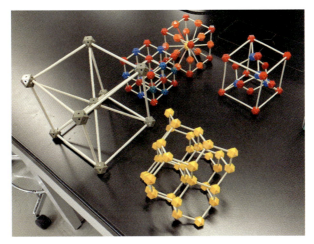

Figure 5-1-1 ▶ Crystal structure model

pared in the same way as those for sighted students.

(3) Trace Experiment

A preliminary experiment was conducted with all parties involved, except for Ms. Amakawa. The following is a description of what we confirmed.

- Ms. Amakawa would be able to perform the overall operation of the X-ray diffraction experiment (sample preparation and sample setting) without any problems.
- As it was a specialized experiment and did not focus on PC operation, Ms. Amakawa would not operate the PC, and the setting of measurement conditions and analysis would be performed by a co-experimenter in the same group (the TA would provide explanations regarding operation details).
- The obtained X-ray diffraction patterns would be confirmed using a tactile copy, and the tactile copies of data yielded during the experiment will be made on the spot. The data to be used for explanation would be tactile copied and listed in advance.
- Regarding the research assignment to be conducted during the measurement waiting time, the assignment would be translated into Braille, and diagrams would be explained by the TA by having Ms. Amakawa touch a tactile copy,

a model, or an actual device. Answers to assignments would be entered in BrailleSense and communicated verbally to the TA to confirm their correctness. Ms. Amakawa would input the numerical values into Excel on her own computer and create the respective graph (the TA would check Ms. Amakawa's graph on the screen, and if the graph is correct, hand her a tactile copy of the example answer made in advance to check it).
* Because touching Si single-crystal samples may affect measurement, Ms. Amakawa would touch Si wafers that were prepared separately to confirm the results.

(4) Observations on the Experiment Day (Week 1)

◆ Explanation before the start of the experiment

On the day of the experiment, we asked Ms. Amakawa to come to the laboratory ~30 min before sighted students so that the faculty members could interview her, the TA could explain the contents of the experiment and experimental equipment, and she could actually touch the inside of the X-ray diffractometer and check its structure (Figure 5-1-2). Using a crystal structure model, we explained to her regarding crystal planes and Miller indices as well as the research assignment.

Figure 5-1-2 ▶ Checking the X-ray diffractometer

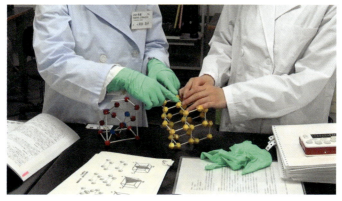

Figure 5-1-3 ▶ Using a crystal structure model to work on the research assignment

◆ **Addressing the research assignment**

Answers to the research assignment were entered into BrailleSense while communicating them verbally to the TA to confirm their correctness (Figure 5-1-3).

◆ **Measurement of single-crystal and glass substrates**

The co-experimenter measured Si(100) and Si(111) single-crystal substrates and glass substrate. We prepared a small piece of Si wafer separately for Ms. Amakawa and asked her to check it by touching it with her gloved fingertips. Similarly, we asked her to confirm the shape of the glass substrate by touching it with her gloved fingertips.

◆ **Sample preparation and setting up the instrument and measurement conditions**

The NaCl sample was prepared by Ms. Amakawa. She took the NaCl powder from the sample bottle into a mortar using a medicine spoon and ground it using a pestle. Although she did not seem to know the amount of sample on the medicine spoon, she took the necessary amount of sample, while an assistant checked the amount, and then she ground the sample (Figure 5-1-4). We asked her to check the degree of the grinding of the sample with her gloved fingertips. Ms. Amakawa placed the required amount of ground NaCl into the depression of the glass sample plate and then used a sample packing glass plate to pack the top surface of the sample evenly. The co-experimenter placed the samples in the X-ray

Figure 5-1-4 ▶ Crushing of NaCl sample

diffractometer, set the measurement conditions by operating the PC, and performed measurement. The co-experimenter prepared the Si powder sample and performed measurement.

◆ Analysis of measurement results and research assignment

Data analysis and research assignments were the primary tasks in the afternoon. First, each task of data processing (smoothing, background removal, and Kα_2 removal) was explained to Ms. Amakawa using an enlarged tactile copy of a part of the diffraction pattern as an explanatory material. By touching graphs with her fingertips, she seemed to be able to fully recognize differences in diffraction patterns at each data processing stage. She entered her notes into BrailleSense as she listened to the explanation.

The co-experimenter operated the measurement PC, processed the data, and printed out the measurement data for all five samples. Moreover, the assistant printed the data with only Kα_2 being removed (before the last peak detection) and made tactile copies of all nine data of the five samples. Ms. Amakawa obtained the numbers and figures for axes that needed to be indicated, and Ms. Hamada added these to the vertical and horizontal axes of the resulting graphs in Braille.

She continued to work on the research assignment while exchanging opinions with her co-experimenters to complete the assignment. She worked on the

Figure 5-1-5 ▸ Working on the research assignment

assignment while entering her answers and notes into BrailleSense. For each diffraction peak of NaCl, she used her own PC (Excel) to calculate the theoretical values of relative intensities (Figure 5-1-5). The co-experimenter and TA read out the values and assisted with input when necessary. The day ended with the completion of the research assignment.

(5) Observations on the Experiment Day (Week 2)

Originally, students were to work on the assignment from home as a response to the COVID-19 pandemic. However, Ms. Amakawa and Ms. Hamada came to the laboratory in the second week to work on the assignment and data analysis with the TA because we considered that it would be difficult for Ms. Amakawa to work on the home assignment by herself.

In the first half, she checked the diffraction peaks in the diffraction spectra by touching the tactile copies of the measured data, and the TA assisted her in entering the numerical values into the PC to compile data. She also worked on the text assignment. She seemed to have difficulty in understanding the 3D structure of NaCl while touching the model, such as how easy it is for NaCl to cleave. Ms. Hamada created a specific crystal surface by attaching two types of round felt stickers to a piece of paper for Ms. Amakawa to touch. She also cut the (fragile)

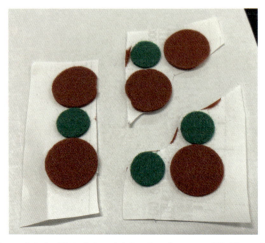

Figure 5-1-6 ▶ Material explaining the cleavage of NaCl crystal

surface while providing additional explanations (Figure 5-1-6).

In the second half, she worked on issues related to Si and $BaTiO_3$ while touching crystal structure models.

(6) How to Confirm the Understanding Level

Understanding of the topic was confirmed through a Zoom-based examination and oral presentation.

(7) Comments

Because it was difficult for Ms. Amakawa to check the amount of reagent in the prepared reagent bottles and on the spoon, we felt that it was necessary to be very careful when handling highly hazardous reagents. As far as possible, we tried to read out the formulas and numerical values during the examination. When other students mentioned equation numbers in their comments, we read out the equations again and explained the meaning of the equations. Assisting a visually impaired student in an experiment was a meaningful experience. We thought that being able to understand the other person's position and give an appropriate explanation is a skill that can be used in any field.

(Original text by: Ito, partly revised by Akanuma)

5 -2 Logic Circuit
(Experiments in Applied Physics A, Electricity)

(1) Outline of Experiment

The objective of this experiment was to understand the operating principles of logic circuits, which are the basis of digital processing devices, by measuring the static and dynamic characteristics of several basic logic circuits and finally by combining these circuits to create and understand circuits that perform logical processing. For each experiment subject, students proceeded in the following order: 1) building a logic circuit, 2) connecting and setting up measuring equipment, and 3) measuring and recording. In the first week, they conducted experiments on five subjects, and in the second week, they performed experiments on two subjects and created and verified the assigned circuits.

Normally, the experiment is conducted in pairs, but this time, Ms. Amakawa did all operations and recording. In this experiment, the terminals of many components lined up on the device surface were connected with lead wires according to the circuit diagram, and the device was actually operated to measure the logical values (1 or 0) and voltage values. Key challenges were how to enable Ms. Amakawa to recognize complex schematics, to find and connect the desired terminals from a large number of component terminals, and to understand measurement results.

(2) Advance Preparation

◆ Experimental equipment and supporting devices

Logic circuit experiments were conducted using a dedicated practice board. This device had built-in logic circuit components, and a circuit was to be built and verified by connecting many-component terminals lined up on the panel with lead wires. First, preparations were made for two anticipated problems.

(1) Information on the layout of each component in the device and arrangement of terminals

The symbols and names of each logic component were printed on the panel of the experimental device, and internal connections to the connection terminals were also printed. The experimenter had to connect lead wires between the terminals following the circuit diagram in the printed text.

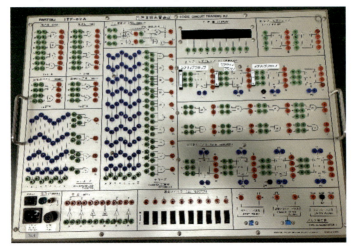

Figure 5-2-1 ▸ Logic circuit practice board

For this experiment, we prepared the following to identify the information through nonvisual means.

(a) A layout drawing of components used was prepared, and a tactile copy of the drawing was made and provided to Ms. Amakawa.

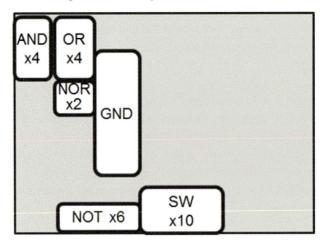

Figure 5-2-2 ▸ Example of the layout of the practice board used in experiments (for the first experiment)

(b) The area of the board containing components not used in experiment was covered with plastic panels to reduce the amount of information on components and terminals.

Figure 5-2-3 ▶ Practice board covered with plastic panels

(c) Logic component symbols were made out of wires (tin-plated wires) and affixed onto the board using a tape.

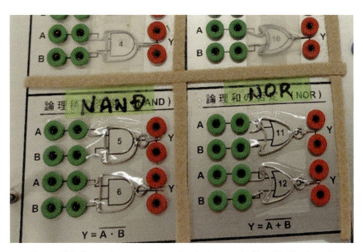

Figure 5-2-4 ▶ Logic symbols made of wires and affixed to the board

(d) The component names in Braille were affixed to logical component areas on the board.

(2) Output logic value determination method

In the first week of the experiment, logic values (1 or 0) and voltage values were measured. We wanted her to be able to determine logic values by herself, though the TA was to read the voltmeter display and communicate the voltage value. For this purpose, the following two methods were prepared.

(a) Determination by the presence or absence of sound (1: beep, 0: silence).
(b) Determination by the presence or absence of LED light emission (1: on, 0: off) + light emission detector (sound output).

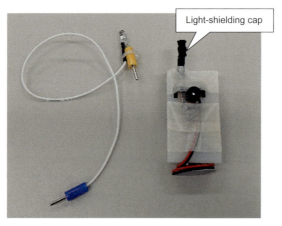

Figure 5-2-5 ▶ LED indicator and light emission detector

Although the device in (a) was convenient for measuring output at a single location, it was not suitable for simultaneous measurements at multiple locations in close proximity, so it was used in combination with (b). A light-shielding cap was attached to (b) to prevent light interference from nearby LEDs.

◆Measuring instruments

The three measuring instruments used in this experiment were a digital multimeter (DMM), a function generator (FG), and an oscilloscope (OSC), all of which are general-purpose instruments used in electrical experiments. Assuming that Ms. Amakawa would operate all measuring instruments and that the TA would read the set values and measured values in the numerical form, the following preparations were made for each measuring instrument.

(1) DMM

The measurement cable was a pair of positive and negative wires, with the negative wire normally connected to the reference ground (GND). Both connections had alligator clips and were usually distinguished by their color. For this occasion, a narrow felt sticker was wrapped only on the positive wire at the base of the alligator clip to distinguish it from the other. In the second week of the experiment, three DMMs were used simultaneously, so the two cables of each DMM were bundled together with a cable band, and we wrapped one, two, and three felt stickers around the positive wire so that each DMM could be distinguished by touching the alligator clips.

Figure 5-2-6 ▶ DMM with a felt sticker wrapped around the cable (from left to right: one sticker, two stickers, and three stickers)

As the buttons of DMM included the "DC voltage (DCV)" button and three buttons for "display range (U/D/AU)," we thought that Ms. Amakawa could operate the DMM by putting felt stickers on these buttons to distinguish them from other buttons and by writing abbreviations in Braille. The experimental manual also included a diagram showing the position of these buttons on the operation panel, and a Braille diagram was provided.

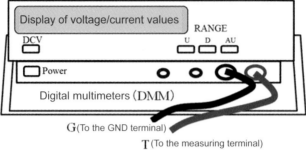

Figure 5-2-7 ▸ Example of DMM manual description (provided as a Braille diagram)

(2) FG

A common signal generator was used. Like the DMM, both of its positive and negative cables have alligator clips on the ends so that they can be distinguished by the presence or absence of a felt sticker. Additionally, as the setting only required pressing a few buttons, we marked the buttons to be used with felt stickers and Braille. When setting signals, the display showed operation items and set values, which the TA read and communicated to Ms. Amakawa so that she could perform the settings.

(3) OSC

This was a challenging experiment in which multiple waveforms of logic signals were displayed on a display screen, and students had to read time differences between waveforms. Normally, a cursor was displayed for waveform measurements, and the time information was displayed when the cursor was aligned with the positions to be measured, and the time difference between two points was measured in this way. For this occasion, we asked Ms. Amakawa to attempt data acquisition using a combination of the following two methods.

- Print out the image data of the displayed waveform (PNG format), remove unnecessary information from it, add additional information such as scales, and make a tactile copy. This would give her a rough idea of the shape of waveforms.
- Output the displayed waveforms as numerical data (csv format), load them in Excel after completing the experiment, and read the time difference between the two sets of numerical data arranged in the chronological order by focusing on the details of the waveforms.

◆ Preliminary explanatory materials

In the past, information about relevant logic circuits and an overview of the experiment have been provided using PowerPoint (PPT) in about 30 min. A video based on the PPT was also made for this year's on-demand experiment, and prior learning was requested. For this occasion, we prepared explanatory materials based on this PPT for the same purpose. The previous PPTs used a lot of diagrams and animations for the ease of understanding explanations, but many of them were changed to text-based explanations. Following is a list of points that were particularly noted in this preliminary explanation.

(1) Figures should be changed to simple ones, and explanations and comments in the figures should be brief.
(2) Additional explanations should be added in the "Notes" column to compensate for the brevity of figures and explanations in figures.
(3) Be careful not to over-explain.
(4) The arrangement of components on the practice board and how to use supporting tools should be provided as prior information.
(5) To avoid the need to refer to pre-experiment materials during the experiment, all information needed during the experiment should be written in the experimental manual, and this should be stated in pre-experiment materials.
(6) We should tell Ms. Amakawa what we want her to prepare before the day of the experiment.

◆ Experimental manual

The previous experiment manuals used many photographs and diagrams in their explanations, but this one was almost completely redesigned to use only simple tactile drawings (Braille diagrams) and Braille. To aid in her understanding, we tried to standardize the explanation format for each experiment as much as possible, following the structure below.

(1) Outline of the experimental subject

Brief explanation regarding the purpose of the experiment, what will be measured, and how to summarize the results.

(2) Equipment arrangement

A simple layout diagram showing how measuring instruments and other equipment used in each subject were arranged was provided. We asked her to confirm the arrangement by touching it at the beginning of the experiment so that she

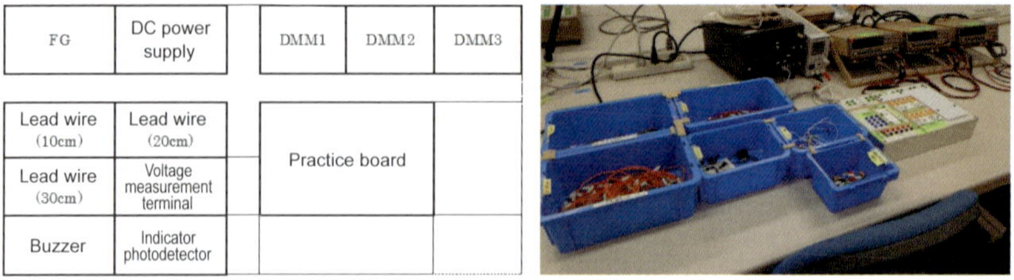

FG	DC power supply	DMM1	DMM2	DMM3
Lead wire (10cm)	Lead wire (20cm)	Practice board		
Lead wire (30cm)	Voltage measurement terminal			
Buzzer	Indicator photodetector			

Figure 5-2-8 ▶ Examples of component layout diagrams and actual layouts

could proceed with the experiment as efficiently as possible.

(3) Measuring instruments

We asked Ms. Amakawa to identify the buttons and knobs on the control panels of measuring instruments used for each experiment and to understand their approximate positional relationship. We also asked her to check the clips at the end of the measurement cables and differences among the probes of each channel. If any initial settings were required, we asked her to set them initially, but power supply and signals should be turned off at the beginning of the experiment.

(4) Experimental procedures

For tasks in which measurements were made after assembling the logic circuit according to a circuit diagram, the circuit diagram was provided. In addition to simplifying the circuit diagram, a list of connecting terminals that were to be connected to each other was shown separated by ";" (semicolon) (as it was unpredictable whether she would build the circuit mainly from the circuit diagram or wiring information, both were prepared and ready).

After completing the circuit, measuring instrument was connected and the power supply was turned on. Next, the measurement values were acquired, some of the input was changed, the next measurement was taken, and so on, with the process being repeated. The sequence of steps was shown using bullet points. All experimental data were compiled in a table, which was also included in the manual. The manual included a description regarding how the equipment was to be turned off and cleaned up after completing each part of the experiment.

◆ Assignment

The assignment was to design a circuit to compute the product of two four-bit binary numbers as an application of the logic circuit studied in the first week's experiment. The circuit diagram shows the necessary IC components, and the initialization section is provided as a pre-wired "semi-completed circuit"; however, it must be completed by adding 25 or 26 additional wires. The algorithm for designing the circuit was explained to students through diagram-based explanations and animated videos. While assignment A was required of all students, this time, we prepared the following new methods instead: (1) and (2).

(1) How to think about multiplication circuits (Braille transcription material)

The algorithm for the calculation method using logic circuits has been explained primarily in the text format.

(2) Multiplication circuit connection table (Excel)

Even if she understood the algorithm and connection of components, it was difficult to draw them on circuit drawing. Thus, we prepared a tool that represents the connection between terminals as a list. There were 26 unconnected terminals in Excel, and one terminal at a time was selected from the list of 23 terminals and pasted. Although there were many unconnected terminals, we thought that once the connection pattern for one bit was known, the rest was not as difficult as expected because the same pattern was repeated.

The method used for entering data into this connection table was designed in such a way that Ms. Amakawa could listen to explanation using the "cell text-to-speech" function of Excel, and the selected cell was read out loud at the time of connection so that she could work easily. In addition, the created terminal connections were converted to IC pin numbers using a conversion table and displayed.

Because the circuit for this assignment was rather large and complicated, she could not use the large "practice board" with a wide space between terminals that

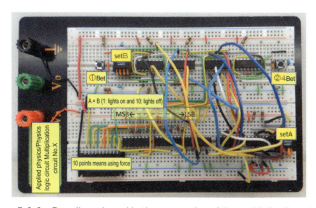

Figure 5-2-9 ▶ Breadboard used in the connection of the multiplication circuit

she had used in previous experiments but had to do detailed work with thin jumper wires on a small breadboard. Even if circuit connections were ready, it would have been difficult for her to complete wiring on a semi-finished breadboard without assistance.

Thus, after consulting with Ms. Amakawa, we decided to proceed by selecting from the following methods.

(1) Connect by herself at first, and switch to (2) when it becomes difficult due to tangled wiring.
(2) Ms. Amakawa will read values, and the TA will connect wires.
(3) The TA connects wires based on the connection table that has been prepared, and Ms. Amakawa only verifies wiring (the same applies if there is not enough time to complete the experiment).

(3) Pre-experiment

Because many experiments were similar and repetitive, we did not follow all procedures as they were, but traced only some of them. In particular, we prepared measuring instruments and experimental equipment in such a way that Ms. Amakawa could use them with minimal assistance, and we asked her opinions and advice on the equipment we had prepared for this purpose.

The following is a description of the practice board, measuring instruments, experimental procedures, and assignments.

◆ Experimental equipment and supporting devices

Following is a list of comments and modifications made for the preparation of the practice board used in the first week's experiments.

(1) There was no problem with respect to covering the areas containing components not used in the experiment with plastic panels.
(2) She appreciated the logical component symbols made of wires, but it would be easier to understand if the names of the components (in Braille) were included.
(3) The boundaries of each component area should be clearly indicated, and the component names should be written in Braille in the upper left corner of the area to make it easy to find them.

→ The boundaries were marked by cutting felt stickers into long, thin strips and affixing them, and the Braille labels were affixed in the upper left corner of each area to indicate component types.

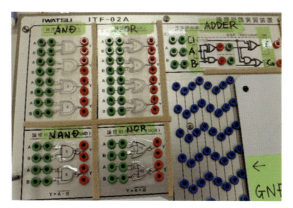

Figure 5-2-10 ▶ Practice board with felt stickers and Braille labels to clearly indicate component types

(4) When we told her that we had prepared two methods for determining logical values: (a) sound and (b) LED light emission + light emission detector, she verified them as very good.

Other preparation

(a) A laptop computer will be used to record the measurement results, so space for it should be secured on the lab desk.

(b) Prepared the tactile copy machine in the laboratory so that it can be used immediately during the experiment.

◆ **Measuring instruments**

The suggestion to place Braille labels next to buttons and knobs was deemed unnecessary because in this experiment, the number of buttons and knobs used for this occasion was small and therefore it was considered easy to remember them after listening to the explanation once. Ms. Hamada commented that excessive care was not helpful for Ms. Amakawa, and we decided to use only felt stickers to mark positions. Changes we made to the DMM measurement cables and oscilloscope probes were well received.

The following two methods of acquiring waveform data with an oscilloscope were also sufficient.

(1) Output the displayed waveforms as image data, process them, and print them in a tactile chart.
(2) Output the displayed waveforms as numerical data, and load them in Excel after the experiment is completed to obtain the necessary data.

◆ **Experiment procedure**

Although we had planned to have Ms. Amakawa experience all experiments, we had resigned ourselves to the fact that doing Experiment 2 (building a breadboard with individual components) in the first week would be difficult. However, Ms. Hamada had brought a large breadboard that had been prepared for Ms. Amakawa in Basic Experiments in Science and Engineering 1B "Electronic Circuits Workshop", so we urgently considered whether we could use it to accommodate her.

In Experiment 2, while sighted co-experimenters could choose either TTL-NAND or CMOS-NAND and then measure them together, only CMOS-NAND could be prepared for Ms. Amakawa. As it turned out that CMOS-NAND could be made using this large breadboard, we printed out a tactile copy of the circuit diagram and added it.

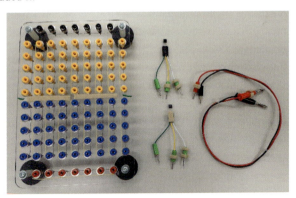

Figure 5-2-11 ▸ Large-size breadboard and adapted components and cables

(4) Observations on the Experiment Day (Week 1)

◆ **Regarding circuit diagrams**

Circuit diagrams were primarily Braille diagrams from the manual, while some were tactile copies prepared on the day of the experiment.

Initially, she had a hard time distinguishing between the straight lines of a rectangle indicating a flip-flop from those of wiring.

When we explained to her that flip-flops were distinguished by rounded corners, she said "I see" and seemed to be able to identify them somewhat more easily after that. Additionally, it was effective to draw connection points with large black circles.

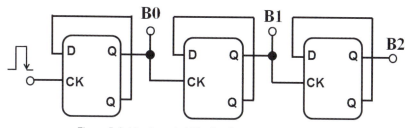

Figure 5-2-12 ▶ Rounded flip-flop frame and wiring diagram

◆ About circuit wiring (connection)

Once her fingertips left wiring, she seemed to have a hard time finding the same place again because she had to follow wiring again. Therefore, the entire wiring process was completed by holding down circuit terminals and wiring

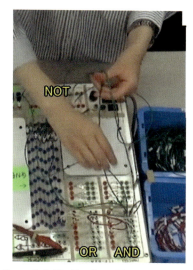

Figure 5-2-13 ▶ Tracing wiring with a finger

points with her fingers while moving on to the next operation. When connecting terminals one after the other, it seemed difficult to trace connections and find an available terminal.

Initially, it took a long time to connect wires, but once she got the hang of it, she could accelerate the process. There were almost no mistakes, and wiring could be done almost without error.

When building a circuit, it is common to roughly arrange and connect components according to the circuit diagram so that the circuit is easy to follow later, but in the Amakawa's case, the arrangement on the diagram was completely irrelevant.

◆ Experimental equipment and supporting devices

In Experiment 3.2, the building of the CMOS-NAND circuit, the circuit was built using the large-size breadboard provided in the Basic Experiment. Furthermore, we printed out a tactile copy of the circuit diagram and had Ms. Hamada add Braille to it on the day of the experiment; thus, we managed to get it ready in time.

At first, she seemed puzzled, and we were concerned that she was not making progress. However, she seemed to get used to it, and when the circuit was completed, it worked correctly and there were no wiring errors.

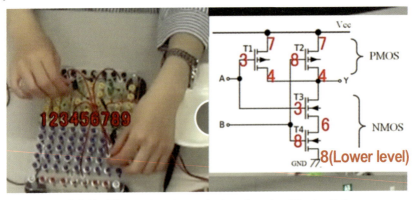

Figure 5-2-14 ▸ Wiring using a large-size breadboard and its circuit diagram

Experiment 3.3 was rather complicated, and she initially had to pause and seemed to be at a loss with respect to finding a connection point when there was no vacant terminal at the point where she wanted to make the connection. Once she figured out how to find it, she proceeded with wiring smoothly. Following are notes on the actual identification of logic circuits on the practice board and techniques used for measuring logic values prepared by the laboratory.

- It seemed difficult to distinguish between different types of logic components using wire symbols, so she relied mostly on Braille.
- She followed connections between the input and output terminals of logic symbols by following wires, so the logic symbols made of wires were useful in this respect.
- She chose to use the "LED + photo detector" method for identifying logical values among the two methods we had prepared.

◆ How to record experimental data

Ms. Amakawa was planning to use BrailleSense, which she had brought with her, to record the data, but when we explained the Excel file we had prepared, she chose to use it to record the experiment data.

(5) Observations on the Experiment Day (Week 2)

◆ Electrical characteristics of TTL and CMOS-NAND circuits (Experiment 3.6)

The arrangement of component terminals on this experimental circuit was different from that of the experimental circuit used in the first week, so it took some time to initially set up the measurement circuit. Although this information was included in preliminary explanatory materials, it was still difficult when it came to the actual use of the equipment because she was not familiar with its operation. From the latter half of Experiment 3.6 to Experiment 3.7, the same equipment was used to set up the measurement circuit, and she completed operations much faster in later stages.

Connecting multiple clips to a single measurement terminal also seemed a bit difficult. When the expected results could not be obtained or when the measured values became unstable, she did not rely on the TA but actively tried to solve the problem by following wiring and checking the results.

The preparation of many clips on measuring instruments with different numbers of felt stickers indicating each of them seemed to be effective, and she could distinguish and use them with no difficulty. The cables of measuring instruments were bundled with cable ties when they were longer than necessary, and this also seemed to be effective. There were a few minor problems in the first "3.6 (1) Measurement of TTL input/output characteristics," which caused some delays; however, the latter two parts, namely (2) and (3), proceeded smoothly.

◆ NAND switching characteristics (Experiment 3.7)

Assembling of the experimental circuit went smoothly as she had become accustomed to it. During the process of acquiring and recording data, she frequently rubbed and stretched her wrists and fingers. Reading Braille and typing into BrailleSense may also be tiring tasks.

The numerical data were saved in the csv format on a USB memory stick and loaded into Excel. However, it was found that the data were not displayed properly because they exceeded the width of Excel columns. For this reason, we temporarily took the acquired data, adjusted column widths on the spot, and gave them back to her.

◆ Assignment A "Multiplication Circuit" (Experiment 3.8)

In Assignment A, students were asked to think about the wiring of a multiplication circuit. For this occasion, instead of preparing a circuit diagram, Ms. Amakawa was asked to prepare a table, considering unconnected terminals and terminals to which they should be connected.

Specifically, the task involved selecting one of the possible connection destinations for unconnected terminals and then copying and pasting them to create a connection table, as shown below. This process was performed by having her listen to the explanatory text in Excel using the cell text-to-speech function.

The connection table that Ms. Amakawa had actually prepared had some incomplete parts (one of the additions was wrong, and the Carry input of the least significant bit was wrong); therefore, we instructed her first thing in the afternoon before starting Experiment 3.7.

This circuit was wired by the staff with jumper wires according to the connection table corrected during the course of Experiment 3.7. After the completion of Experiment 3.7, we asked her to verify operation by herself to ensure that multiplication was done correctly in four different patterns.

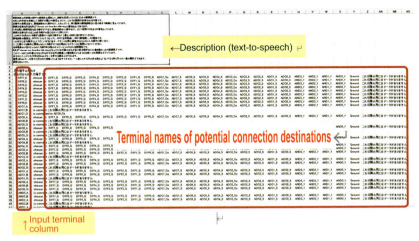

Figure 5-2-15 ▶ Prepared circuit wiring connection table for Assignment A

◆ **Assignment D: "Ternary Counter Circuit" (Experiment 3.8)**

When we asked her if she wanted to try further assignments as we had a little extra time, she said "Yes, I do" and seemed quite motivated. She said she was prepared for the experiment to be extended until around 6:00 p.m., so we decided to conduct Assignment D as well.

(6) How to Confirm the Understanding Level

The level of understanding of this subject was checked through examination and a report.

(7) Comments

There were a lot of trials and errors already from the preparation stage, and she spent more time than sighted students, but at the end of the experiment, Ms. Amakawa herself commented, "It was interesting," which made us feel that our hard preparation work has been rewarded.

(Original text by: Itaki, Yamamoto)

5 -3 Optical Circuit Elements
(Experiments in Applied Physics A, Electricity)

(1) Outline of Experiment

The final purpose of this experiment was to understand the principle of the operation of an external modulator, which is indispensable for ultrahigh-capacity optical transmission using dense wavelength division multiplexing (DWDM). In the first week of the experiment, students learn the basics of Mach–Zehnder optical interferometer, and in the second week, they understand the characteristics of Mach–Zehnder-type LN optical modulators.

In the first week, students operate the optical components of a Mach–Zehnder interferometer, such as prism reflectors, detectors, half-wave plates, and quarter-wave plates, to observe the wavelength of the light source (calculation) and polarization state and to measure the relationship between the polarization state (linear, circular, or elliptical) and output light intensity.

Students mostly perform operations such as using micrometers to slide optical components and adjusting the angles of the half-wave plate, quarter-wave plate, and analyzer to change and detect the polarization state.

In the second week, students use a Mach–Zehnder-type LN optical modulator to determine the relationship between the applied voltage and response of the output light in TM and TE polarization and calculate the half-wave voltage, extinction ratio, and insertion loss in both polarization states.

The main operations performed by students are the adjustment of the polarization controller to create TM and TE polarization and operation of the function generator (FG) to adjust the voltage applied to the optical modulator.

In the first and second weeks, it was difficult for Ms. Amakawa to set those measurement conditions that had to be set visually, so the staff members performed this task. Moreover, the staff read the measurement data and entered them in Excel, Ms. Amakawa adjusted the micrometer and analyzer, and the resulting waveforms were provided in a tactile copy so that she could understand the characteristics of the data.

(2) Advance Preparation

The main tasks in this experiment were experimental operations (adjusting the scales of the detector and wave plates and changing the applied voltage) and recording the results (reading the measurement data on digital multimeters and oscilloscopes and writing them).

Normally, students would work in pairs and divide up tasks; however, this time Ms. Amakawa would be conducting the experiment alone, so we decided to have Ms. Amakawa carry out experimental operations and have a staff member record the results. In addition to experimental operations, we considered asking her to fill in the data by telling her displayed values. However, because she would have to take her hand off the device when filling in the data, it was a special Excel sheet, and reading and writing data were not crucial to the experiment, so we decided to have a staff member fill in the data in the sheet while telling her the displayed values simultaneously.

For scale alignment, thin felt stickers were attached to the typical values of the half-wave plate, quarter-wave plate, and detector so that the scale could be adjusted via tactile sensation.

The wave plates and detector used in the experiment would become unusable if the lens parts were touched directly by a person, so the key issue was how to help her get a sense of these parts. However, we had an interferometer for display in addition to the one used in the experiment, so we decided to have her touch that

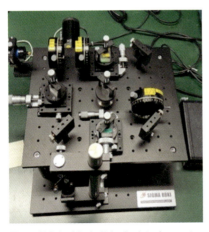

Figure 5-3-1 ▶ Mach–Zehnder interferometer

Figure 5-3-2 ▶ Analyzer with thin felt stickers

while wearing gloves. In addition, there was a detector part that could not be used in the experiment because its lens was already dirty, so we asked her to actually touch it to understand the position of the part that should not be touched in the actual equipment.

For other experimental equipment, felt stickers were attached to the buttons of the function generator that Ms. Amakawa planned to use, and the layout diagram of these buttons was provided as the Braille translation material so that she could operate the device. As for how to share the output results, the oscilloscope waveform images were temporarily exported as csv files, which were edited by staff members to create black-and-white diagrams that were easier to understand when made into tactile copies. For the Excel file specific to the experiment, the color of markers on the plot was changed to black, and the shape and size of the markers were adjusted to easily differentiate between them when printed as tactile charts.

A new experiment manual was prepared by extracting elements as text strings as the original manual contained many images and by dividing diagrams in such a way that two light paths overlap into two diagrams for the ease of understanding.

(3) Observations on the Experiment Day (Week 1)

After explaining the outline of the experiment to Ms. Amakawa, we started by describing the structure of the experimental apparatus verbally while having her actually touch the interferometer used for display so that she could understand the structure of the device and positional relationship of lenses.

◆ Optical axis adjustment: Experimental operation (1)

As the adjustment of the optical axis was a task that required checking the two light spots projected on the wall and adjusting them to a position where interference fringes were visible, Ms. Amakawa had difficulty in doing this, so a staff member performed adjustment.

Figure 5-3-3 ▶ Touching the interferometer on display and checking the relative positions of parts

◆ Wavelength measurement of light sources: Experimental operation (2)

Ms. Amakawa was asked to operate a micrometer with a thin felt sticker on it to confirm the feeling of aligning with a tape mark. Though she struggled to align tapes in the first few minutes, she seemed to be able to operate it without difficulty as she became accustomed with the operation.

Figure 5-3-4 ▶ Reading the felt sticker on the micrometer with her hand

◆ Polarization (extinction ratio) experiment

Angles were adjusted using felt stickers attached to the wave plates and detector, results were output, and data were read. Toward the end of the experiment, Ms. Amakawa seemed to have mastered the operation so well that she was able to correct herself when she made a mistake (turned a wave plate that did not need to be turned).

Figure 5-3-5 ▶ Operating the wave plate and detector with ease

Figure 5-3-6 ▶ Reading a graph printed using a tactile copy machine

(4) Observations on the Experiment Day (Week 2)

After explaining the outline of the experiment to Ms. Amakawa, we asked her to touch the layout and wiring of the entire device and confirm the flow of light.

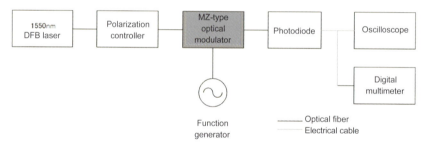

Figure 5-3-7 ▶ System diagram of optical modulator experiment

We explained that optical fibers are very delicate and that an incorrect connection to a connector can damage equipment so that optical fiber connections will be done by the staff. We also explained to her that the polarization controller used to generate TE and TM polarizations must be adjusted in real time while checking waveforms output to the oscilloscope and that the staff must perform this adjustment as well. It was decided that Ms. Amakawa would operate the function generator, which adjusts the voltage applied to the optical modulator.

Figure 5-3-8 ▶ Overall view of the equipment actually used

Figure 5-3-9 ▶ Function generator with felt stickers

As the actual experimental operation consisted only of operating the function generator (turning the dial), Ms. Amakawa attempted to create her own graphs from the measurement data entered in Excel in the second week of the experiment. The graph was then printed out using a tactile copy machine without any processing, and she was asked to confirm how the results were printed.

While the graph itself provided very good and expected data, it was created using a sheet without templates, so the adjustment of titles, axes, etc. was inadequate, and the impression was that the results were not easy to understand from the graph that she made.

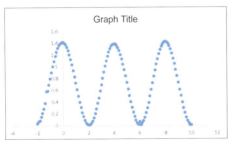

Figure 5-3-10 ▶ Graph made by Ms. Amakawa

Figure 5-3-11 ▶ Checking the tactile copy of the graph (created by herself)

(5) How to Confirm the Understanding Level

The level of understanding of this subject was checked through examination and a report.

(6) Comments

In the first week of the experiment, Ms. Amakawa was the only student, so there was plenty of time for us to deal with any problems on the spot. As for the experiment in the second week, Ms. Amakawa herself tried to make a graph for the first time, and it went well, so we thought that it would be a good opportunity to gradually increase the number of things she would perform. Although there may be some difficulties when performing the same tasks as everyone else in a group, she completed this experiment without any major difficulties, partly because it was conducted on her own.

(Original text by: Itaki)

5-4 Magnetization Measurement
(Experiments in Applied Physics A, Physical Properties)

(1) Outline of Experiment

In this experiment, a ferromagnetic zinc–nickel ferrite $Ni_{1-x}Zn_xFe_2O_4$ ($0 \leq x \leq 0.7$) was used to obtain a magnetization curve at room temperature utilizing a vibrating sample magnetometer (VSM), and the temperature change of magnetization was measured when ferrite was heated. Students also obtained magnetization curves for commercially available magnetic tapes, floppy disks, etc., and measured coercivity, spontaneous magnetization, residual magnetization, etc. Through these experiments, students deepen their understanding of phase transition phenomena.

As with sighted students, specimen preparation was omitted in 2021 academic year to deal with the COVID-19 pandemic, and only measurement experiments with the VSM—at room temperature and when specimens were heated—were conducted in one day.

In the magnetization measurement experiment using a VSM, an X–Y recorder displayed the magnetization curve. However, as this is a precision instrument and cannot be checked by touch, we ensured that the measurement status was communicated as much as possible in real time through verbal explanations by the assistant.

The analysis of magnetization curves and temperature changes involved drawing tangent lines on a paper, but we were careful not to provide any more assistance than necessary.

(2) Advance Preparation

The following preparations were made before the trace experiment.

- The Braille translation of board notes and the VSM manual.
- Created a model of the crystal structure (various types of moles in the model represent different atoms, Figure 5-4-1).

5 Applied Physics

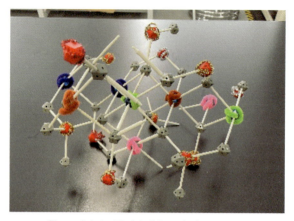

Figure 5-4-1 ▸ Model of the spinel structure

(3) Trace Experiment

The trace experiment was conducted in advance by Ms. Hamada, who was assisting in the experiment, the TAs, and the staff. Ms. Amakawa was asked to come to the laboratory before the class started on the day of the experiment to confirm the following things.

- Specimen holder (Figure 5-4-2)
- Main unit operation buttons in the VSM and X–Y recorder operation (Figures 5-4-3 and 5-4-4)
- We decided to attach Braille labels and felt stickers to the buttons necessary for operation, and Ms. Hamada attached them after completing tracing (Figure 5-4-5).

Regarding information explaining the experiment written on the whiteboard, Ms. Amakawa will use this information, together with other texts transcribed in Braille, while sighted students will use the information on the whiteboard as well as its transcription. The crystal structure will be explained using a model made by the TA (Figure 5-4-1). The TA assisted with explanation using the tactile copy and molecular model.

This experiment was conducted jointly by 2–4 students. A group of 2–4 people worked in turns. Specifically, the two tasks of mounting specimens and operating the buttons on the main unit were performed in turn, with Ms. Amakawa

Figure 5-4-2 ▶ Specimen holder

Figure 5-4-3 ▶ Main unit operation buttons in VSM

Figure 5-4-4 ▶ X–Y recorder

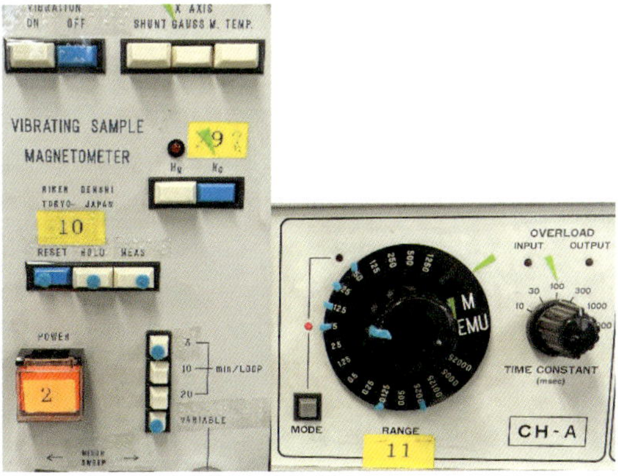

Figure 5-4-5 ▶ Examples of Braille labels and felt stickers (blue)

performing the same tasks. The following is a description of the support provided to Ms. Amakawa for the experiment, which was decided upon consultation with Ms. Hamada.

- The specimen was to be mounted on the holder with screws and then lightly secured with a tape, and this task was to be performed by Ms. Amakawa without any changes.
- For button operations that needed to be performed while looking at the display on the main unit, Ms. Amakawa would operate the buttons, while the TA

read the display out loud.

- Operation of the buttons on the X–Y recorder and setting of the pen were also to be performed by Ms. Amakawa. The positioning of the recorder's chart paper was to be performed by the TA as it was necessary to align it while looking at the LED lights on the board, and it was not essential to the nature of the experiment.
- Before measurement, the vertical axis scale was adjusted by turning the scale knob from the state in which the pen part of the recorder touched the top edge of the recorder at the maximum magnetic field to the scale one level higher. Adjustment was made by placing a piece of paper on the top edge and checking whether the pen part of the recorder touched the top edge or not.
- The actual measurement operation to obtain the magnetization curve was to be performed by Ms. Amakawa as it was mainly a button operation. The measurement results were to be photocopied, and Ms. Hamada was to make tactile copies of them on the spot using a raised line drawing board (using tactile copy machines would emphasize the grid lines in the chart paper, making it difficult to distinguish the graphs from them).
- Normally, one of the group members would take the raw data home and share them by making copies; however, for this occasion, we decided to make copies in the laboratory and distribute them to sighted students and Ms. Amakawa on the spot.
- In addition to measurement operations mentioned above, heating measurement involved raising and lowering the furnace, which was to be performed by Ms. Amakawa. Sighted students were also instructed by the TA to adjust the vertical position, so Ms. Amakawa was to do the same while the TA monitored the vertical position.
- All data obtained on the day of the experiment were to be converted into the PDF format and sent to Ms. Amakawa.

The following is a description of the support provided to Ms. Amakawa for the analysis work, which was decided upon consultation with Ms. Hamada.

- As with sighted students, only one analysis was to be performed; the rest was to be done at home.
- To analyze the magnetization curve, it is necessary to read the height and width of the graph. Therefore, the graph and a part of the reference axis

would be made as a tactile chart, and each would be measured with a braille ruler. The height of the graph was then calculated by comparing measurements (sighted students read squares and calculate the graph height, etc.).

- The graph depicting the temperature dependence of magnetization required drawing a tangent line from the inflection point, which Ms. Amakawa was able to do. However, the accuracy may not be high; therefore, the results obtained by other students of the same group were to be used.
- Sighted students would have made a plot of "doping x" vs. "molar saturation magnetization σ_{mol}" at home, but we decided that Ms. Amakawa would not make this plot because it would have the same form as in a figure of the text, and she could imagine it by observing the figure.

(4) Observations on the Experiment Day

Most experimental procedures could be performed normally using felt stickers and other means. Meanwhile, the analysis work, which is usually done at home by each student, was done in the laboratory because assistance was needed.

◆ Explanation before the start of the experiment

On the day of the experiment, we asked Ms. Amakawa to come to the laboratory before the start of the experiment and confirmed and explained the following information in advance.

- The TA explained the entire device, and Ms. Amakawa confirmed the positions of necessary components by touching them (operation buttons, sample holder, disk brake for fixing the vibratory apparatus, electromagnets, etc.).
- She performed the installation of the Ni standard sample under the guidance of the TA and was able to do so without any problems. Disk brake operation did not appear to be a problem.
- The TA explained each operation button and the X–Y recorder while Ms. Amakawa touched them to understand how they work (from operating each button to adjusting the scale of the lock-in amplifier and cutting the chart paper).
- The TA explained the shape of the furnace and method used for adjusting its position, and Ms. Amakawa actually adjusted the furnace by raising and lowering it.

 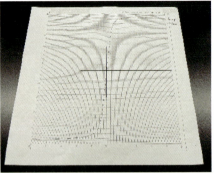

Figure 5-4-6 ▶ Specimen mounting

Figure 5-4-7 ▶ Example of the tactile chart of room temperature measurements (the cross at the center denotes the tactile line using the tape)

The following is a description of the experimental work.

◆ Room temperature measurement

First, the TA explained operation to sighted students while they measured the Ni standard specimen in a parallel direction. The TA provided the verbal explanations of the recorder's operation simultaneously.

A co-experimenter wrote notes (sample name and scale) on the chart paper. Thereafter, Ms. Amakawa and her co-experimenters took turns for mounting specimens and starting measurement by operating buttons (5 min per measurement) (Figure 5-4-6). In between measurements, the TA gave lectures. The TA verbally explained the operating status of the recorder. At the end of the room temperature measurement, the specimen was weighed on a balance. The values were read out by the TA and recorded by a co-experimenter. The room temperature measurement ended about 20 min later than planned. For the measurement data, the staff copied each measurement result, and Ms. Hamada converted the graphs into the respective tactile form using a raised line drawing board and also attached a tape to a part of the axis to make it tactile (Figure 5-4-7). Ms. Amakawa checked them in her spare time.

For the lecture, Ms. Amakawa used the Braille version of the lecture, and the co-experimenters used printed lecture materials. The crystal structure was explained using a model.

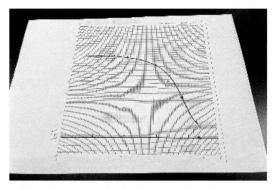

Figure 5-4-8 ▶ Example of the tactile chart of heating measurement

◆ Heating measurement

Ms. Amakawa, with explanations from the TA, conducted initial specimen mounting, furnace position adjustment, and button operation. Furnace position adjustment was carried out without any problems. Thereafter, measurements were repeated by Ms. Amakawa and her co-experimenters, who took turns for mounting specimens and starting measurements by operating buttons (40 min per measurement).

In between measurements, the TA gave lectures. Analysis was conducted after the lecture. The magnetization (M) – temperature (T) graph of heating measurement was made tactile by attaching a tape instead of using a raised line drawing board as this the former easier to understand (Figure 5-4-8).

The analysis work is described below.

Regarding the analysis of the room temperature measurement results, the saturation magnetization, residual magnetization, and coercivity were measured by estimating the height and width of the tactile graph with a ruler and comparing the values with the length of a portion of the tactile axis.

Regarding the heating measurement results, Ms. Amakawa read the inflection point by touching the taped tactile graph and drew a tangent line from the inflection point. Ms. Amakawa placed a ruler on the tangent line, and the TA drew the line. Ms. Hamada attached a felt sticker at the intersection of the tangent line and axis (Curie temperature), and Ms. Amakawa read the position of the felt sticker with a ruler. Regarding the Curie temperature of $x = 0.2$, which was analyzed first, the value obtained by Ms. Amakawa was 480°C and that by her co-experimenters was 485°C. Thus, the accuracy of her measurement was confirmed to be satisfactory. Even among sighted students, a difference of ±5°C is possible. Therefore, Ms. Amakawa and her co-experimenters analyzed subsequent specimens in the same manner to confirm the values.

Though it was planned during the trace experiment that only the results of one specimen would be analyzed in the laboratory as usual and the rest would be done at home, it was decided that Ms. Hamada and the TA would need to help Ms. Amakawa while checking with her about the necessary axes, etc.; therefore, all results were analyzed in the laboratory. For this reason, the experiment ended about 1 h later than usual. The raw data of the measurement results were later converted into PDF files and sent by the laboratory staff.

(5) How to Confirm the Understanding Level

The level of understanding of this subject was checked through a Zoom-based examination and a report.

(6) Comments

Due to the COVID-19 pandemic, Ms. Amakawa conducted experiment this time with one co-experimenter, instead of the usual five, and specimen preparation that was conducted during the first week in previous years was omitted. The amount of experimental manipulation per person was greater in this case than when the experiment was conducted by five persons. The explanation for the crystal structure using a model seemed to be understood after several exchanges of questions with the TA, and the model was also helpful for sighted students.

Because of the large size of the whole device, it may have taken time to grasp the overall picture, and it is possible that she could not grasp anything other than the parts that she had operated. As we did not place importance on the structure of the entire device this time, we did not make any special preparations. However, considering the fact that sighted students could see the device with their eyes helped them understand it to some extent, so it might have been a good idea to prepare a reduced-size schematic of the entire device so that she could understand the entire structure easily.

(Original text by: Akanuma)

5 –5 Infrared Absorption Spectroscopy
(Experiments in Applied Physics A, Physical Properties)

(1) Outline of Experiment

A vacuum line was operated to generate HCl and DCl, which were introduced into a cuvette in the gaseous form. Then, these were measured with a Fourier-transform infrared spectrophotometer (IR) to obtain the infrared absorption spectra. By analyzing the obtained spectra, students gained a better understanding of the vibrational and rotational energy levels of diatomic molecules and spectroscopic measurements.

In the first half of the experiment, Ms. Amakawa initially would confirm the principles of the experiment using materials translated into Braille and a molecular structure model. Next, she would operate a vacuum line to collect the target substance in a gas cuvette and measured it using infrared spectroscopy. We paid attention to allow her to understand the overall picture of the vacuum line and flow within the line.

In the second half, analysis work was performed based on the spectral data obtained in the first half. Initially, the group reviewed the analysis method, and then each student analyzed the data using a PC. Finally, the obtained results were reviewed by the entire group. As it required preparing graphs and entering mathematical formulas in Excel, Ms. Amakawa's laptop computer with its text-to-speech function and the support of the staff were important.

(2) Advance Preparation

To explain the principle of the experiment, we prepared a Braille translation in advance and used molecular structure models to illustrate the vibrations and rotations of molecules (Figure 5-5-1). Using models, the staff could not only tell her how molecules move, but they could also check her understanding by having her move the model herself.

A tactile copy of the entire vacuum line was made because it was necessary for her understanding of it (Figure 5-5-2) and for operating the vacuum line with an understanding of the movement of gases. As tactile copying requires

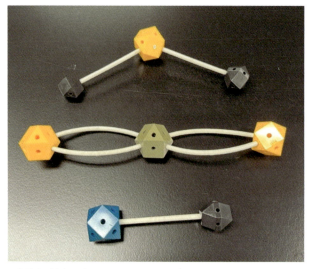

Figure 5-5-1 ▶ Molecular structure models (from the top, H_2O, CO_2, and HCl)

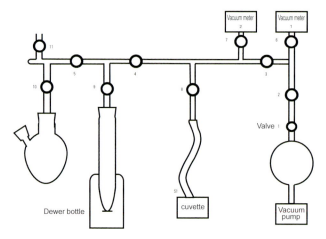

Figure 5-5-2 ▶ Overview of the vacuum line

appropriate thickness and size, it was difficult to read the text portion. Therefore, Braille labels were used for stopcock numbers and other letters. Felt stickers were attached to the main body of the vacuum line in the direction of the valve opening for the ease of opening and closing the stopcock.

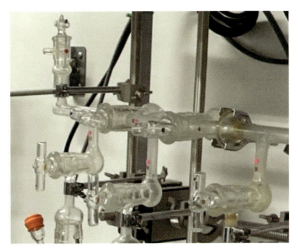

Figure 5-5-3 ▸ Attached felt stickers (pink)

Figure 5-5-4 ▸ Checking the approximate height of liquid nitrogen

Only the following aspects of operations were changed.

- A guide for determining the height when operating a liquid nitrogen lab jack was provided to Ms. Amakawa.
- A spare vessel with a Teflon cock, etc. was prepared as an example of the reaction vessel assembly.
- The value of the pressure gauge was read out each time it changed.

(3) Observations on the Experiment Day

Because this was a group experiment conducted by several students, it was necessary to assign roles to each student. Ms. Amakawa performed the following operations.

- Mounting of the reaction vessel
- Stopcock open/close operation
- Mounting of a Dewar bottle containing liquid nitrogen

The three co-experimenters shared responsibility for the following operations.

- Mounting of the collection vessel (same operation as for the reaction vessel)
- Stopcock open/close operation
- Injection of sulfuric acid into the reaction vessel
- Mounting of gas cuvette

Because sulfuric acid is highly hazardous, other students were in charge of its handling. In addition, the co-experimenters were in charge of the window panel of the gas cuvette because touching it was prohibited, but Ms. Amakawa confirmed operation using a sample gas cuvette during preliminary explanation. Thanks to prior confirmation, there were no difficulties in each operation. PC operation for spectrum measurement was performed by the co-experimenters, and the meaning and operation of parameters to be set were explained verbally each time.

In the afternoon, students analyzed the obtained data in their PC (individually). Initially, the spectral data were explained using a text, and the analysis task was described based on the text and an Excel file sent in advance (paper materials were given to sighted students). Because it was difficult for her to grasp the entire Excel file, we spent extra time to explain it to her.

The staff assisted her in the analysis process performed in her personal PC as follows.

- Reading out each value
- Operational assistance for approximate curve creation

- Tactile copy of the created approximate curve

After completing analysis, a diagram of the complex shape (a diagram comparing harmonic oscillators and Morse potential) was used to explain the results. After explanation to the whole group, Ms. Amakawa could grasp the concept and understand the content through an individual explanation.

(4) How to Confirm the Understanding Level

Understanding regarding this subject was determined through an examination and oral presentation.

(5) Comments

Although it took her a little longer than it would for other students to find explanations in the text, she could understand explanations without problems. It seemed difficult for her to follow explanation when pages changed quickly. She understood the spectral data immediately by just touching it. Moreover, she understood that peak positions were very close and that there were two peaks just by touching, even in areas that were almost completely squashed in the tactile copy.

Although we spent more time on verbal explanations than usual, the experiment was completed in about the same amount of time as for other groups because experiment and analytical operations went very smoothly. After the written and verbal explanations during the afternoon, we provided her with several individual explanations, but we felt that if she understood the content, there would be no problem even without detailed explanations.

(Original text by: Takano)

5-6 High-Temperature Superconductivity
(Experiments in Applied Physics A, Physical Properties)

(1) Outline of Experiment

In this experiment, a sample of high-temperature superconductor $YBa_2Cu_3O_7$ was prepared, and its electrical resistance was measured while cooling it with liquid nitrogen to demonstrate the zero-resistance phenomenon and experience the Meissner effect through a magnetic levitation experiment. In addition, the same experiment was performed on a specimen in which Y in $YBa_2Cu_3O_7$ was substituted with Gd and Cu with Zn at different ratios, and the results were compared to discuss the mechanism of superconductivity.

As with sighted students, specimen preparation was omitted in 2021 academic year due to the COVID-19 pandemic, and only the measurement of electrical resistance and magnetic levitation of specimens prepared in the laboratory in advance were conducted in a single day.

In the electrical resistance measurement experiment, students were responsible for mounting the specimen in the specimen holder and applying the silver paste. As Ms. Amakawa could not visually check the position of the silver paste, we were careful about what type of assistance to provide to her and to what extent.

In the magnetic levitation experiment, it was necessary to put the specimen in a specific place on the magnet in liquid nitrogen; however, as it was not possible to check it by touch, we were careful about how much assistance we should provide. Moreover, as it was not possible for her to visually confirm the state of levitation, we considered taking alternative means of experiencing it as much as possible.

(2) Advance Preparation

The following preparations were made before the trace experiment.

- The Braille translation of the information on the whiteboard and of the manual for electrical resistance measuring instruments

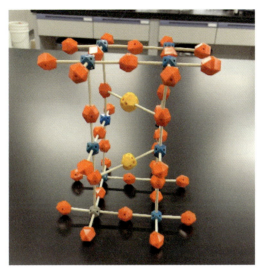

Figure 5-6-1 ▸ Structural model of YBa$_2$Cu$_3$O$_7$

- Created a model of the crystal structure (each atom in the model represents an atom of a different size, Figure 5-6-1)

(3) Trace Experiment

The trace experiment was conducted in advance by Ms. Hamada, who was assisting in the experiment, the TAs, and the staff. Ms. Amakawa was asked to come to the laboratory before the class started on the day of the experiment to confirm the following things.

- A set of electrical resistance measuring instruments (Figure 5-6-2)
- Magnet for magnetic levitation, specimen, and specimen holder (all can be touched with bare hands; Figures 5-6-3 and 5-6-4)
- Attachment of the specimen holder to the probe

As the valve of the vacuum exhaust system was the same as that used in infrared spectroscopy, a felt sticker was attached in the same way as in that experiment (Figure 5-6-5). Information written on the whiteboard was translated into Braille and was used to explain the experiment to Ms. Amakawa, together with

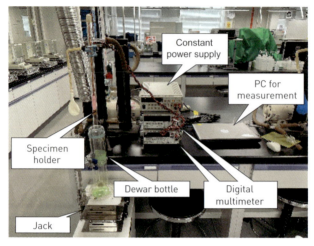

Figure 5-6-2 ▶ A set of electrical resistance measuring instruments

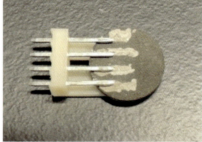

Figure 5-6-3 ▶ Magnet for magnetic levitation   Figure 5-6-4 ▶ Specimen and specimen holder

Figure 5-6-5 ▶ Felt stickers on the vacuum exhaust system

other texts in Braille, while information on the whiteboard was utilized to explain the experiment to sighted students. The crystal structure was explained using a model (Figure 5-6-1). The TA assisted with explanations using Braille materials and models.

In this experiment, 4–5 students individually measured one specimen per person. Normally, the process starts with the preparation of sample for electrical resistance measurement (applying silver paste) by two or three students who have finished performing electrical resistance measurement early, and the rest begins with magnetic levitation. While Ms. Amakawa was expected to do the same, we planned to conduct magnetic levitation first because applying the silver paste may take time. In principle, Ms. Amakawa also was to perform all operations. The TA was to assist her in difficult operations. The following is a description of the support provided to Ms. Amakawa for experiment that was decided upon consultation with Ms. Hamada.

◆ **Specimen preparation for electrical resistance measurement**

It was expected that she could insert specimen into the specimen holder without any problem, so she did so.

Normally, after mounting the specimen in the holder, the terminal and specimen were fixed with a silver paste to ensure conductivity. While the silver paste was usually applied with a toothpick, Ms. Amakawa could not check the position of the paste because she could not touch the area where it was applied. Therefore, we decided to use an upside-down holder for applying the silver paste, and by aligning the holder for paste application with a ruler, we could apply the paste to four places simultaneously (Figure 5-6-6). In reality, it was difficult to apply the paste evenly to all necessary areas using this method. However, according to Ms. Hamada, it was important for Ms. Amakawa to recognize the difficulty of the work, so this method was used for this experiment. After Ms. Amakawa completed task, the TA would make changes if necessary.

It was expected that drying the silver paste with a hair dryer would not be a problem. However, as a distance of ~30 cm was required, she used a ruler to keep the distance and align the dryer.

The TA measured the width, thickness, and distance between terminals using calipers as the silver paste would come off if the applied points were touched (as caliper operation was not important in this experiment).

Figure 5-6-6 ▶ Silver paste application with ruler support

◆ Regarding magnetic levitation experiment

The magnetic levitation experiment comprised two parts: zero-field cooling, in which the sample was cooled in liquid nitrogen in the absence of a magnetic field and then placed on a magnet, and cooling in a magnetic field, in which the sample was placed on a magnet and then cooled using liquid nitrogen. We decided to use bamboo tweezers to set the specimen in place in liquid nitrogen because they are easier to grip than resin tweezers that are usually used.

For the position adjustment of the specimen in the liquid nitrogen container, rulers were placed as supports, as shown in Figure 5-6-7, and the specimen was placed within the range of rulers and in front of the magnet. Cooling was considered complete when liquid nitrogen bubbles stopped appearing, but it was difficult to observe bubbles and to hear sound due to the noise level of the surrounding equipment; therefore, the TA confirmed cooling while explaining verbally.

To adjust the position of the sample on the magnet, a ruler was placed on the support in the same way as when inserting the sample, the sample was moved forward from the insertion position and lifted up and inserted when it touched the magnet (the TA provided verbal support for positioning).

We decided to use a toothpick to check if the specimen was levitating : if it was levitating, repulsion could be felt; if not, it would not move even when pushed because it was in contact with the magnet and; if it repelled and flew away

Figure 5-6-7 ▸ Using rulers as support

to another place, the specimen was gone. It was decided that Ms. Amakawa would use the specimen with x = 0 because the specimen with x = 0 and no element substitution levitates highly and was easy to check.

◆ **Regarding electrical resistance measurement**

Ms. Amakawa was to attach the specimen holder with the specimen to the probe (practiced on the morning of the day of the experiment with a dummy).

The TA was to check if the values of multimeters and other instruments in the measurement system were not disturbed (if so, the TA was to repair the silver paste).

The TA was to operate the PC on behalf of Ms. Amakawa, providing a Braille translation of the information on the screen and verbally explaining what was being done (as with sighted students, once the conditions were entered into the PC, one measurement was taken; a resistance value R of approximately $10^{-3} \, \Omega$ was acceptable).

Before cooling with liquid nitrogen, a vacuum pump was used to evacuate the glass tube in which the probe was mounted, and the specimen was replaced with helium gas. Ms. Amakawa performed all helium replacement operations (essentially only opening and closing valves, while referring to a manual for operation).

The electrical resistance measurement while cooling was performed in a software using a dedicated program. It was a program that automatically measures resistance when the temperature difference ΔT from the previous measurement becomes 0.5 K or more. After starting measurement in the software, the height of the Dewar bottle filled with liquid nitrogen was raised with a jack, and the glass tube with the probe attached was gradually immersed in liquid nitrogen to continuously measure resistance while lowering the temperature of the specimen. Ms. Amakawa gradually raised the jack and adjusted the cooling rate so that ΔT would be ~1.0 K. Numerical values such as ΔT, current temperature, and resistance were read out by the TA.

The following is a description of the support provided to Ms. Amakawa for the analysis work, which was decided upon consultation with Ms. Hamada.

- While sighted students performed analysis at home, Ms. Amakawa analyzed all data in the laboratory because she needed the tactile copies of the data.
- In principle, the raw data were transferred to Ms. Amakawa's PC, and she worked on it.
- Specific analysis tasks included entering the specimen size, changing the unit of resistivity, preparing graph, reading the transition temperature (roughly locating the position with a tactile copy and finding the exact value from a table), displaying the slope of the approximation line, and correcting the slope for each graph. The TA assisted with any operation that was necessary for correction and could not be performed.
- It was planned to create tactile copies by stacking four copies for x = 0 to 1.0, dividing them into pairs (the number of copies would be decided on the spot depending on whether they could be distinguished by touch), and stacking four copies for y = 0 and 0.03 (x = 0 and y = 0 are the same); additionally, copies were created with their slope corrected (about eight copies in total were planned).

All data obtained on the day of the experiment were to be converted into a PDF format later based on the Excel file received during tactile copying and sent to Ms. Amakawa.

(4) Observations on the Experiment Day

Most experimental operations could be performed as planned, with the use of support devices, felt stickers, etc. However, the following procedures were changed to alternative methods.

- The assistant (TA) operated the PC for the electrical resistance measurement device. The TA read out the measured values on the screen, and Ms. Amakawa operated the jack to cool the specimen accordingly.
- In data analysis, it was necessary to superimpose multiple graphs on Excel. However, Ms. Amakawa could not select axes, so each graph was created by Ms. Amakawa and then copied and pasted by the TA.

◆ Explanation before the start of the experiment

On the day of the experiment, we asked Ms. Amakawa to come to the laboratory ~30 min beforehand to confirm the following information and to listen to a preliminary explanation.

- She touched and checked the specimen, specimen holder, and probe and practiced mounting the specimen and attaching the specimen holder to the probe.
- The TA explained the entire equipment, and she checked it by touching and operating it (probes, the Dewar bottle, measuring instruments, such as digital multimeters, and the jack).
- The TA explained regarding helium replacement operation, including components such as valves, piping, and pumps, and Ms. Amakawa confirmed the operation by touching the entire system.
- She touched and checked the magnet used for magnetic levitation and bamboo tweezers as well as practiced holding a dummy specimen with the tweezers. Because the specimen in liquid nitrogen cannot be touched by hand, it was difficult to adjust its position with the tweezers to the place where the specimen was to be placed. Ms. Hamada and the TA held the ruler against the support and gave verbal instructions to Ms. Amakawa as she clamped the specimen and released it in the liquid nitrogen or on the magnet.

Sighted students listened to explanation regarding the experiment while

Figure 5-6-8 ▶ Silver paste application

Figure 5-6-9 ▶ Specimen after silver paste application

looking at the writing on the whiteboard, and Ms. Amakawa listened to the explanation while reading the Braille transcription of the writing on the whiteboard. Ms. Amakawa did not ask any questions and did not seem to need any particular assistance. The experimental work is described below.

◆ Specimen preparation

For silver paste application, Ms. Amakawa used a special ruler for positional support and the upside-down specimen holder as an application tool, both of which were considered during the trace experiment (Figure 5-6-8). Initially, she was perplexed, but after several attempts, she confirmed the adhesion of the silver paste in two inner positions. Therefore, we changed the original plan and decided to use a ruler support and a toothpick to apply the silver paste onto two outer positions. Application appeared to be fine, and the TA made some minor adjustments afterward, just like for sighted students (Figure 5-6-9). After adjustment, the TA confirmed with a tester that there were no conductivity problems.

The drying process with the dryer took 10 min, as planned during the trace experiment, with a ruler keeping the distance to specimen. After drying, sighted students measured the thickness, width, and distance between terminals with calipers, while Ms. Amakawa measured only the thickness (Ms. Amakawa used the calipers, and the TA read the values). The width and distance between terminals were measured by the TA because it was necessary to measure them without touching the specimen and holder and because it was not a task that was essential

Figure 5-6-10 ▶ Confirmation of magnetic levitation with a toothpick

to the nature of the experiment.

◆ Regarding magnetic levitation experiment

Magnetic levitation was first performed with multiple sets of magnets and zero field cooling. Ms. Hamada and the TA assisted in positioning with rulers via verbal instructions. It seemed difficult to place the specimen in the liquid nitrogen with the tweezers and to put it on the magnet inside the liquid nitrogen. Levitation was confirmed by the absence of falling sound when the specimen was placed on the magnet and by pushing the specimen with a toothpick. Especially, she seemed to be able to feel the repulsive force by pushing the specimen with a toothpick. Subsequently, magnetic field cooling was performed using multiple magnet pairs, and zero magnetic field cooling and magnetic field cooling were performed using a flat plate and a ring-shaped magnet. The conditions were such that it became more difficult for magnets to levitate in the latter half of the experiment. Additionally, because the levitation time and height decreased, magnets sometimes fell before or while being touched with the toothpick, so she had to do several attempts. Cooling in a ring-shaped magnetic field was particularly weak in terms of levitation; therefore, even after several attempts, she was unable to successfully confirm the results. Thus, Ms. Hamada suggested that she should lightly touch it with a folded sticky note, and eventually she could confirm levitation.

Measurements of the levitation time and height, which were optional for sighted students, were not performed.

◆ Regarding electrical resistance measurement

Initially, the specimen holder prepared in the morning was attached to the probe, and measurement was started. Installation was smooth, thanks to the prior practice.

Operation was conducted in accordance with the operation manual that had already been translated into Braille and sent to Ms. Amakawa in advance. Ms. Amakawa had already entered the operation manual into Braille Sense and proceeded to read it as she conducted the experiment. As she performed operation while understanding the connection of the vacuum line, she could confirm that the glass tube was filled with helium by observing how the balloon became smaller.

While we had sent her a Braille transcription of the PC screen in advance, Ms. Amakawa did not had it with her on the day of the experiment. The TA's detailed verbal explanation of what was on the screen seemed to help her understand. As confirmed in advance, the TA gave a detailed verbal explanation on how to operate the PC, and Mr. Amakawa raised the jack to cool the sample following the TA's instructions. The TA read out changes in the measured values, and Ms. Amakawa also checked with the TA.

She used the structural model of $YBa_2Cu_3O_7$ to confirm the crystal structure. Regarding the handling of the measurement data, the results of electrical resistance measurements were shared via a USB flash drive. The magnetic levitation results were shared in an oral presentation by each student. Ms. Amakawa shared her results by reading the Braille memo and noted the results obtained by sighted students with ease. As only Ms. Amakawa's specimen levitated well, she was asked questions by other students, and she answered them.

◆ Post-experiment analysis

Analysis work is described below.

- She could perform most work of compiling data from multiple Excel files into a single Excel file. Although she created graphs, she struggled with adjusting the axes and combining multiple results into one graph. While sighted students usually created a single graph and then manually selected X and Y values from the Edit Graph menu to create a graph with multiple results, Ms.

Amakawa could not select axes. Therefore, she created individual graphs, and the TA copied and pasted the graphs together to create a graph that combined multiple results. The analyzed data were copied in tactile form, and Ms. Amakawa checked them.

- Because Ms. Amakawa did not use a mouse or touchpad, she could not select the graphs in Excel and needed assistance from the TA.
- The raw data of the measurement results were later converted to the PDF format and sent by the laboratory staff.

(5) How to Confirm the Understanding Level

Understanding regarding the topic was confirmed through a Zoom-based examination and oral presentation.

(6) Comments

At first, we felt nervous because we did not had any previous experience of supporting completely blind students, but at the same time, we wanted to deepen our understanding of completely blind people through this experience. It was a very good experience for us to go through trials and errors during the preparation stage and to find out which operations were essential and how we could help Ms. Amakawa to experience the process. Through explanation on the day of the experiment, we learned that we need to be more specific and explain carefully because we felt that it was difficult to convey results using directives. Through this experience, we felt that we could develop the ability to think about and care for others.

(Original text by: Akanuma)

Main Support Equipment Used in Experiments

This section lists the main support instruments used in each experiment. For example, "weighing reagents," "checking the position of switches on lab equipment," "reading the scale on syringes," "checking color changes," and "reading the graphs of experimental results," all of which involve operations and tasks that are difficult for a completely blind person. Therefore, Ms. Shizuko Hamada and the technical staff provided support to Ms. Amakawa by offering customized experimental equipment and aids such as Braille labels, felt stickers, a balance with a readout function, a tactile copy machine, and a light probe. In this section, we divide operations and tasks into six categories and list experimental support equipment used in Part 3, how it was used, as well as measures that made the performing of experiments possible.

"Visual to tactile conversion": Support for converting visual information into a format that can be understood through touch.

"Measurement support": Support for weighing and other measurements.

"PC support": Support to facilitate smooth PC operation.

"Equipment (part/reagent) identification": Support for the identification of the parts of experimental equipment, reagent containers, etc.

"Visual to audio conversion": Support for converting visual information into audio information.

"Safety considerations": Support for preventing glass equipment, etc. from tipping over or Ms. Amakawa from coming into contact with hazardous areas, etc.

Support Equipment	Support Details	Support Category	Summary
Braille Sense (distributed by Extra Co. Ltd. (Shimizu-ku, Shizuoka city, Shizuoka))	Used to record each experiment as an equivalent of an experimental notebook for a sighted person	Visual to tactile conversion	Ms. Amakawa brought her own. Used to create documents with the Braille keyboard, and utilized as a display device.
Felt sticker	Used to distinguish and locate objects, and utilized as a plot in a graph	Visual to tactile conversion, Measurement support	Approximately 1-mm-thick felt stickers whose backside is sticky.
Raised line drawing board	Used to draw graphs, etc. by tracing a figure with a pen with a hard tip to make it rise	Visual to tactile conversion	A piece of cardboard covered with a rough plastic net is used as a simplified raised line drawing board.
Braillewriter (made by Pioneer Goods Co.(Odawara, Kanagawa))	Used to create Braille labels	Visual to tactile conversion	A set of a pin and a case used to type Braille on papers or labels
Tactile copy machine (PIAF, distributed by KGS Co. (Ogawa, Saitama))	Used to display charts, graphs, etc.	Visual to tactile conversion	A device that heats a black image printed on special thermal foaming papers and creates a tactile shape via foaming
Laptop PC	Data preparation and analysis as well as report writing	PC support	Ms. Amakawa brought her own. Used especially for Word and Excel inputs and management
Braille ruler	Used to measure the size and length of objects in 1-mm units	Visual to tactile conversion	Ms. Amakawa brought her own. Ruler with a scale that can be checked by touch.
Braille label	Used to identify different buttons on the same equipment or devices and on graph axes and other figures	Equipment (part/reagent) identification, visual to tactile conversion	Label printer tape with Braille typed on it using a Braillewriter
Braille graph paper	Used as an alternative of graph papers when plotting graphs	Visual to tactile conversion	A sheet of paper printed in a grid pattern using a Braille printer.
Light probe (distributed by Tokyo Hellen Keller Association Inc. (Shinjuku-ku, Tokyo))	Used to determine differences in shading, objects, and the movement or presence of light	Visual to audio conversion	A device that changes the pitch of the sound depending on the intensity of the light entering the light-receiving part.
Balance with a readout function	Used for weighing reagents, specimens, etc. (in 0.01 g units)	Measurement support	Loaned by a School for Visually Impaired. A balance that reads the displayed value when a button is pressed

Support Equipment	Support Details	Support Category	Summary
Plastic syringe with notches cut into it	Used for separating solutions when accurate quantification is not required	Measurement support	A syringe with notches cut into the handle of the plunger side so that a user can dispense up to a certain scale mark by placing a finger on the notches.
Tray	Used to prevent beakers and other containers from tipping over	Safety precautions	Plastic disposable trays with holes or other modifications.
NonVisual Desktop Access (NVDA) http://www.nvda.jp	Used to enter numbers and other data in Excel files and to check explanatory materials and exercises	PC support	Open-source text-to-speech software for Windows

[Editors]

Administration and Technology Management Center for Science and Engineering, Waseda University

Comprises the Administrative Division, which performs administrative work for the three Schools and graduate Schools of Science and Engineering at Waseda University (Fundamental Science and Engineering, Creative Science and Engineering, and Advanced Science and Engineering), and the Technical Management Division, which provides technical support.

The Technical Management Division has about 100 highly specialized technical staff members, who provide educational support that combines theory and practice and research support through joint-use facilities for research to foster and produce science and engineering talents with practical skills who can contribute to the transformation of society at large.

The three Schools of Science and Engineering place particular emphasis on practical "laboratory education." Technical staff, organized by field, provide technical guidance in collaboration with faculty members in laboratories used across the boundaries of schools and departments. They also offer the centralized, systematic management of equipment and facilities, creating a more advanced and fulfilling educational and research environment.

[Cover Illustration]

Ken Yabuno

Honorary Fellow of Waseda University and a member of the Japan Art Academy.

"Adjusting the Bunsen burner in the laboratory" (front cover), "Nishi-Waseda Campus, Waseda University" (back cover)

Courage and Determination

Techinical Support in Laboratory Education for a Visually Impaired Student

2025年4月10日　初版第1刷発行

編者	Administration and Technology Management Center for Science and Engineering, Waseda University
発行者	須賀晃一
発行所	株式会社 早稲田大学出版部
	〒169-0051　東京都新宿区西早稲田1-9-12 TEL 03-3203-1551 https://www.waseda-up.co.jp/
翻訳協力	株式会社クリムゾン インタラクティブ ジャパン
デザイン	米谷豪
DTP	株式会社 ステラ
印刷・製本	中央精版印刷株式会社

©Waseda University 2025 Printed in Japan
ISBN978-4-657-25002-5

無断転載を禁じます。落丁・乱丁本はお取替えいたします。